FRANCKIE ALARCON

The Secrets
of
Chocolate

A GOURMAND'S TRIP THROUGH A TOP CHEF'S ATELIER

nbm GRAPHIC NOVELS

Nantier · Beall · Minoustchine

N E W   Y O R K

I would like to express my enormous gratitude to Jacques Genin for his warm welcome, his generosity and his chocolates!
And my gratitude also goes out to...
Stéphane Bonnat for an unforgettable and cocoa-flavored trip from Voiron to Peru.
Yannick Lejeune for giving me the opportunity to live, sleep, eat and dream chocolate.
All those big chocolate lovers: Sophie for her patience and her private lessons in Jacques' workshop, Ingrid for her palate and her sharp pen, Elisa for her invaluable advice and her good cheer, and the Aguaruna people for a unique gastronomic and cultural experience.
Jacques Genin's teams for so generously sharing their passion and their know-how with me over the course of an entire year.
Vanadis and my other traveling companions in Peru.
David Chauvel for mentioning my name.
Mom and Grandma for their chocolate-themed memories.
My sister for her Mexican translations.
Marilyne for her help, her talent, and her support throughout my year of culinary discovery!

ISBN 9781681122786
Originally published in French as:
Les Secrets du chocolat by Franckie Alarcon
© Editions Delcourt, 2014
© 2021 NBM for the English translation
Library of Congress Control Number: 2021934461
Translation by Montana Kane
Lettering by Ortho
printed in Turkey
This title is also available wherever e-books are sold (ISBN 9781681122793)

See previews, get exclusives and order from:
NBMPUB.COM
We have hundreds of graphic novels available.
Subscribe to our monthly newsletter
Follow us on Facebook & Instagram (nbmgraphicnovels), Twitter (@nbmpub).

NBM
160 Broadway, Suite 700, East Wing
New York, NY 10038
Catalog upon request

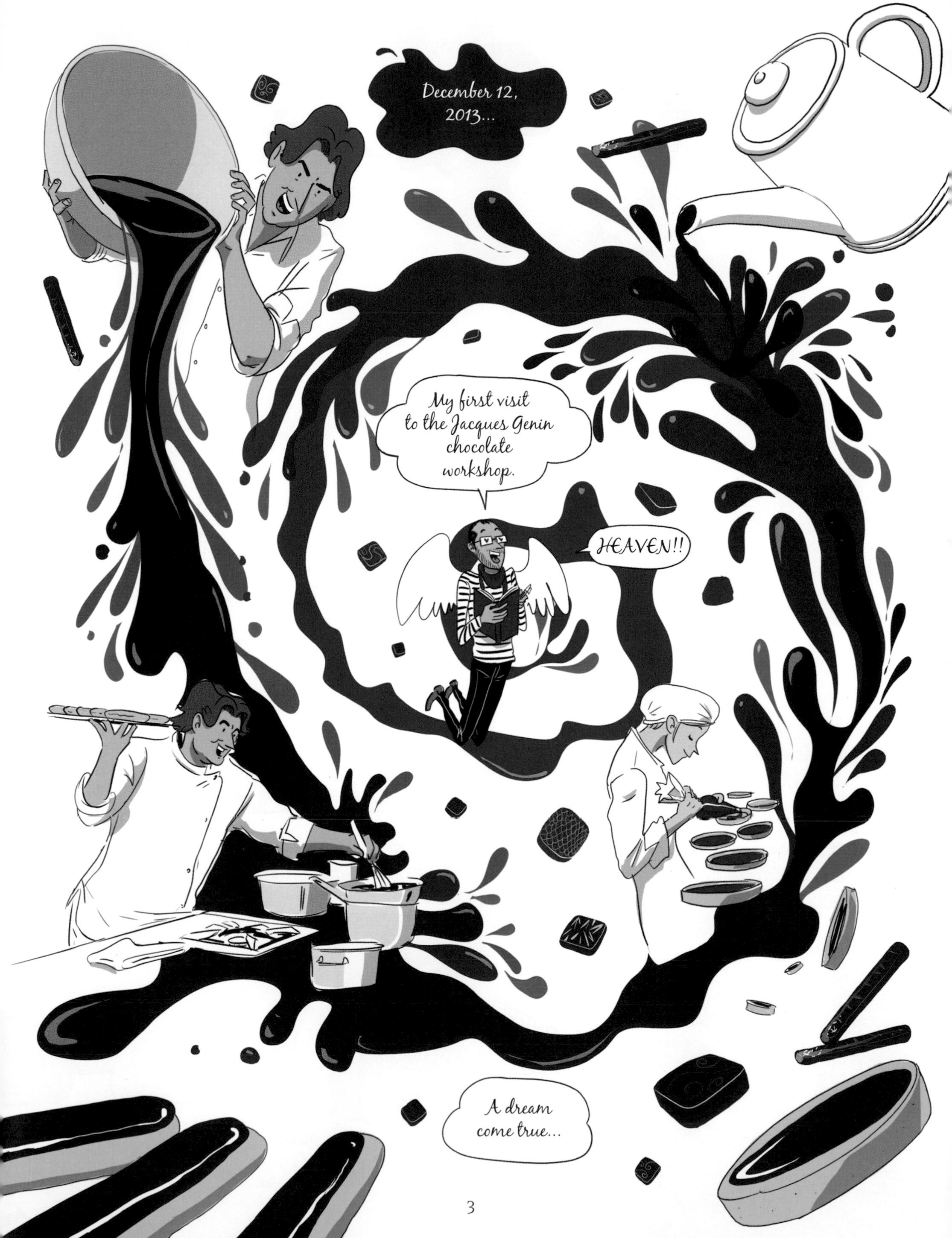
December 12, 2013...
My first visit to the Jacques Genin chocolate workshop.
HEAVEN!!
A dream come true...

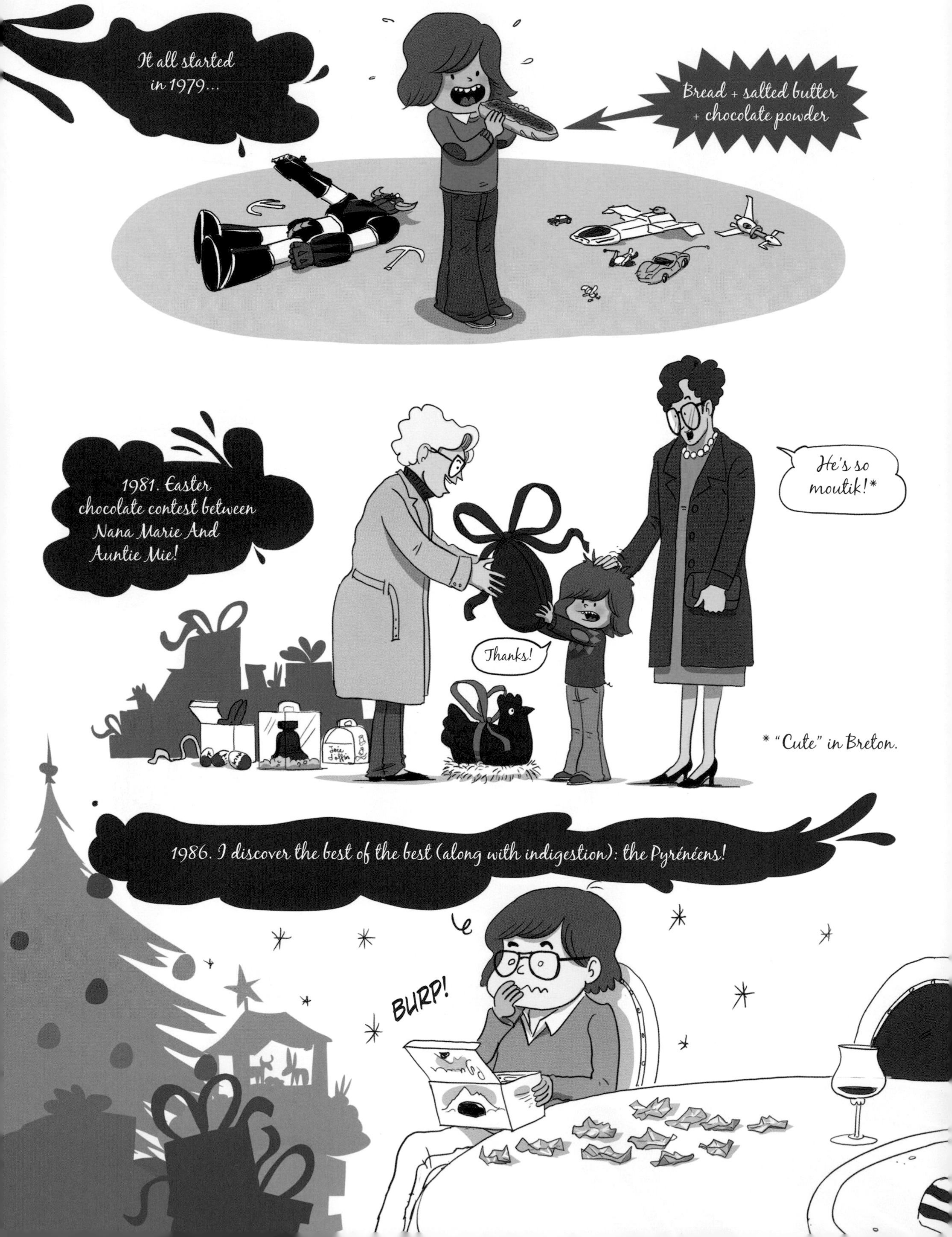
It all started in 1979...
Bread + salted butter + chocolate powder
1981. Easter chocolate contest between Nana Marie And Auntie Mie!
He's so moutik!*
Thanks!
* "Cute" in Breton.
1986. I discover the best of the best (along with indigestion): the Pyrénéens!
BURP!

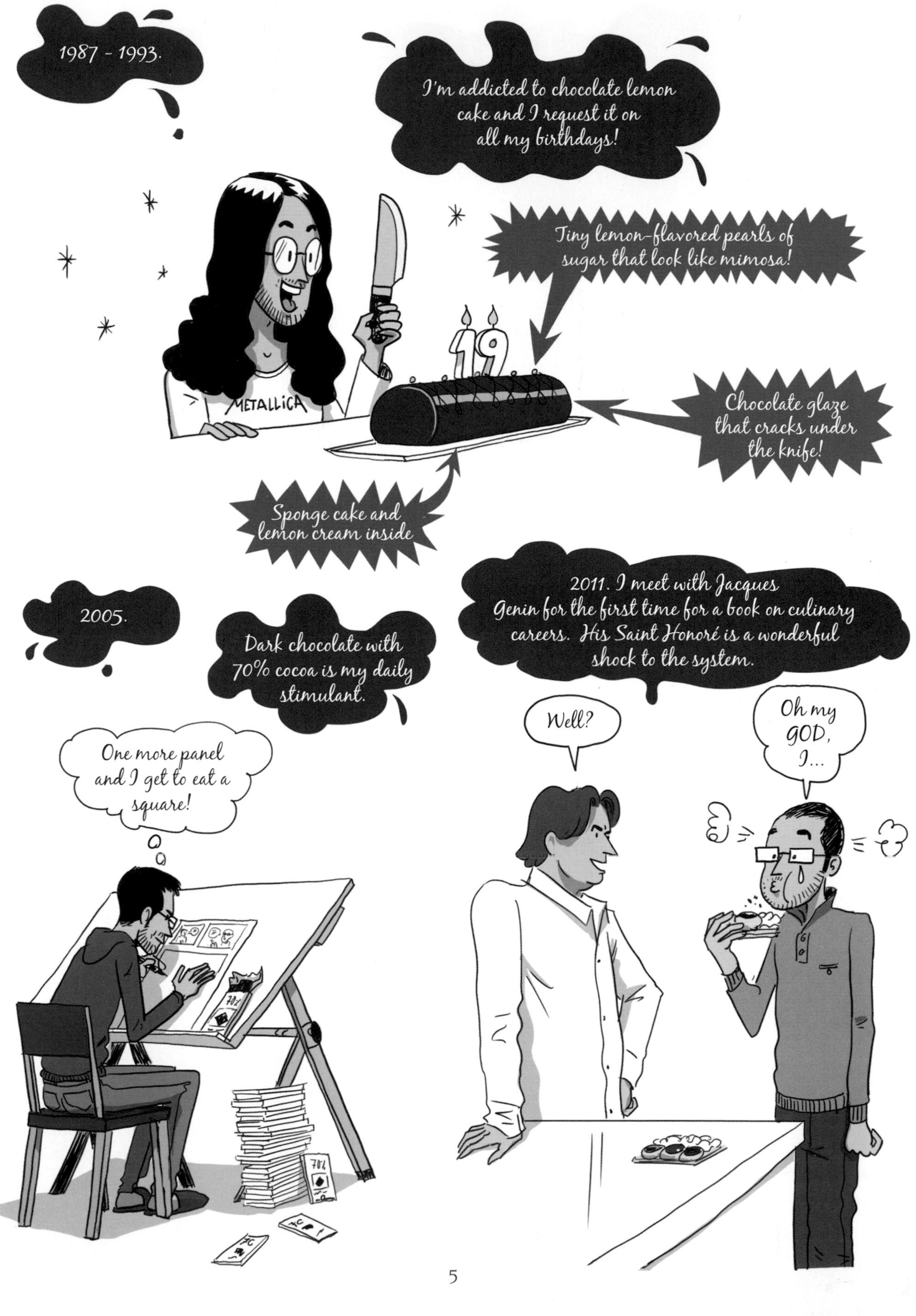
1987 - 1993.
I'm addicted to chocolate lemon cake and I request it on all my birthdays!
Tiny lemon-flavored pearls of sugar that look like mimosa!
METALLICA
19
Chocolate glaze that cracks under the knife!
Sponge cake and lemon cream inside
2005.
Dark chocolate with 70% cocoa is my daily stimulant.
One more panel and I get to eat a square!
2011. I meet with Jacques Genin for the first time for a book on culinary careers. His Saint Honoré is a wonderful shock to the system.
Well?
Oh my GOD, I...

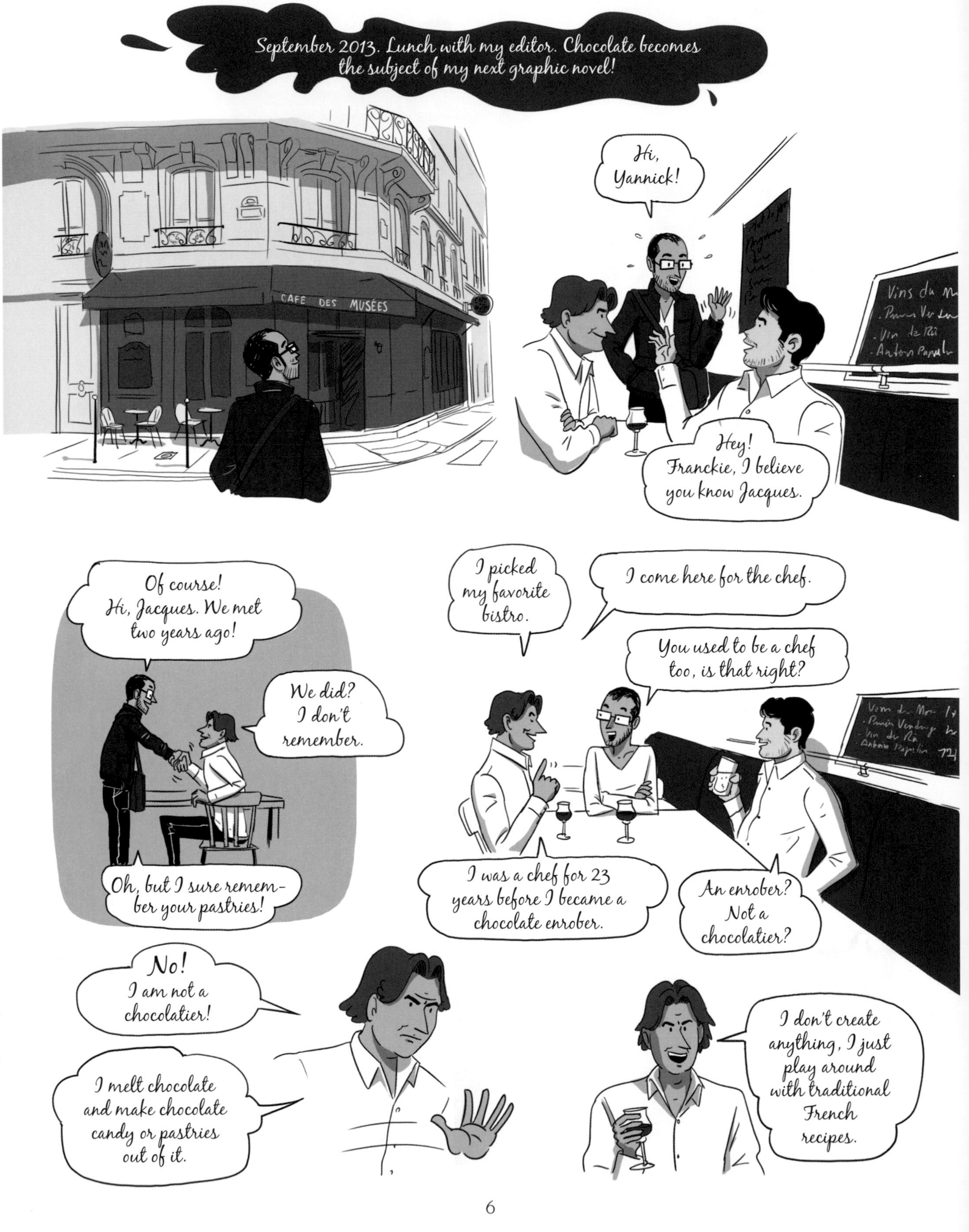
September 2013. Lunch with my editor. Chocolate becomes the subject of my next graphic novel!
CAFE DES MUSÉES
Hi, Yannick!
Hey! Franckie, I believe you know Jacques.
Of course! Hi, Jacques. We met two years ago!
We did? I don't remember.
Oh, but I sure remember your pastries!
I picked my favorite bistro.
I come here for the chef.
You used to be a chef too, is that right?
I was a chef for 23 years before I became a chocolate enrober.
An enrober? Not a chocolatier?
No! I am not a chocolatier!
I melt chocolate and make chocolate candy or pastries out of it.
I don't create anything, I just play around with traditional French recipes.

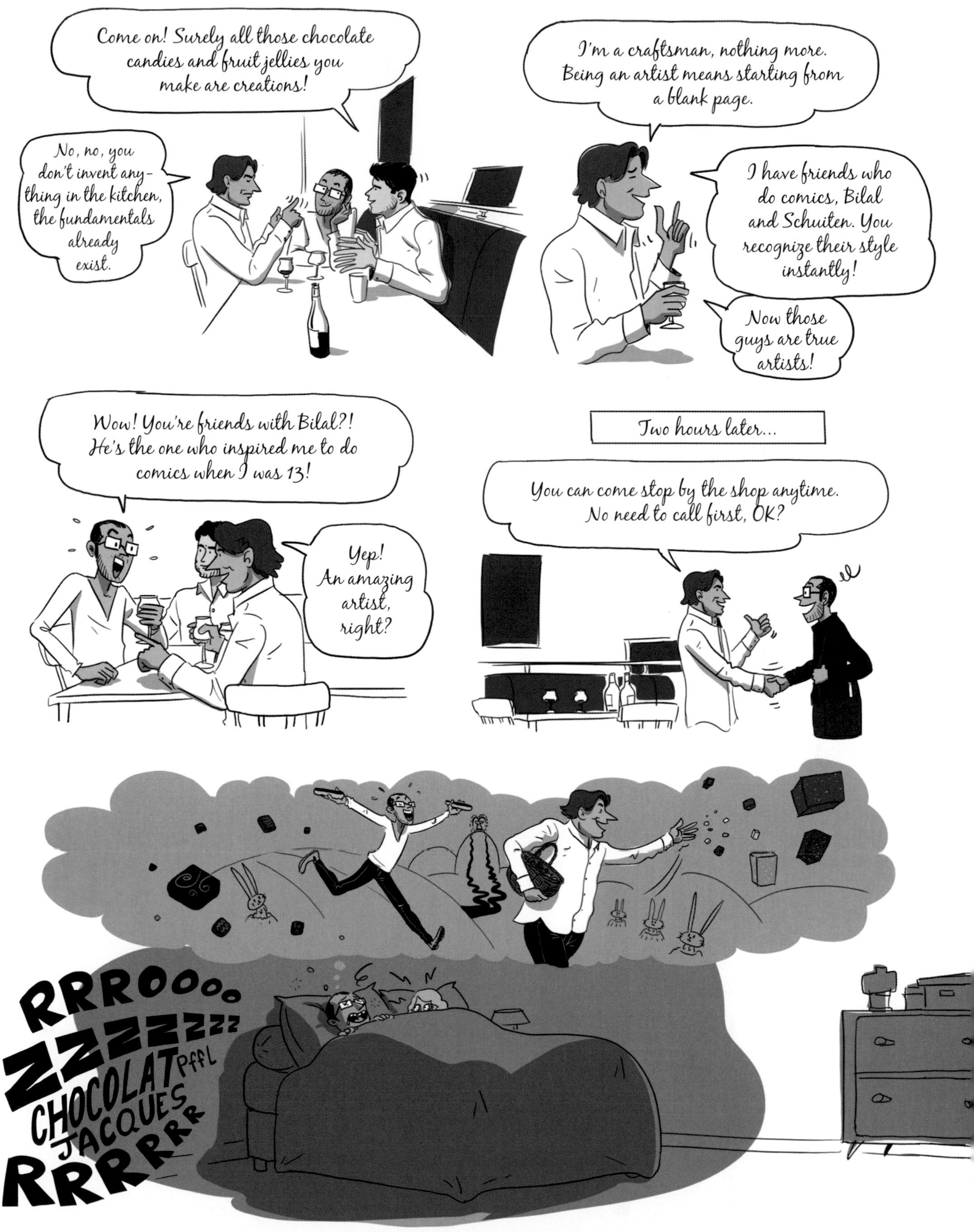
Come on! Surely all those chocolate candies and fruit jellies you make are creations!
No, no, you don't invent anything in the kitchen, the fundamentals already exist.
I'm a craftsman, nothing more. Being an artist means starting from a blank page.
I have friends who do comics, Bilal and Schuiten. You recognize their style instantly!
Now those guys are true artists!
Wow! You're friends with Bilal?! He's the one who inspired me to do comics when I was 13!
Yep! An amazing artist, right?
Two hours later...
You can come stop by the shop anytime. No need to call first, OK?
RRROOOOO
ZZZZZZZZ
CHOCOLAT
PFFL
JACQUES
RRRRRRR

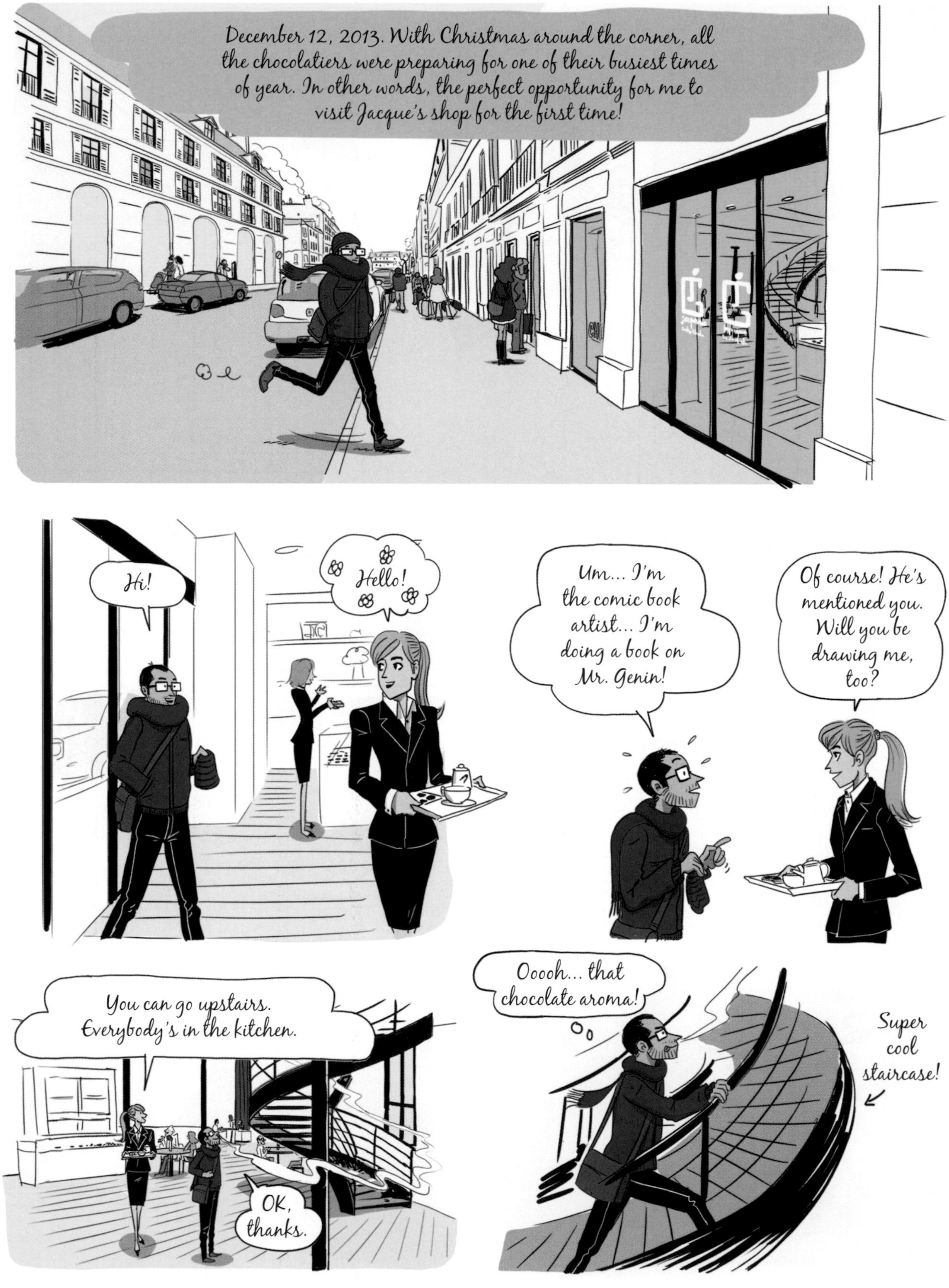
December 12, 2013. With Christmas around the corner, all the chocolatiers were preparing for one of their busiest times of year. In other words, the perfect opportunity for me to visit Jacque's shop for the first time!
Hi!
Hello!
Um... I'm the comic book artist... I'm doing a book on Mr. Genin!
Of course! He's mentioned you. Will you be drawing me, too?
You can go upstairs. Everybody's in the kitchen.
OK, thanks.
Ooooh... that chocolate aroma!
Super cool staircase!

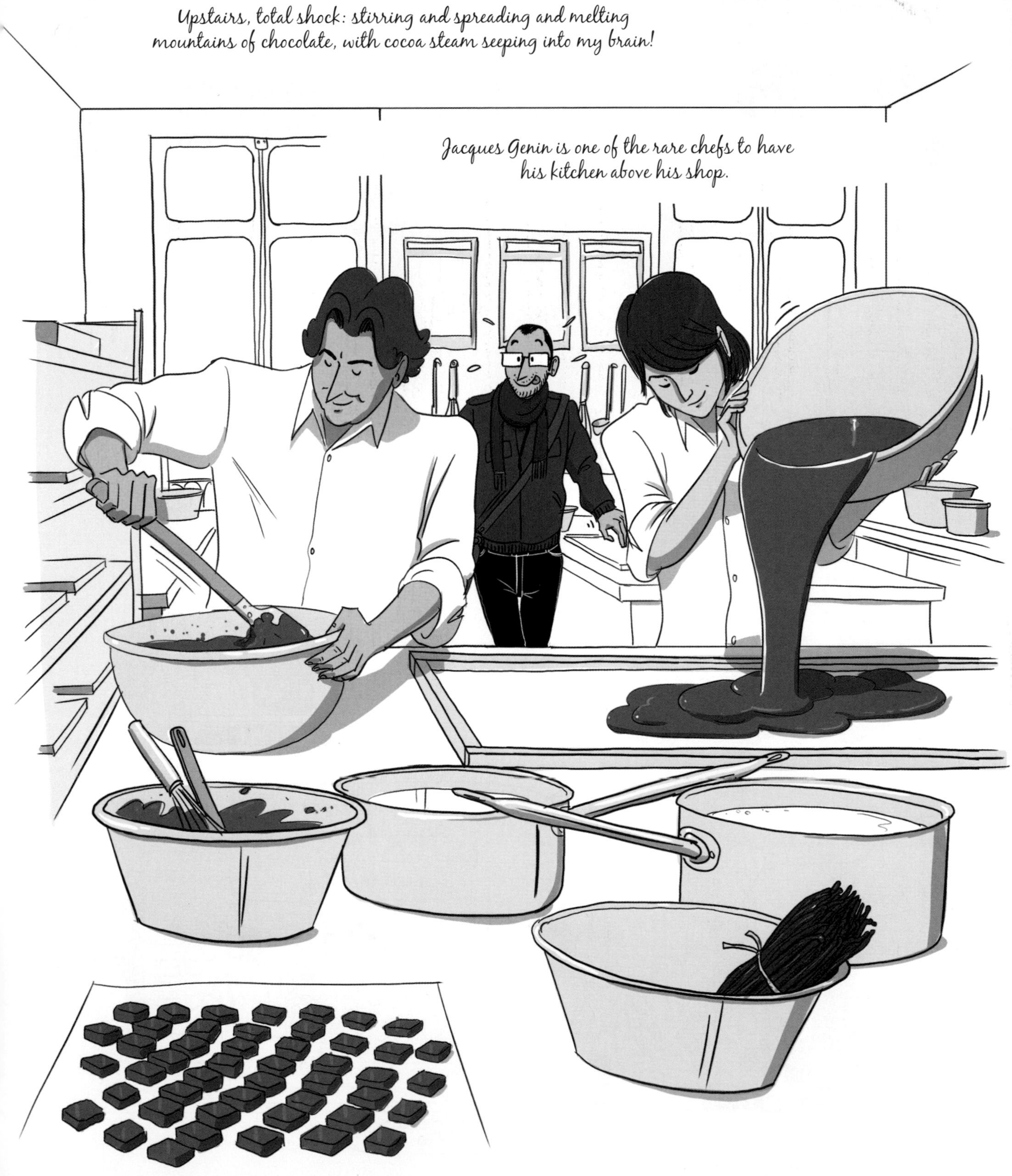
Upstairs, total shock: stirring and spreading and melting mountains of chocolate, with cocoa steam seeping into my brain!
Jacques Genin is one of the rare chefs to have his kitchen above his shop.

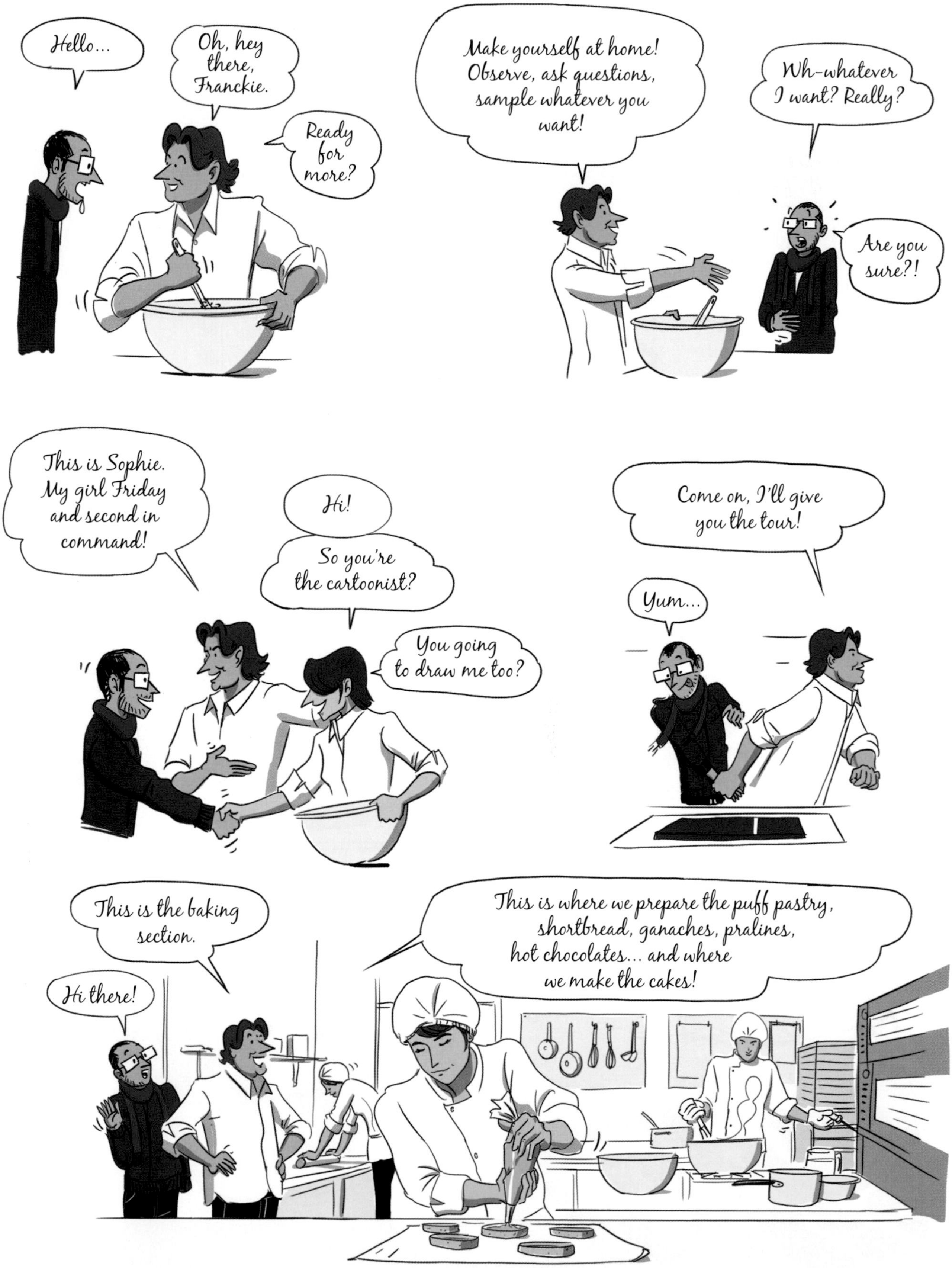
Hello...
Oh, hey there, Franckie.
Ready for more?
Make yourself at home! Observe, ask questions, sample whatever you want!
Wh-whatever I want? Really?
Are you sure?!
This is Sophie. My girl Friday and second in command!
Hi!
So you're the cartoonist?
You going to draw me too?
Come on, I'll give you the tour!
Yum...
This is the baking section.
Hi there!
This is where we prepare the puff pastry, shortbread, ganaches, pralines, hot chocolates... and where we make the cakes!

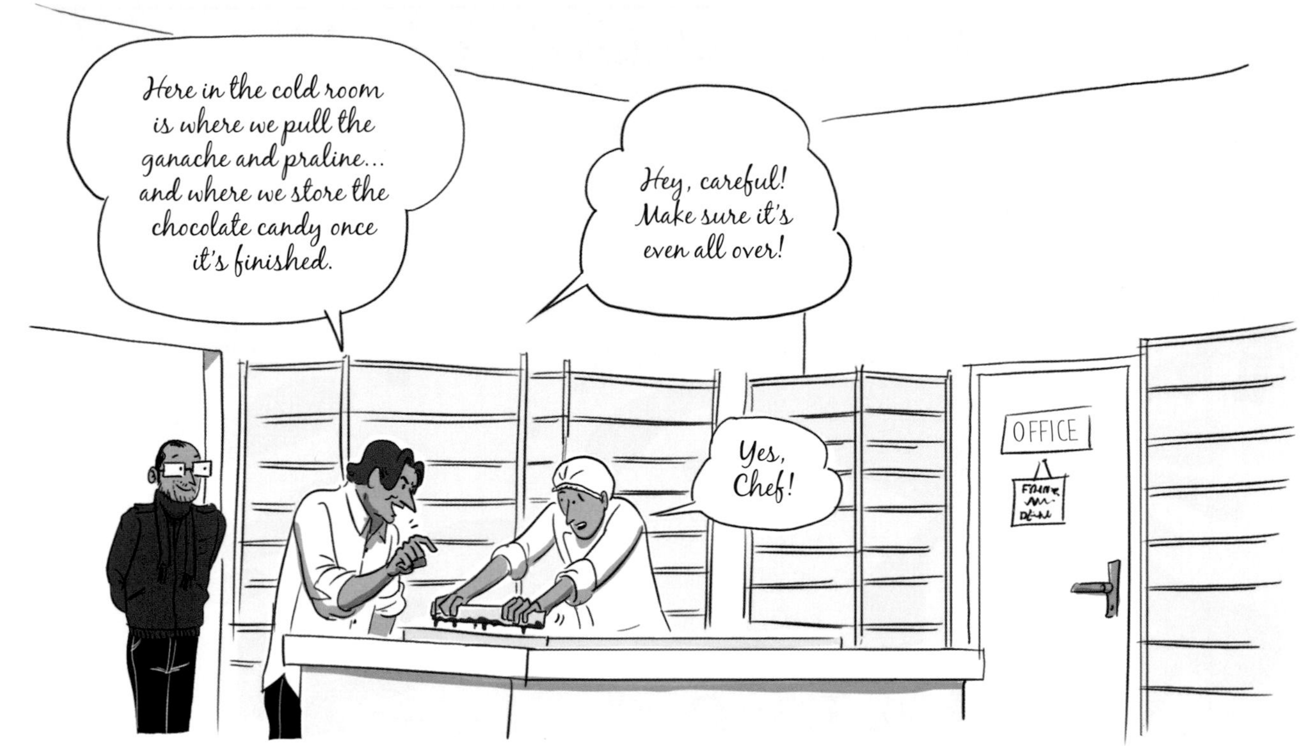
Here in the cold room is where we pull the ganache and praline... and where we store the chocolate candy once it's finished.
Hey, careful! Make sure it's even all over!
Yes, Chef!
OFFICE

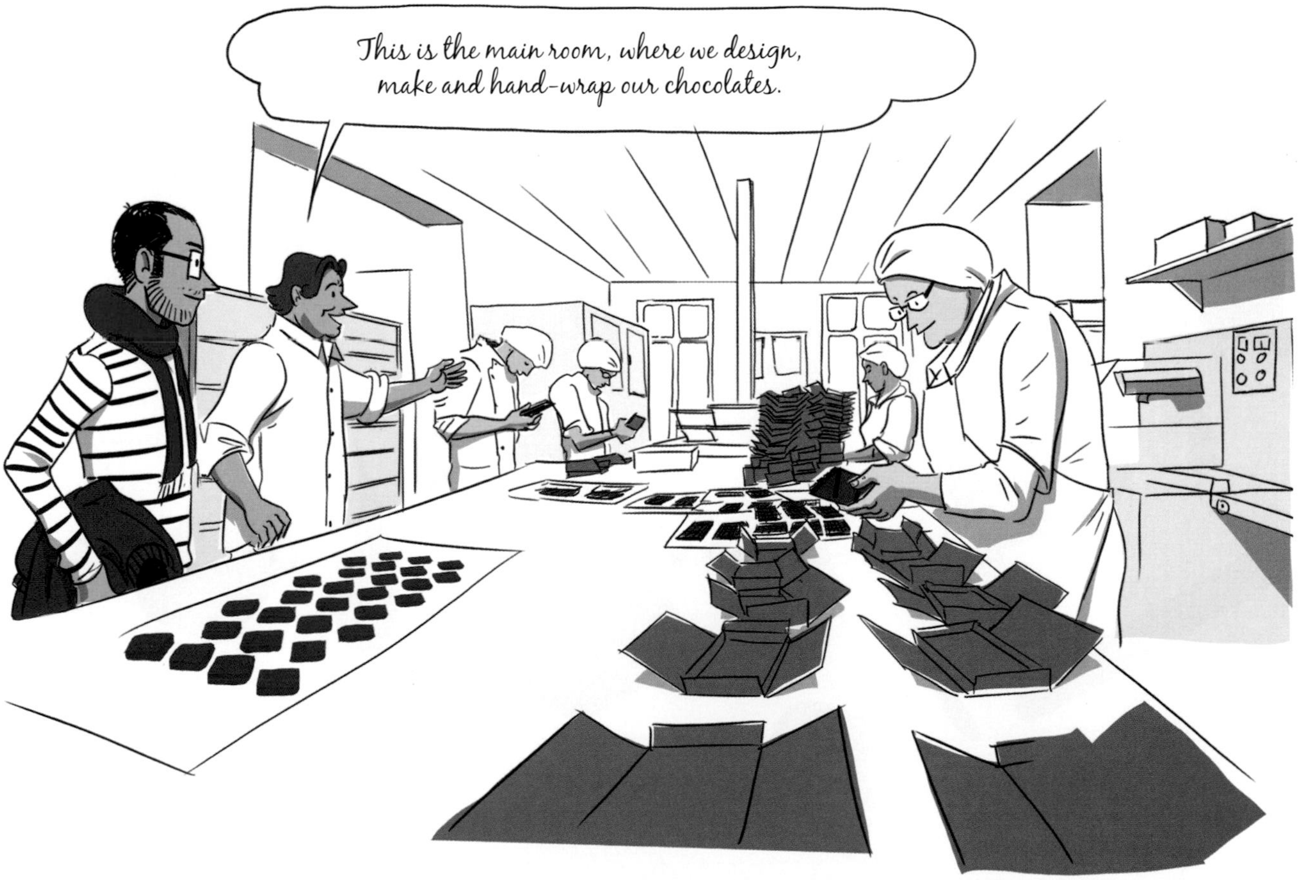
This is the main room, where we design, make and hand-wrap our chocolates.

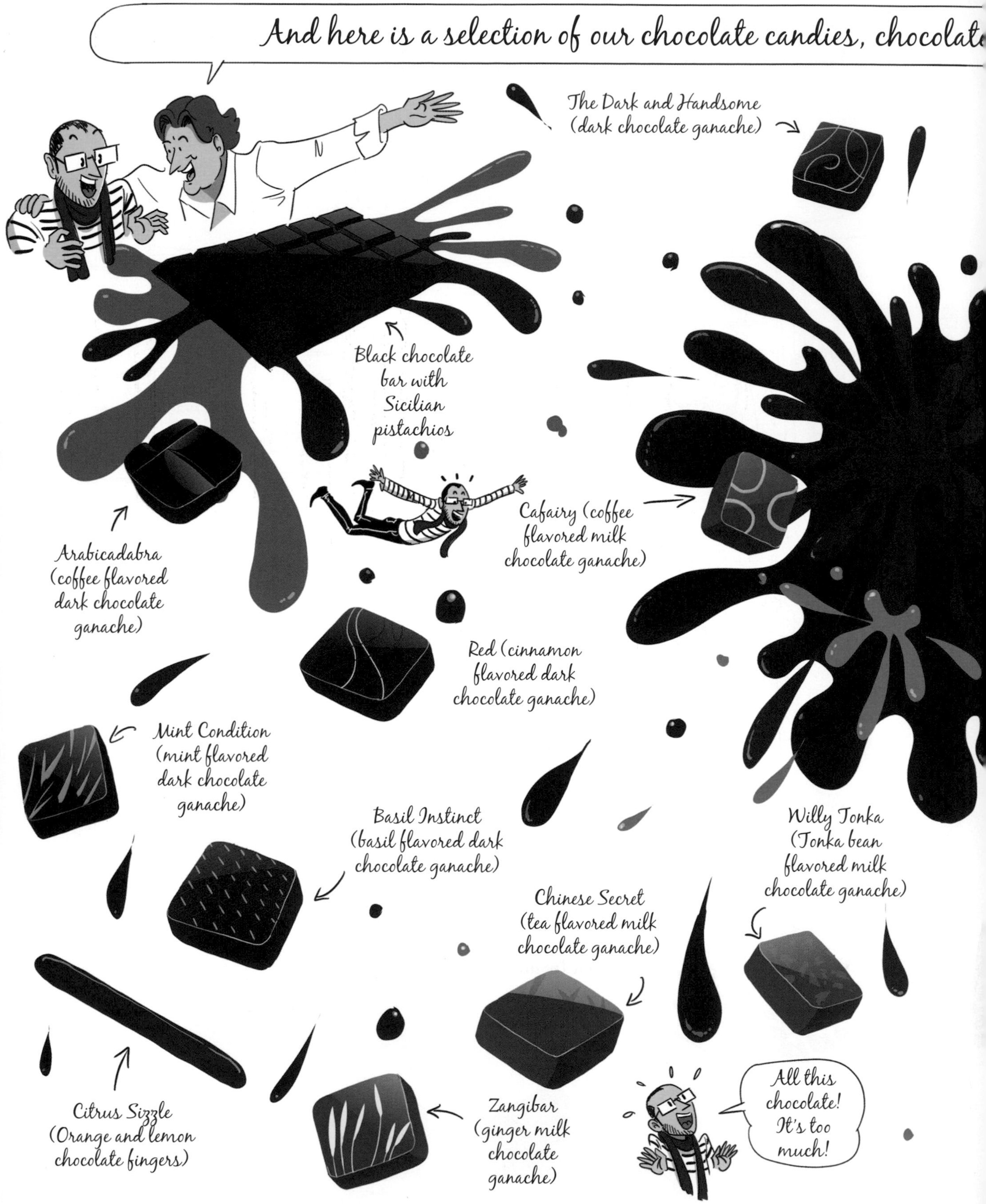
And here is a selection of our chocolate candies, chocolat
The Dark and Handsome (dark chocolate ganache)
Black chocolate bar with Sicilian pistachios
Arabicadabra (coffee flavored dark chocolate ganache)
Cafairy (coffee flavored milk chocolate ganache)
Red (cinnamon flavored dark chocolate ganache)
Mint Condition (mint flavored dark chocolate ganache)
Basil Instinct (basil flavored dark chocolate ganache)
Willy Tonka (Tonka bean flavored milk chocolate ganache)
Chinese Secret (tea flavored milk chocolate ganache)
Citrus Sizzle (Orange and lemon chocolate fingers)
Zangibar (ginger milk chocolate ganache)
All this chocolate! It's too much!

ars, truffles, rochers, mendiants and other sweets...

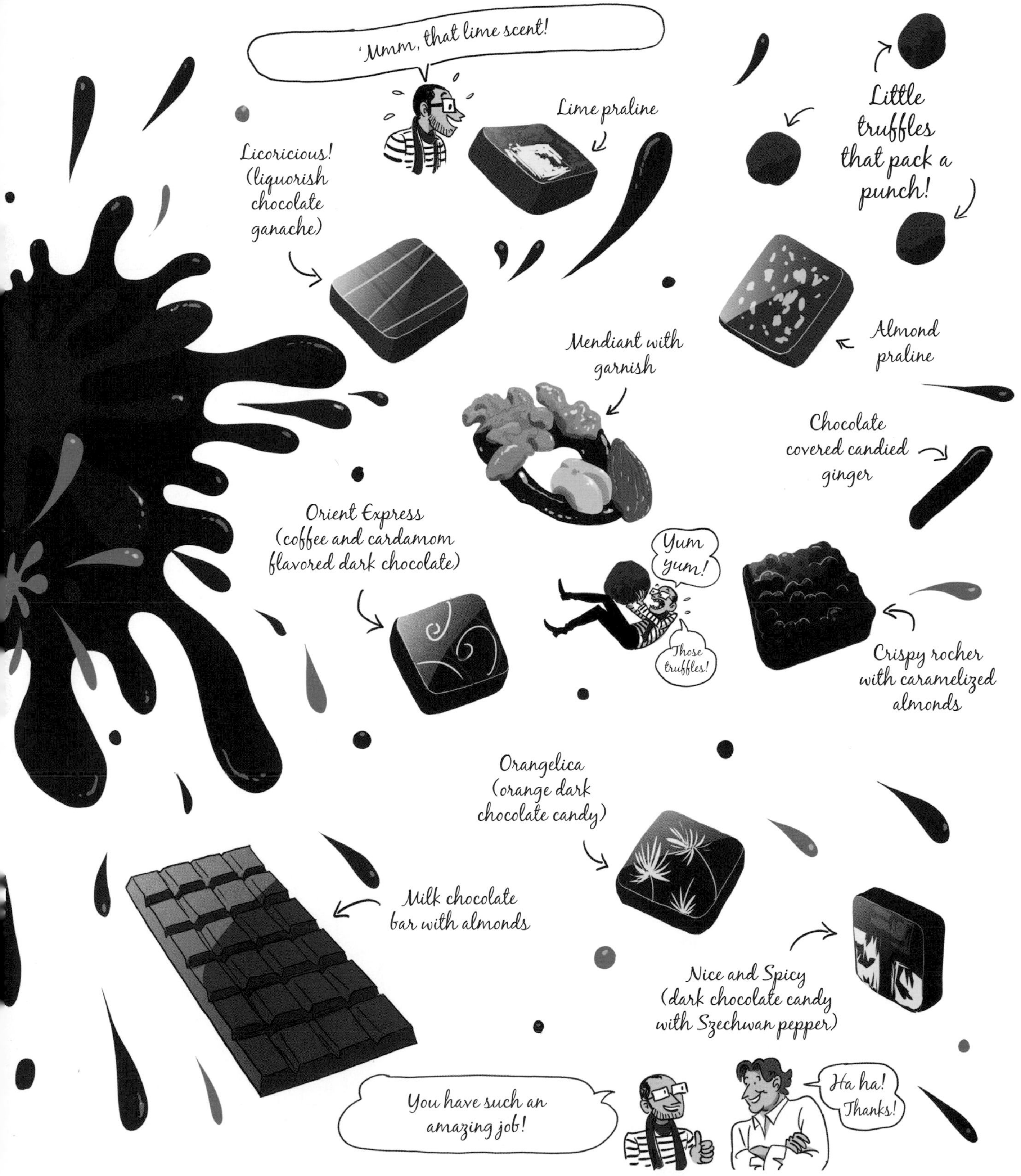

'Mmm, that lime scent!
Lime praline
Little truffles that pack a punch!
Licoricious! (liquorish chocolate ganache)
Almond praline
Mendiant with garnish
Chocolate covered candied ginger
Orient Express (coffee and cardamom flavored dark chocolate)
Yum yum!
Those truffles!
Crispy rocher with caramelized almonds
Orangelica (orange dark chocolate candy)
Milk chocolate bar with almonds
Nice and Spicy (dark chocolate candy with Szechwan pepper)
You have such an amazing job!
Ha ha! Thanks!

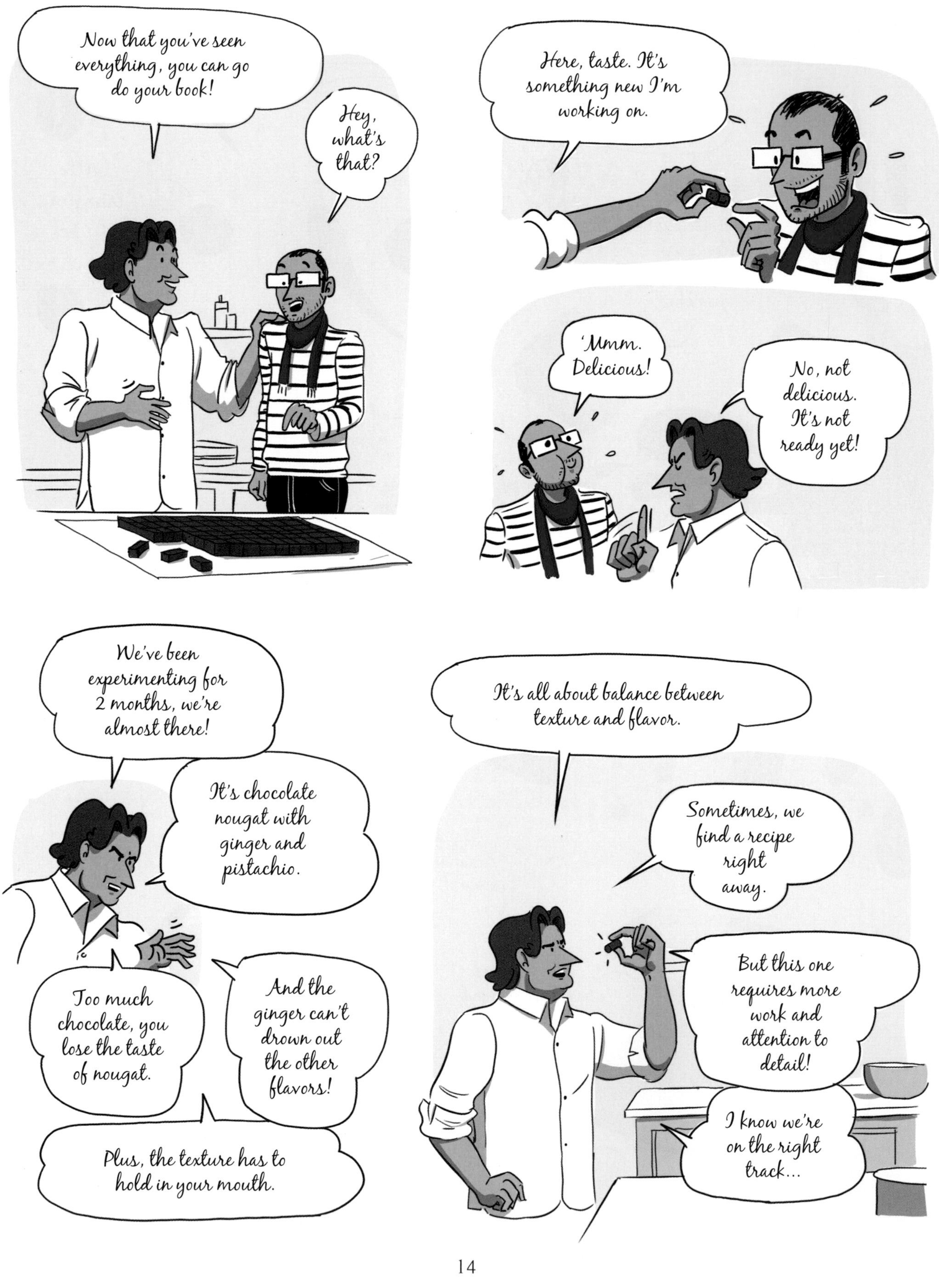
Now that you've seen everything, you can go do your book!
Hey, what's that?
Here, taste. It's something new I'm working on.
'Umm. Delicious!
No, not delicious. It's not ready yet!
We've been experimenting for 2 months, we're almost there!
It's chocolate nougat with ginger and pistachio.
Too much chocolate, you lose the taste of nougat.
And the ginger can't drown out the other flavors!
Plus, the texture has to hold in your mouth.
It's all about balance between texture and flavor.
Sometimes, we find a recipe right away.
But this one requires more work and attention to detail!
I know we're on the right track...

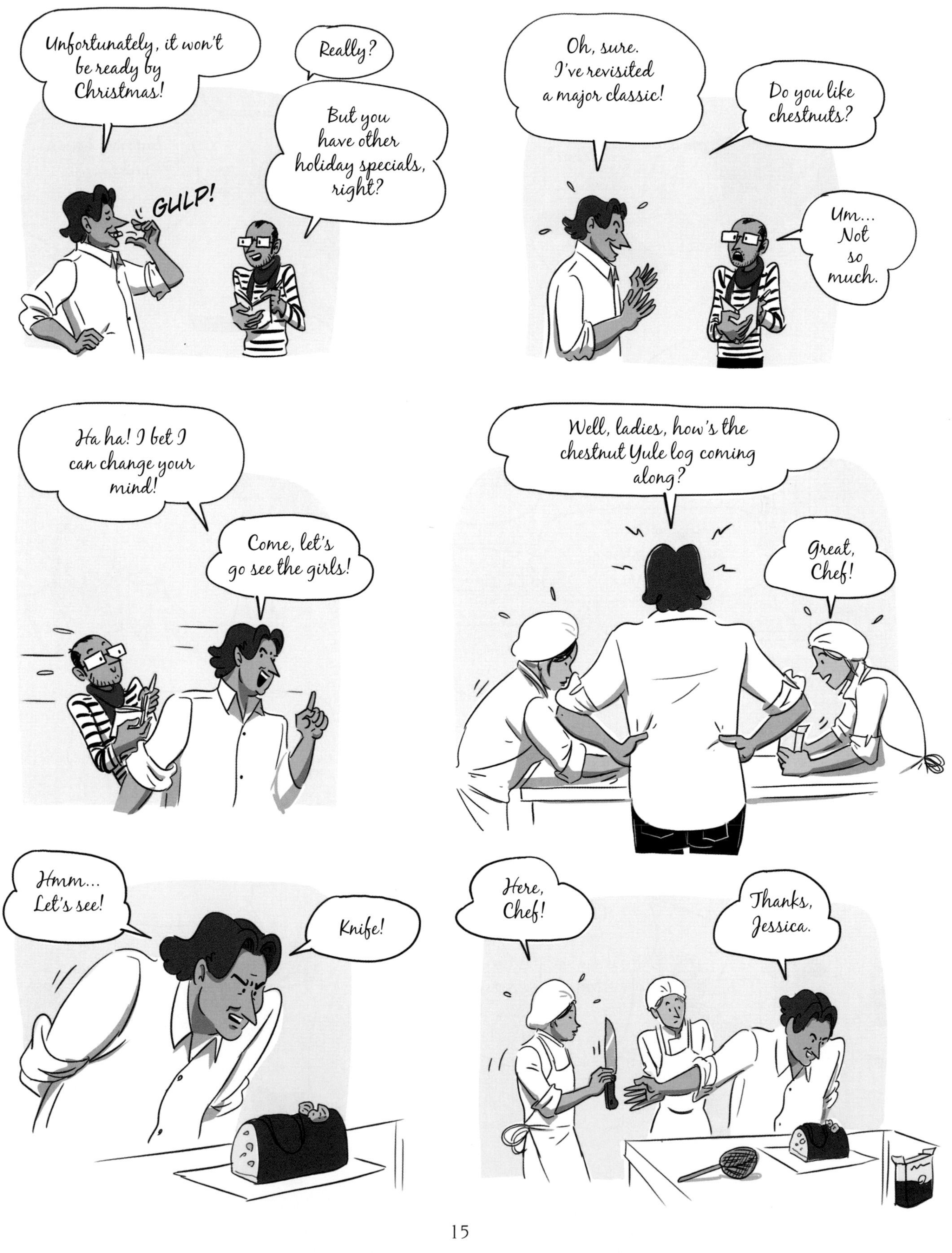
Unfortunately, it won't be ready by Christmas!
Really?
But you have other holiday specials, right?
GULP!
Oh, sure. I've revisited a major classic!
Do you like chestnuts?
Um... Not so much.
Ha ha! I bet I can change your mind!
Come, let's go see the girls!
Well, ladies, how's the chestnut Yule log coming along?
Great, Chef!
Hmm... Let's see!
Knife!
Here, Chef!
Thanks, Jessica.

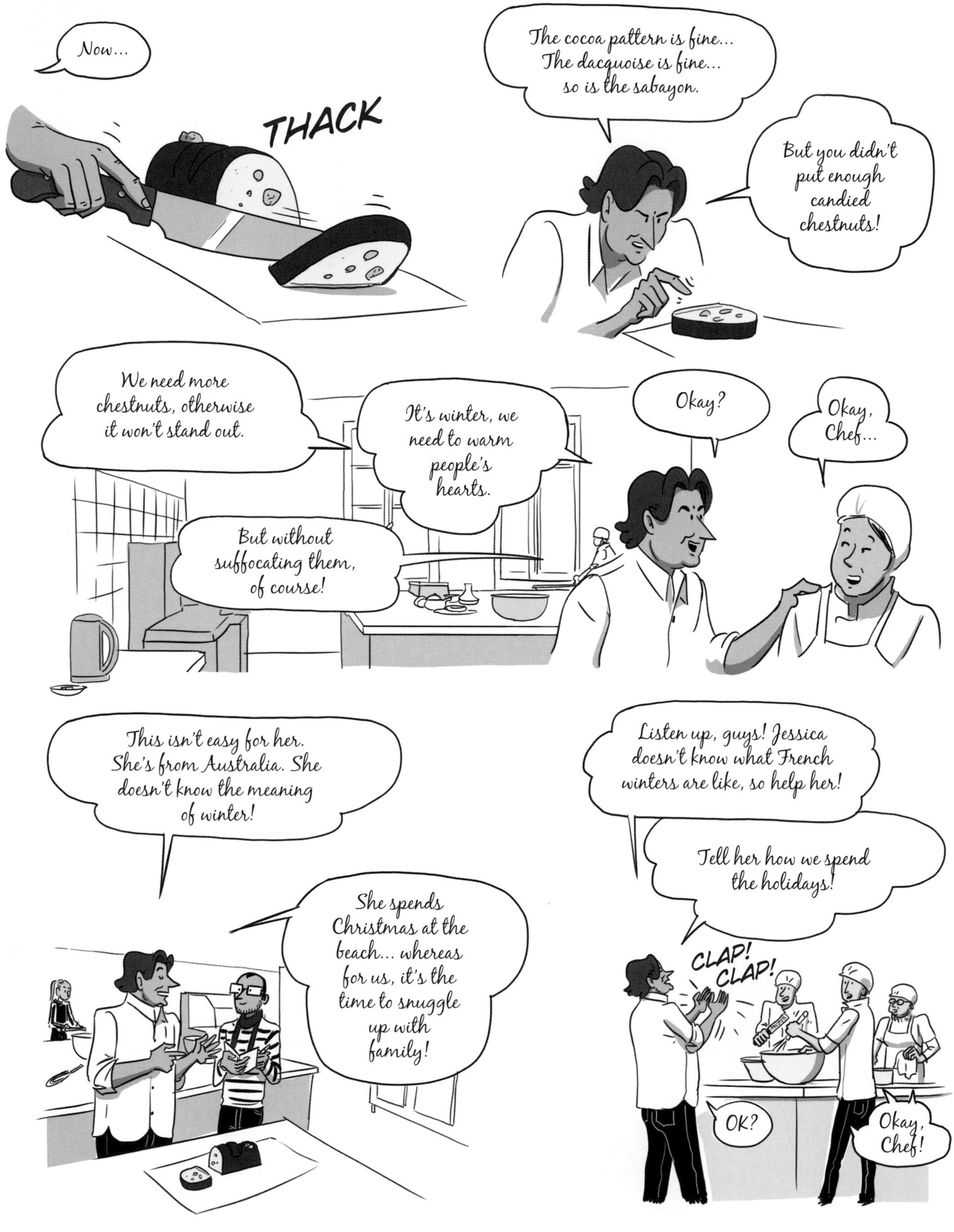

Now...
THACK
The cocoa pattern is fine... The dacquoise is fine... so is the sabayon.
But you didn't put enough candied chestnuts!
We need more chestnuts, otherwise it won't stand out.
It's winter, we need to warm people's hearts.
But without suffocating them, of course!
Okay?
Okay, Chef...
This isn't easy for her. She's from Australia. She doesn't know the meaning of winter!
She spends Christmas at the beach... whereas for us, it's the time to snuggle up with family!
Listen up, guys! Jessica doesn't know what French winters are like, so help her!
Tell her how we spend the holidays!
CLAP! CLAP!
OK?
Okay, Chef!

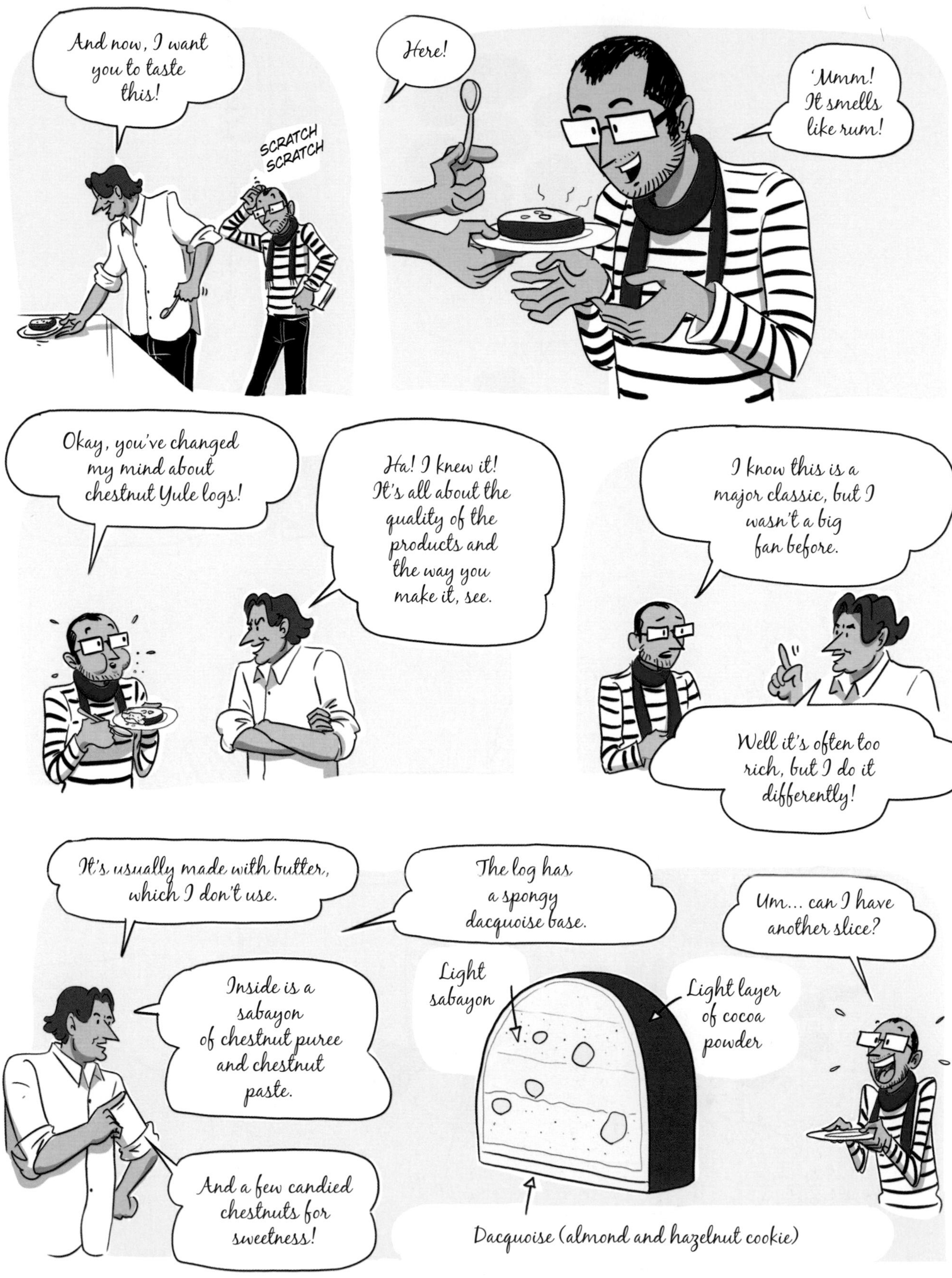
And now, I want you to taste this!
SCRATCH SCRATCH
Here!
'Mmm! It smells like rum!
Okay, you've changed my mind about chestnut Yule logs!
Ha! I knew it! It's all about the quality of the products and the way you make it, see.
I know this is a major classic, but I wasn't a big fan before.
Well it's often too rich, but I do it differently!
It's usually made with butter, which I don't use.
Inside is a sabayon of chestnut puree and chestnut paste.
And a few candied chestnuts for sweetness!
The log has a spongy dacquoise base.
Light sabayon
Light layer of cocoa powder
Dacquoise (almond and hazelnut cookie)
Um... can I have another slice?

Christmas truffles

To conclude our first chocolicious day, Jacques suggested I help him come up with a seasonal recipe!

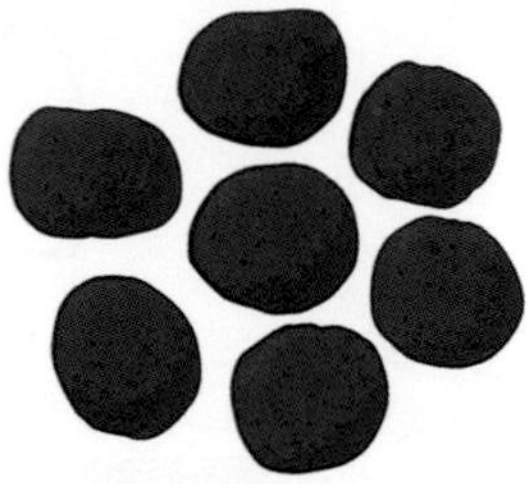

Tip: best to make them the day before.

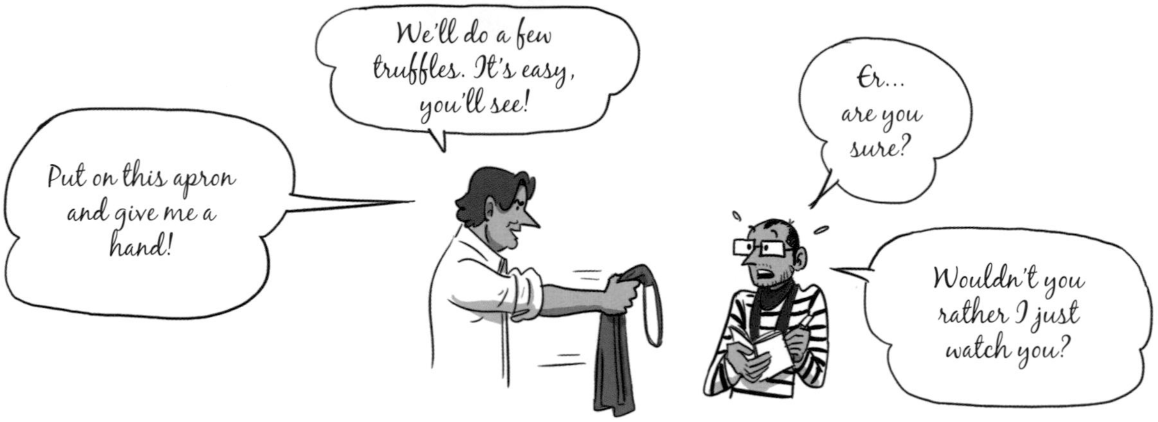
We'll do a few truffles. It's easy, you'll see!
Put on this apron and give me a hand!
Er... are you sure?
Wouldn't you rather I just watch you?

Okay, so, to satisfy a sweet tooth or two, we need:

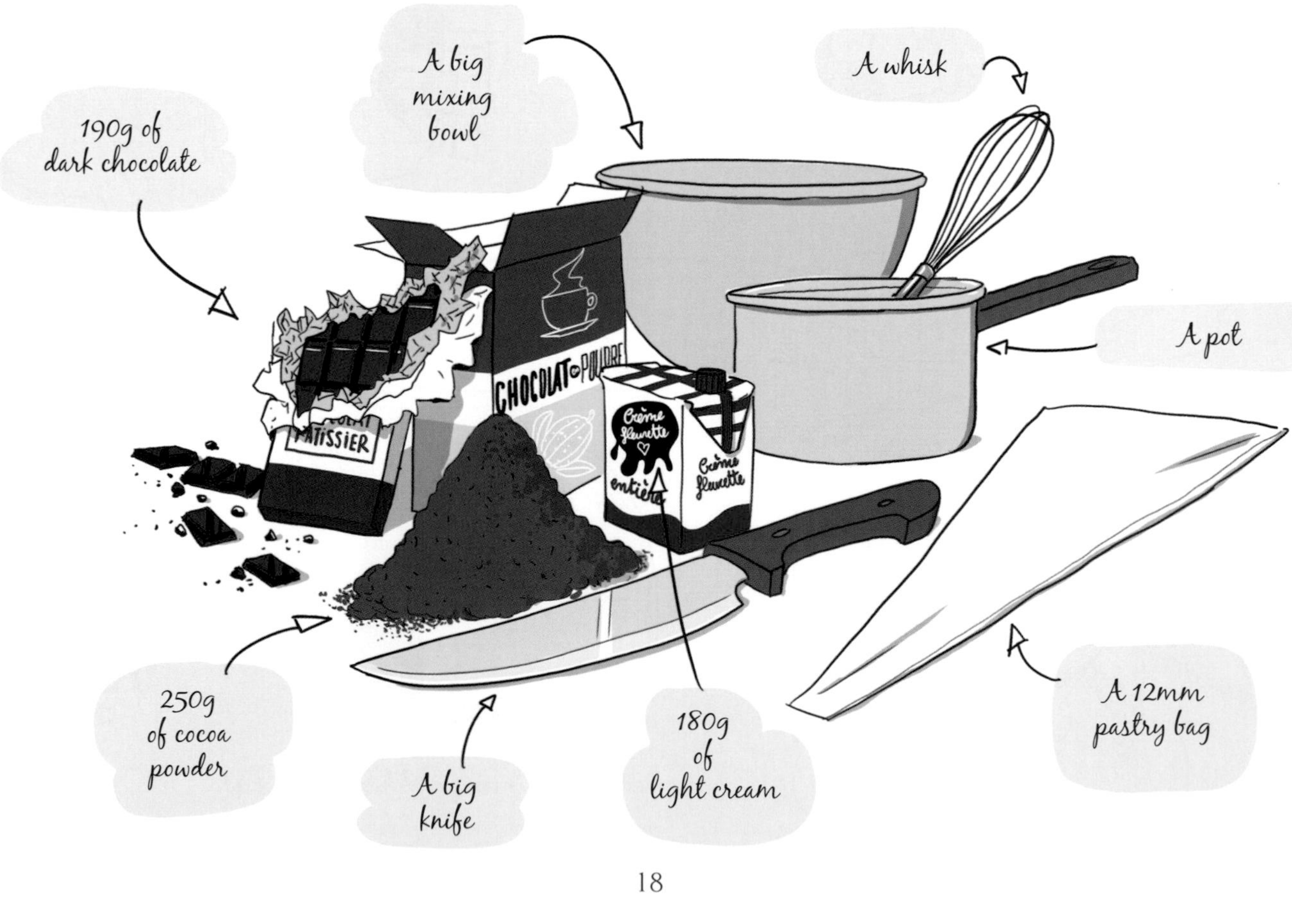
190g of dark chocolate
A big mixing bowl
A whisk
A pot
250g of cocoa powder
A big knife
180g of light cream
A 12mm pastry bag

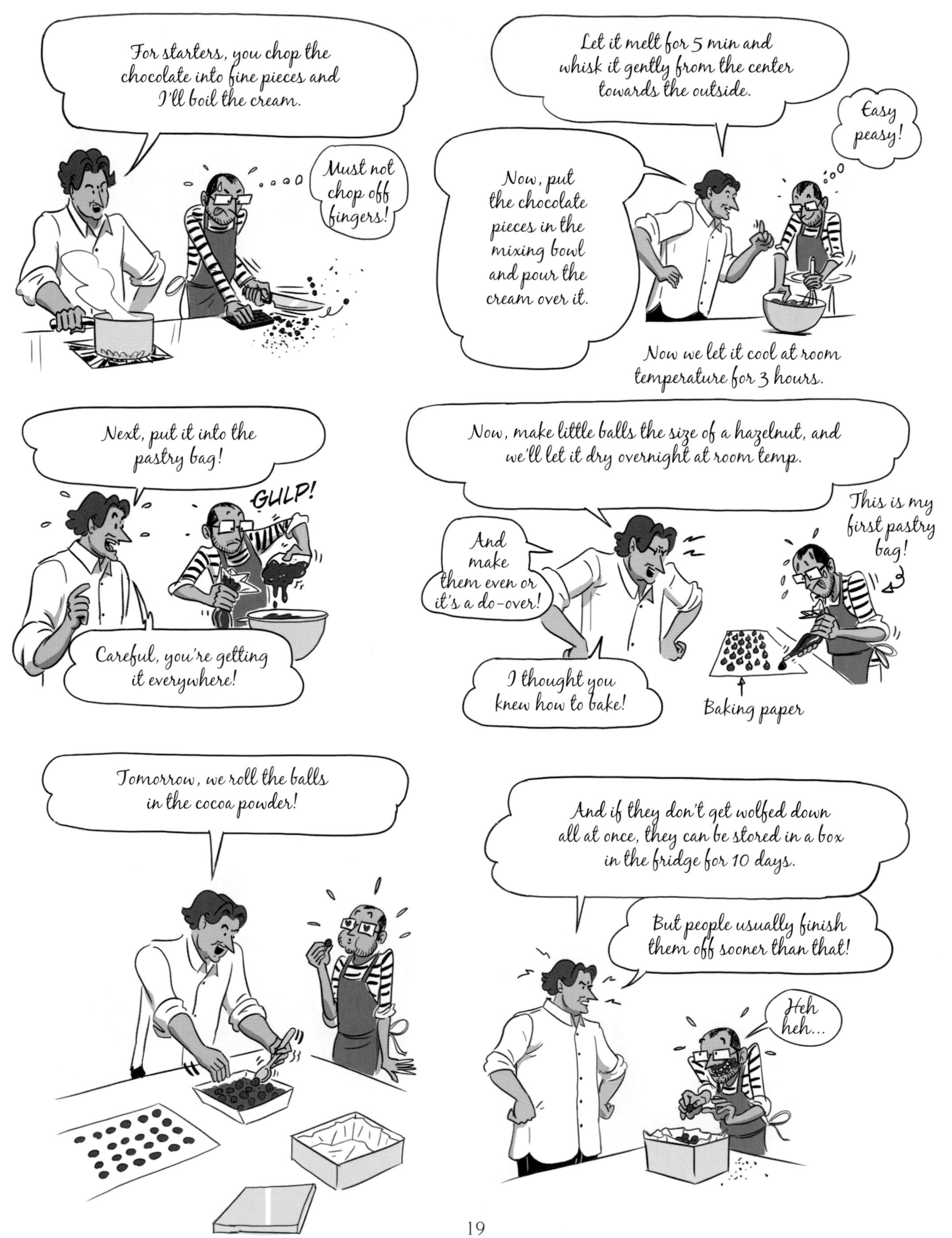
For starters, you chop the chocolate into fine pieces and I'll boil the cream.
Must not chop off fingers!
Let it melt for 5 min and whisk it gently from the center towards the outside.
Easy peasy!
Now, put the chocolate pieces in the mixing bowl and pour the cream over it.
Now we let it cool at room temperature for 3 hours.
Next, put it into the pastry bag!
GULP!
Careful, you're getting it everywhere!
Now, make little balls the size of a hazelnut, and we'll let it dry overnight at room temp.
And make them even or it's a do-over!
This is my first pastry bag!
I thought you knew how to bake!
Baking paper
Tomorrow, we roll the balls in the cocoa powder!
And if they don't get wolfed down all at once, they can be stored in a box in the fridge for 10 days.
But people usually finish them off sooner than that!
Heh heh...

The ordeal known as the pastry bag

If you're like me and have never once held a pastry bag in your hand...

...here are a few tips I stole from Chef Genin!

First, the equipment!

A bag with nozzles

A cake spatula

A clothespin

1. First, insert the nozzle and cut the tip of the pastry bag.

Snip snip!

2. Then, pinch the tip of your bag with the clothespin.

Snap!

3. Fold the top of the pastry bag over

4. Use your spatula to scoop up a lot of filling.

5. Fill up the bag pressing down with your index finger.

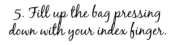

Push down here.

6. Squeeze the bag so as to compress the chocolate.

Hold the bag firmly between your thumb and index finger.

7. Flip the bag upside down and remove the clothespin.

Ponk!

8. Press and turn as you go to gently squeeze out the filling!

Bingo!

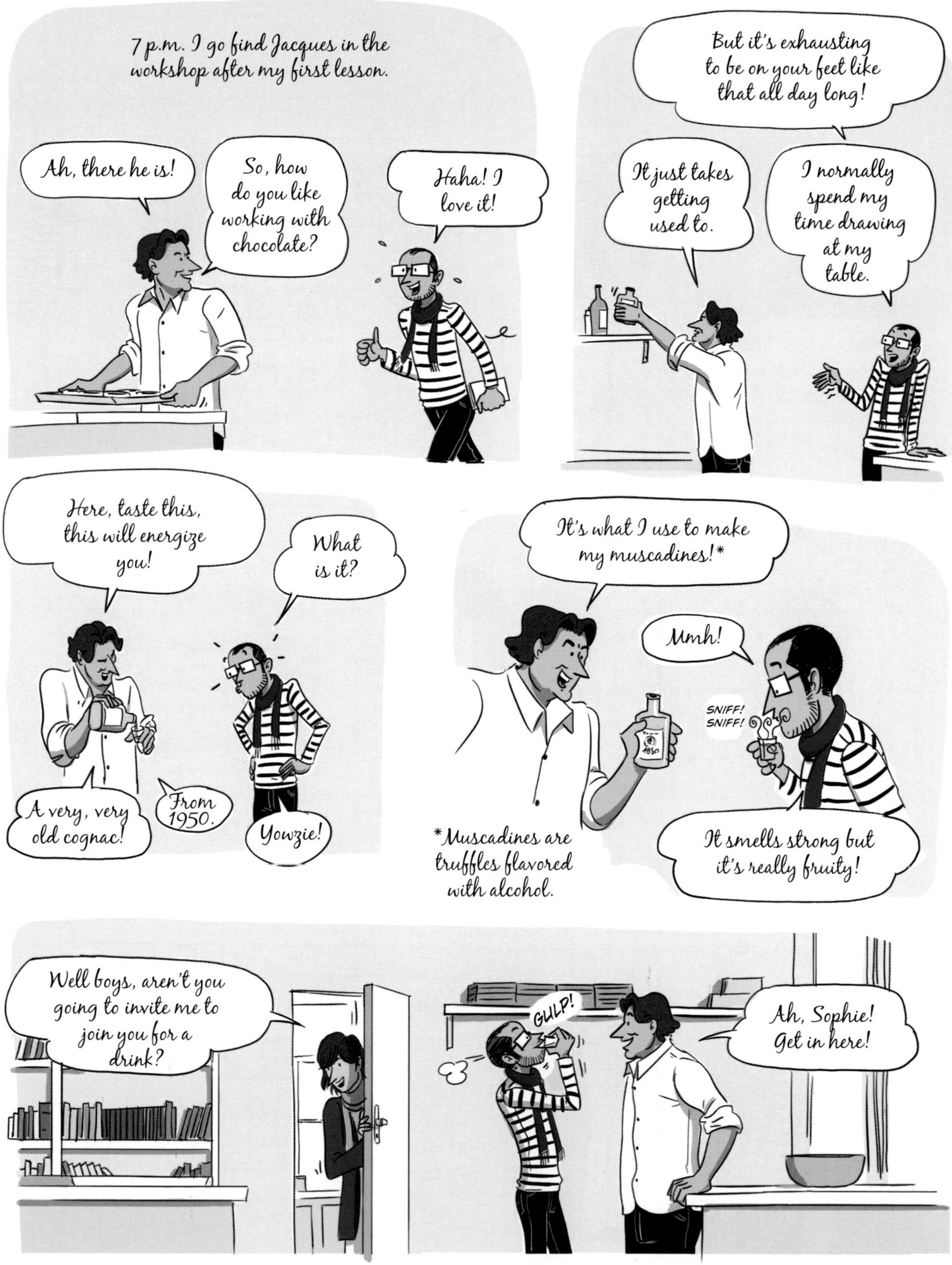
7 p.m. I go find Jacques in the workshop after my first lesson.
Ah, there he is!
So, how do you like working with chocolate?
Haha! I love it!
But it's exhausting to be on your feet like that all day long!
It just takes getting used to.
I normally spend my time drawing at my table.
Here, taste this, this will energize you!
What is it?
A very, very old cognac!
From 1950.
Yowzie!
It's what I use to make my muscadines!*
Mmh!
SNIFF! SNIFF!
It smells strong but it's really fruity!
*Muscadines are truffles flavored with alcohol.
Well boys, aren't you going to invite me to join you for a drink?
GULP!
Ah, Sophie! Get in here!

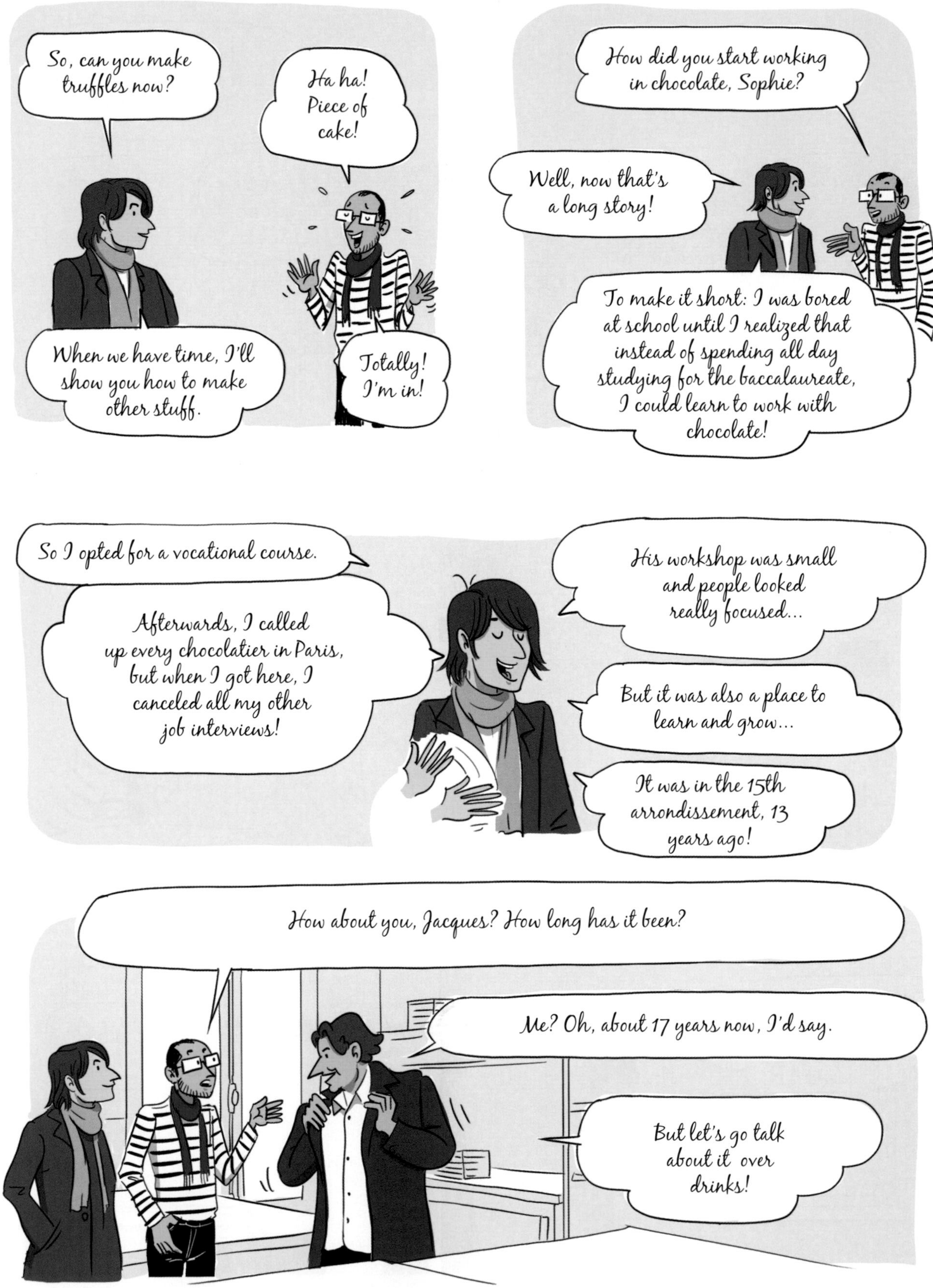
So, can you make truffles now?
Ha ha! Piece of cake!
When we have time, I'll show you how to make other stuff.
Totally! I'm in!
How did you start working in chocolate, Sophie?
Well, now that's a long story!
To make it short: I was bored at school until I realized that instead of spending all day studying for the baccalaureate, I could learn to work with chocolate!
So I opted for a vocational course.
Afterwards, I called up every chocolatier in Paris, but when I got here, I canceled all my other job interviews!
His workshop was small and people looked really focused...
But it was also a place to learn and grow...
It was in the 15th arrondissement, 13 years ago!
How about you, Jacques? How long has it been?
Me? Oh, about 17 years now, I'd say.
But let's go talk about it over drinks!

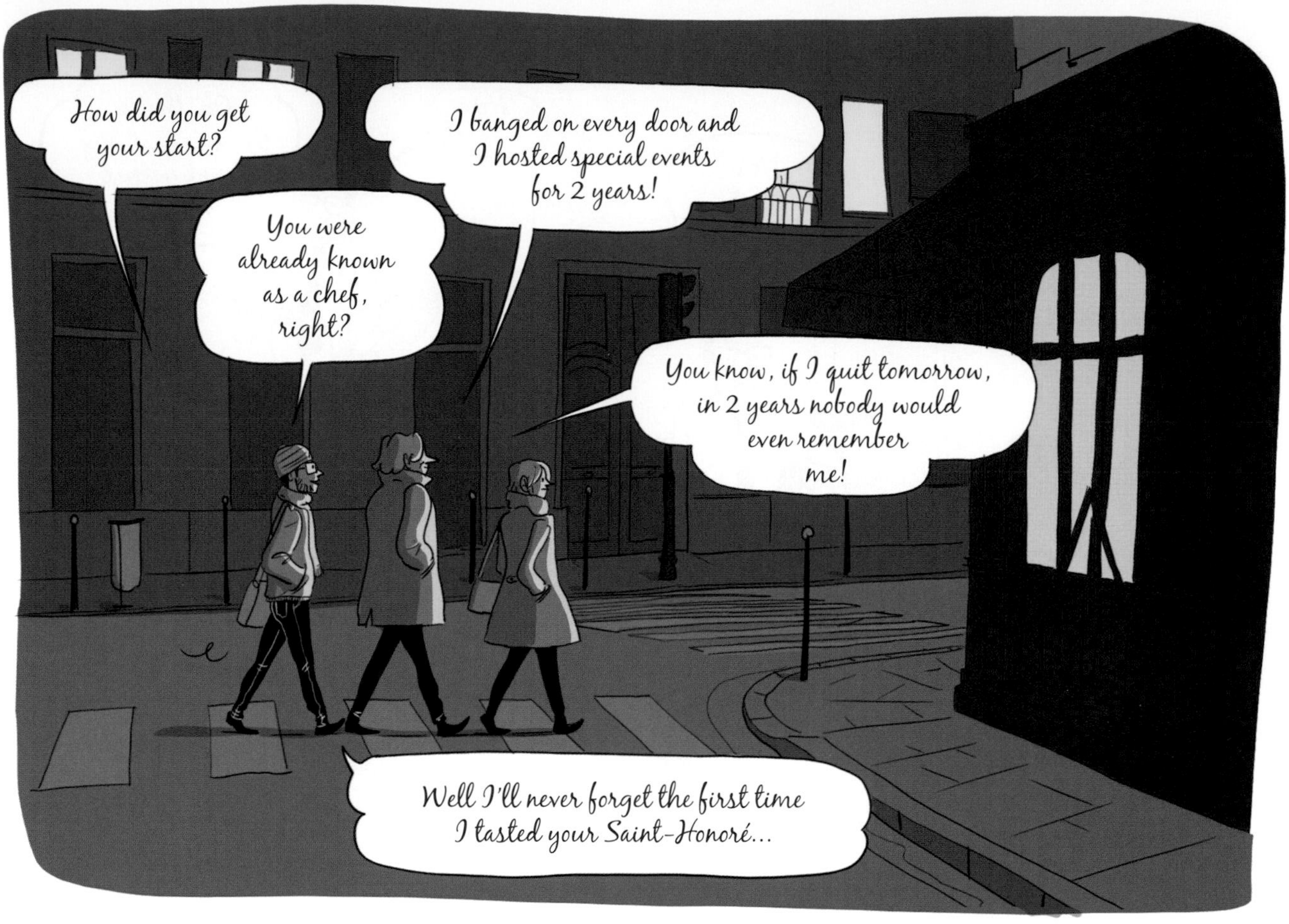
How did you get your start?
You were already known as a chef, right?
I banged on every door and I hosted special events for 2 years!
You know, if I quit tomorrow, in 2 years nobody would even remember me!
Well I'll never forget the first time I tasted your Saint-Honoré...

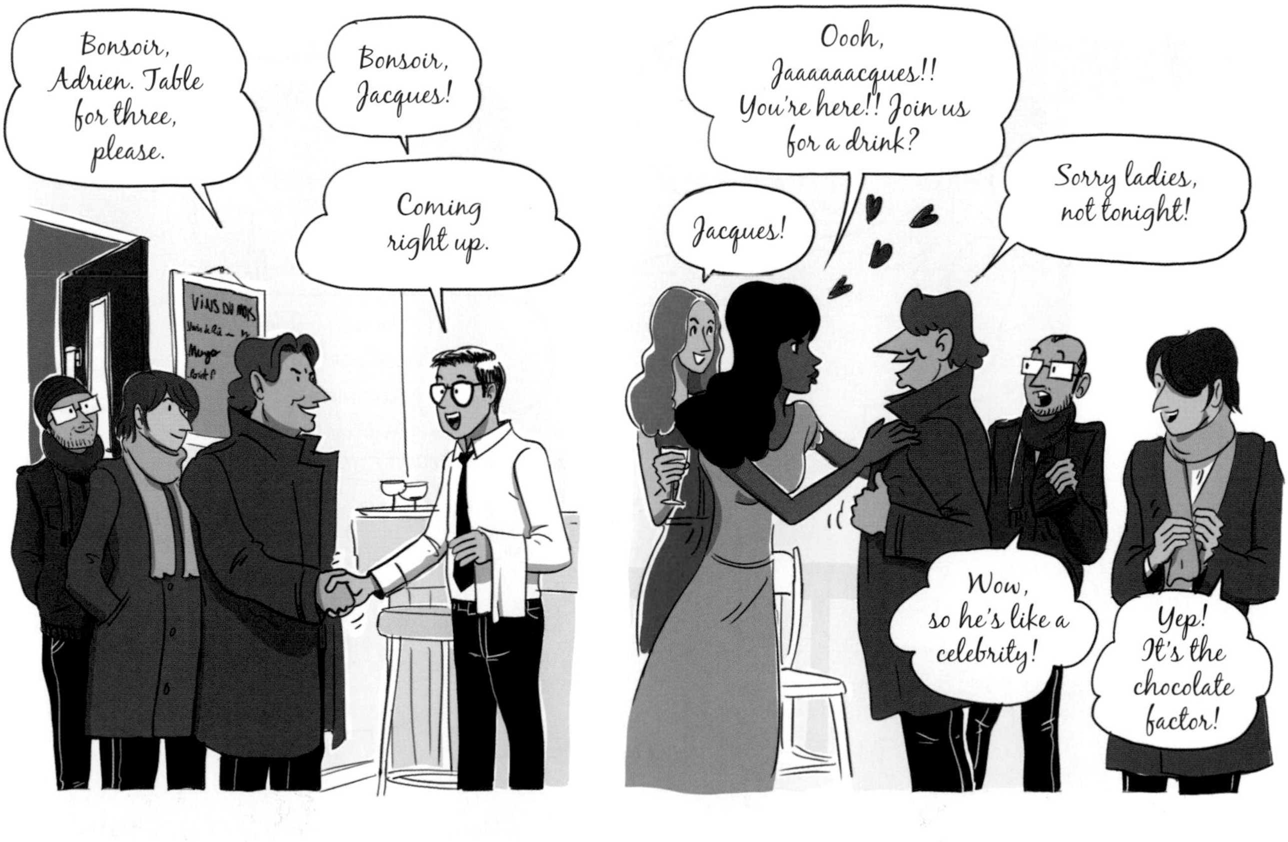
Bonsoir, Adrien. Table for three, please.
Bonsoir, Jacques!
Coming right up.
VINS DU MOIS
Oooh, Jaaaaaacques!! You're here!! Join us for a drink?
Jacques!
Sorry ladies, not tonight!
Wow, so he's like a celebrity!
Yep! It's the chocolate factor!

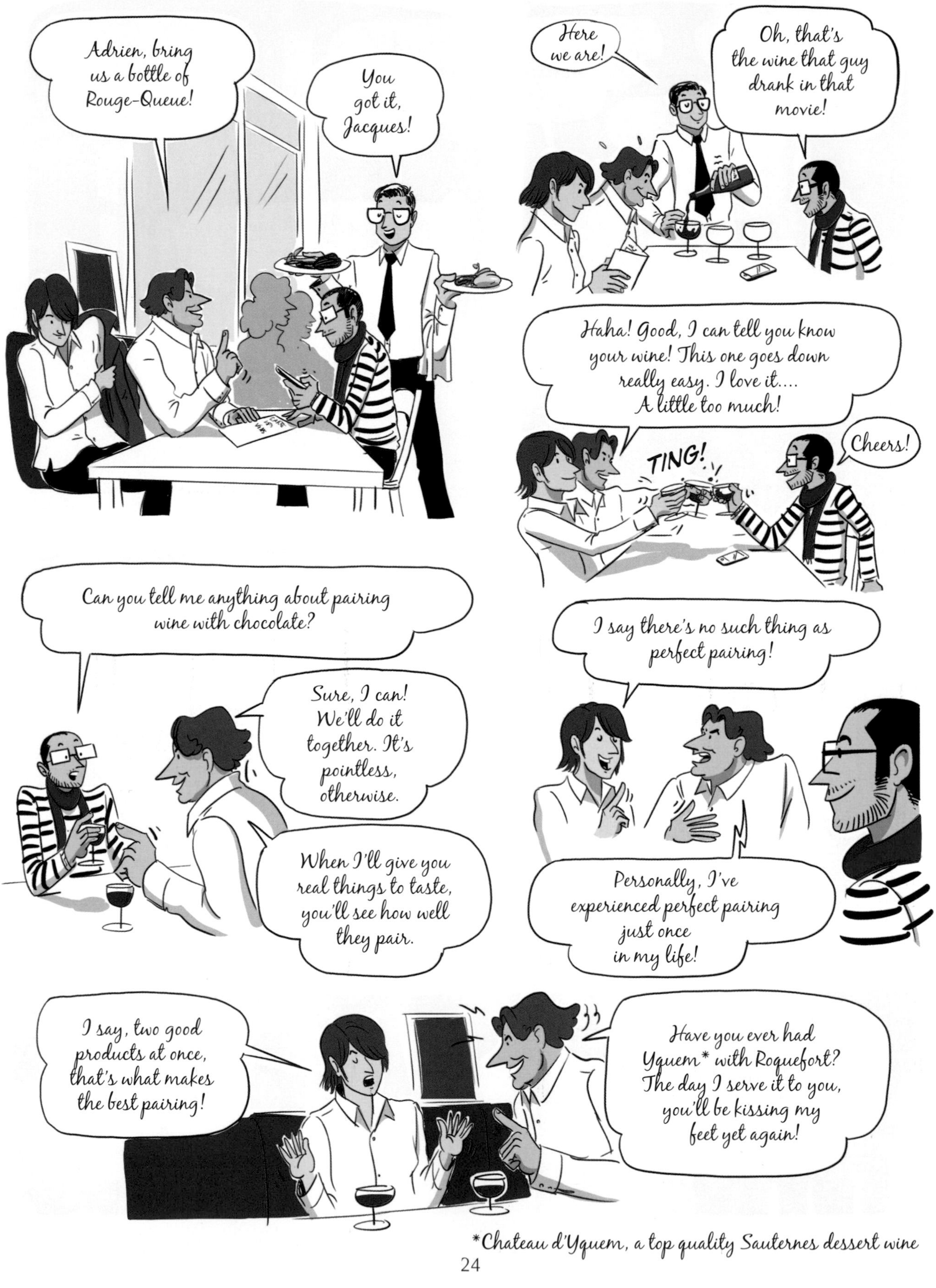
Adrien, bring us a bottle of Rouge-Queue!
You got it, Jacques!
Here we are!
Oh, that's the wine that guy drank in that movie!
Haha! Good, I can tell you know your wine! This one goes down really easy. I love it.... A little too much!
TING!
Cheers!
Can you tell me anything about pairing wine with chocolate?
Sure, I can! We'll do it together. It's pointless, otherwise.
When I'll give you real things to taste, you'll see how well they pair.
I say there's no such thing as perfect pairing!
Personally, I've experienced perfect pairing just once in my life!
I say, two good products at once, that's what makes the best pairing!
Have you ever had Yquem* with Roquefort? The day I serve it to you, you'll be kissing my feet yet again!

*Chateau d'Yquem, a top quality Sauternes dessert wine

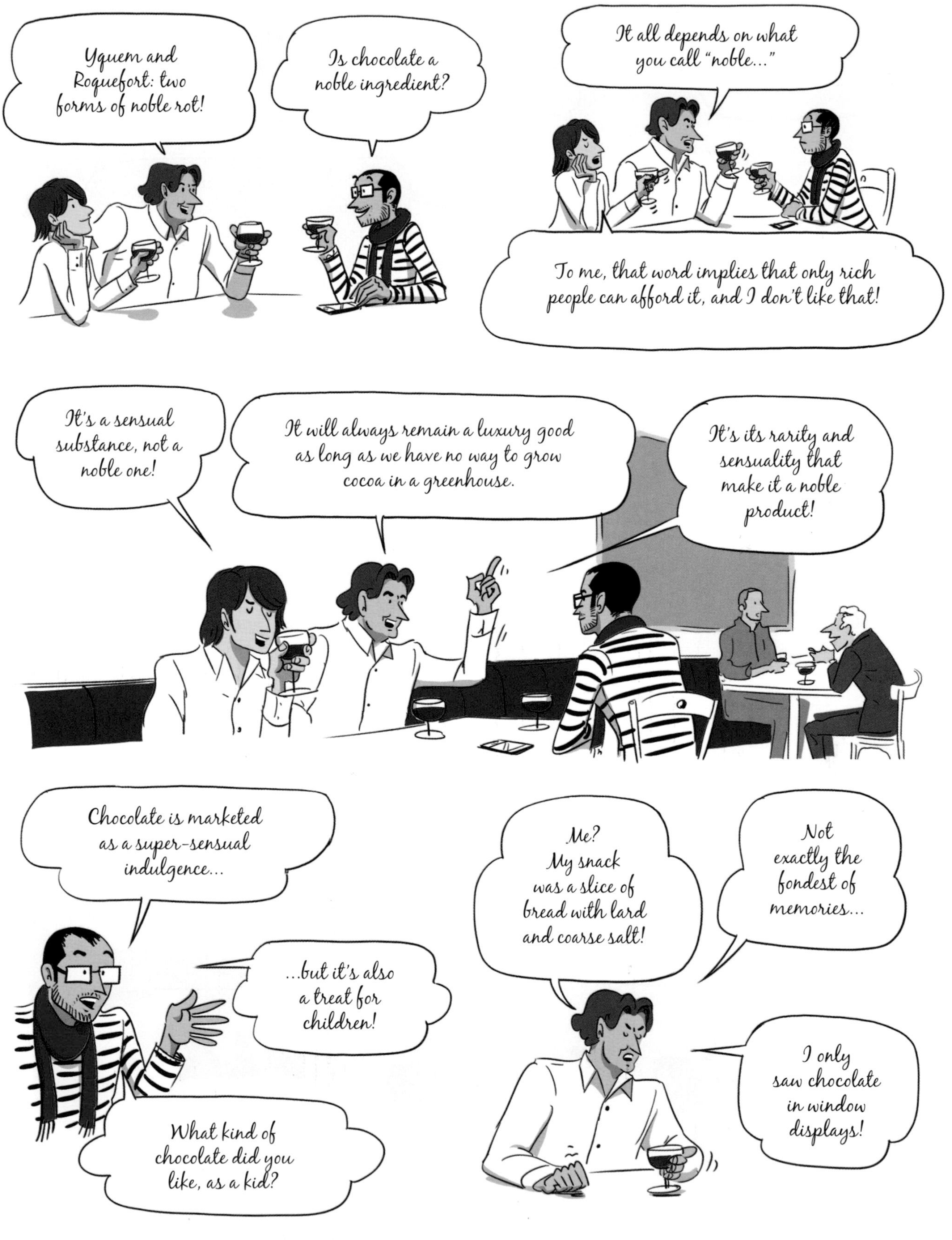
Yquem and Roquefort: two forms of noble rot!
Is chocolate a noble ingredient?
It all depends on what you call "noble..."
To me, that word implies that only rich people can afford it, and I don't like that!
It's a sensual substance, not a noble one!
It will always remain a luxury good as long as we have no way to grow cocoa in a greenhouse.
It's its rarity and sensuality that make it a noble product!
Chocolate is marketed as a super-sensual indulgence...
...but it's also a treat for children!
What kind of chocolate did you like, as a kid?
Me? My snack was a slice of bread with lard and coarse salt!
Not exactly the fondest of memories...
I only saw chocolate in window displays!

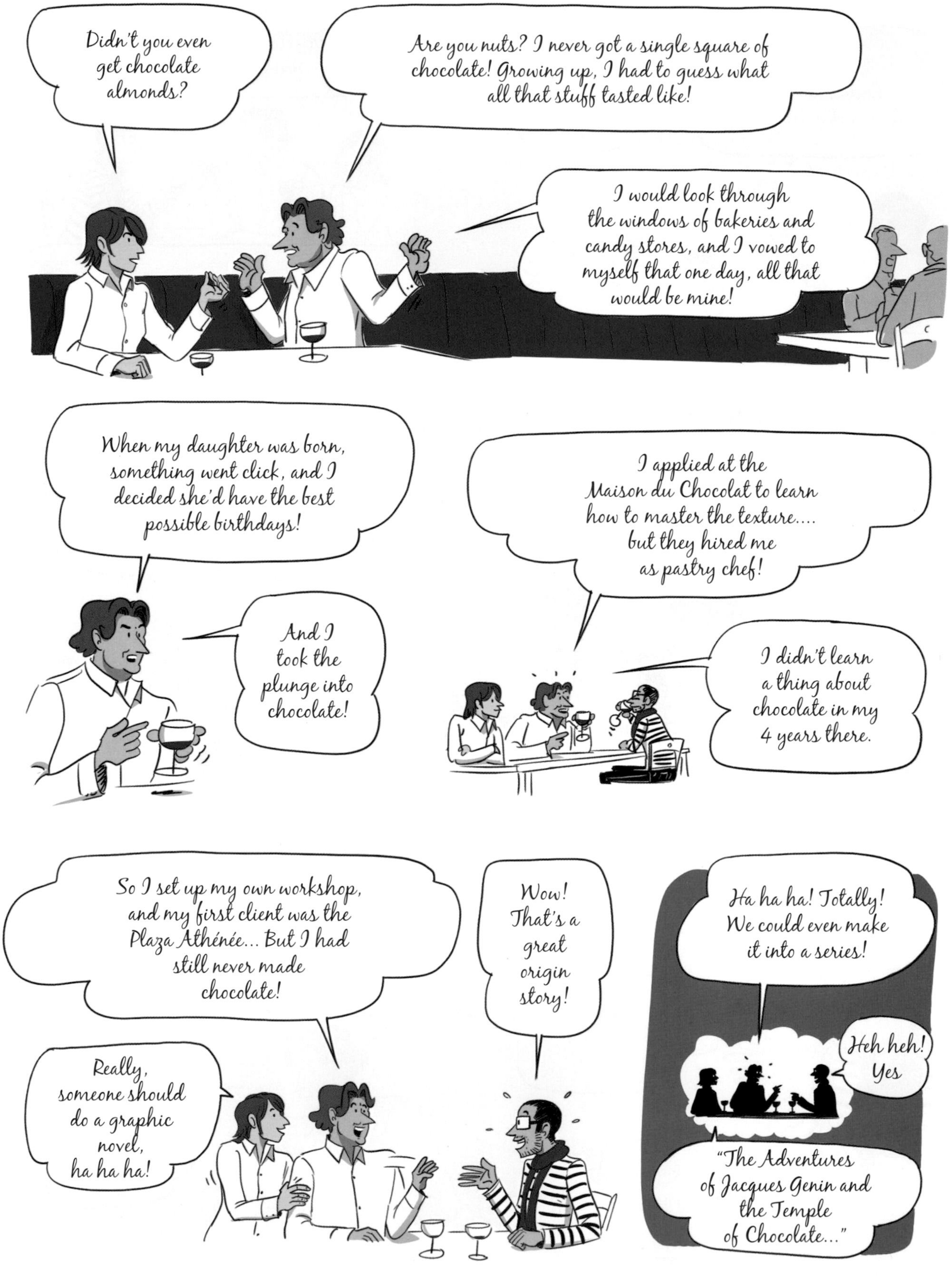
Didn't you even get chocolate almonds?
Are you nuts? I never got a single square of chocolate! Growing up, I had to guess what all that stuff tasted like!
I would look through the windows of bakeries and candy stores, and I vowed to myself that one day, all that would be mine!
When my daughter was born, something went click, and I decided she'd have the best possible birthdays!
And I took the plunge into chocolate!
I applied at the Maison du Chocolat to learn how to master the texture.... but they hired me as pastry chef!
I didn't learn a thing about chocolate in my 4 years there.
So I set up my own workshop, and my first client was the Plaza Athénée... But I had still never made chocolate!
Wow! That's a great origin story!
Really, someone should do a graphic novel, ha ha ha!
Ha ha ha! Totally! We could even make it into a series!
Heh heh! Yes
"The Adventures of Jacques Genin and the Temple of Chocolate..."

CHOCOLATES

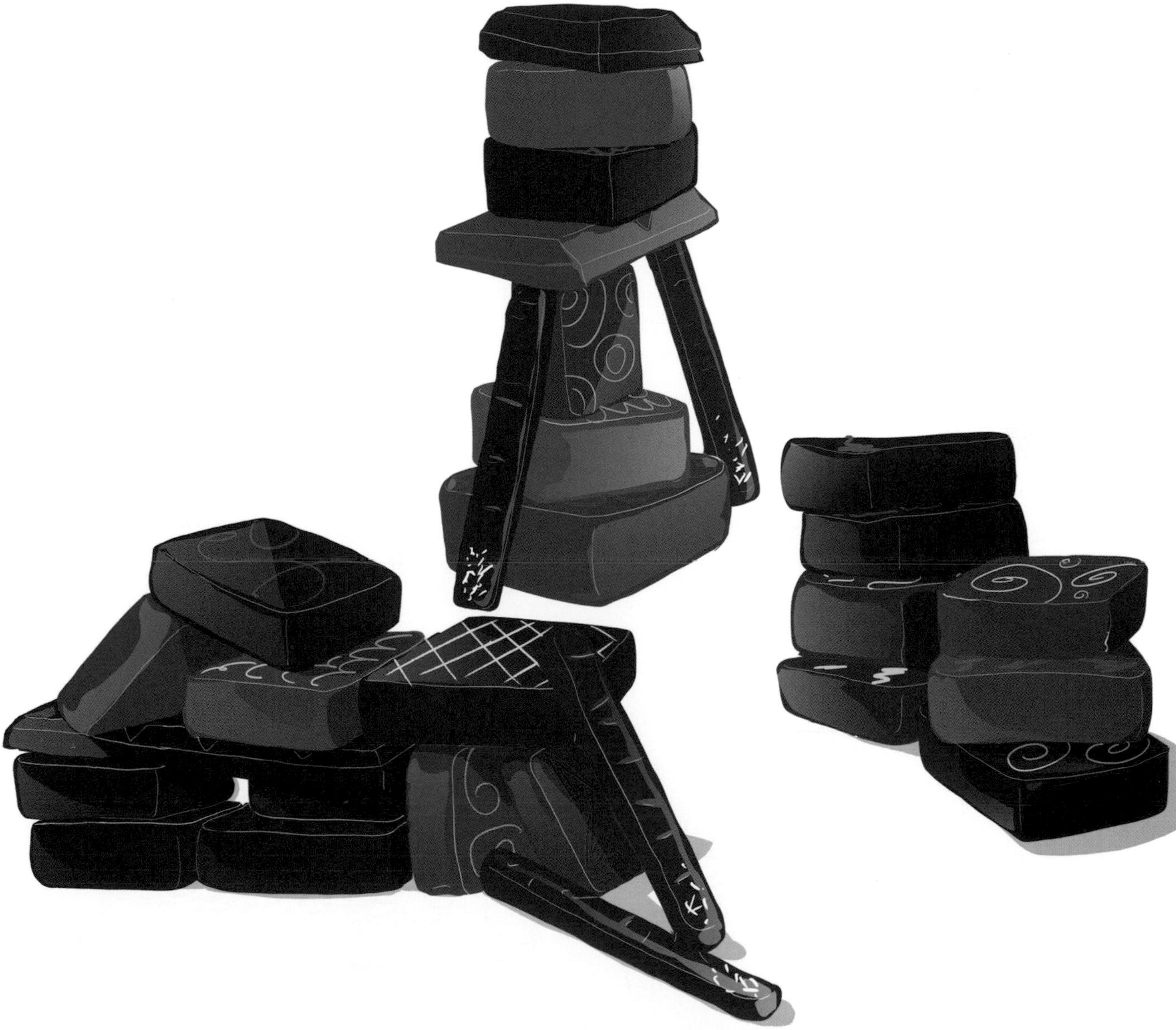

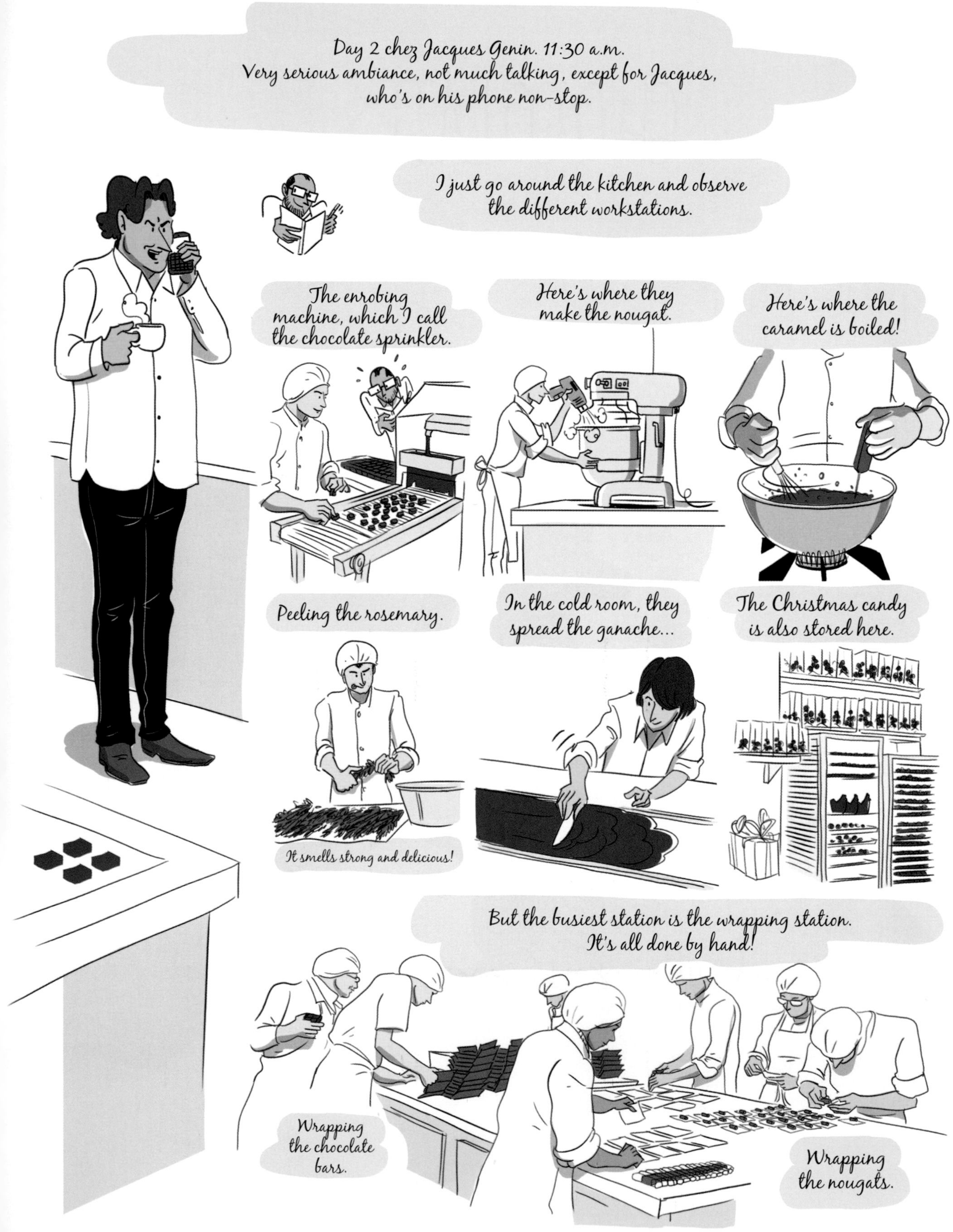
Day 2 chez Jacques Genin. 11:30 a.m.
Very serious ambiance, not much talking, except for Jacques, who's on his phone non-stop.
I just go around the kitchen and observe the different workstations.
The enrobing machine, which I call the chocolate sprinkler.
Here's where they make the nougat.
Here's where the caramel is boiled!
Peeling the rosemary.
It smells strong and delicious!
In the cold room, they spread the ganache...
The Christmas candy is also stored here.
But the busiest station is the wrapping station. It's all done by hand!
Wrapping the chocolate bars.
Wrapping the nougats.

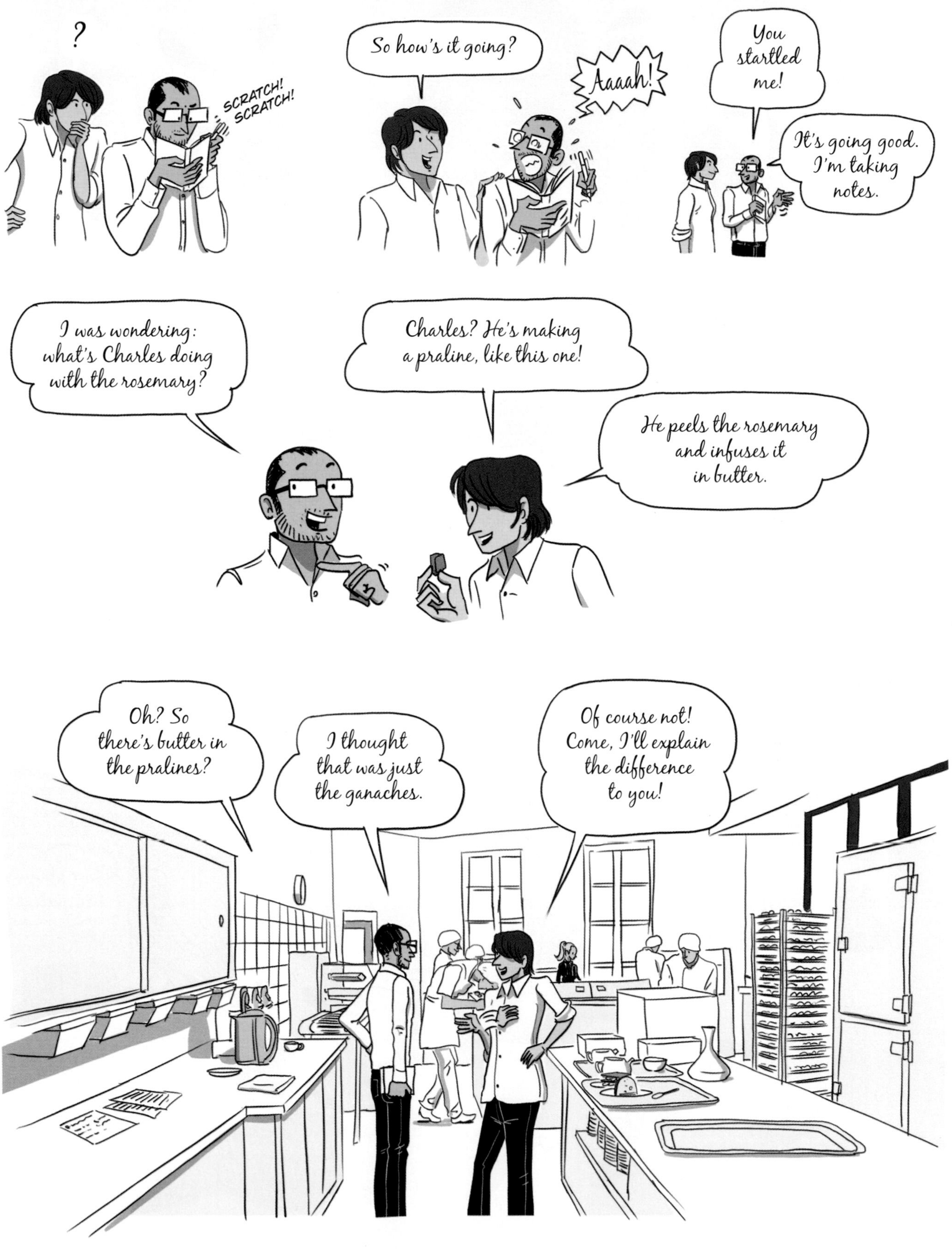
?
SCRATCH! SCRATCH!
So how's it going?
Aaaah!
You startled me!
It's going good. I'm taking notes.
I was wondering: what's Charles doing with the rosemary?
Charles? He's making a praline, like this one!
He peels the rosemary and infuses it in butter.
Oh? So there's butter in the pralines?
I thought that was just the ganaches.
Of course not! Come, I'll explain the difference to you!

Pralines

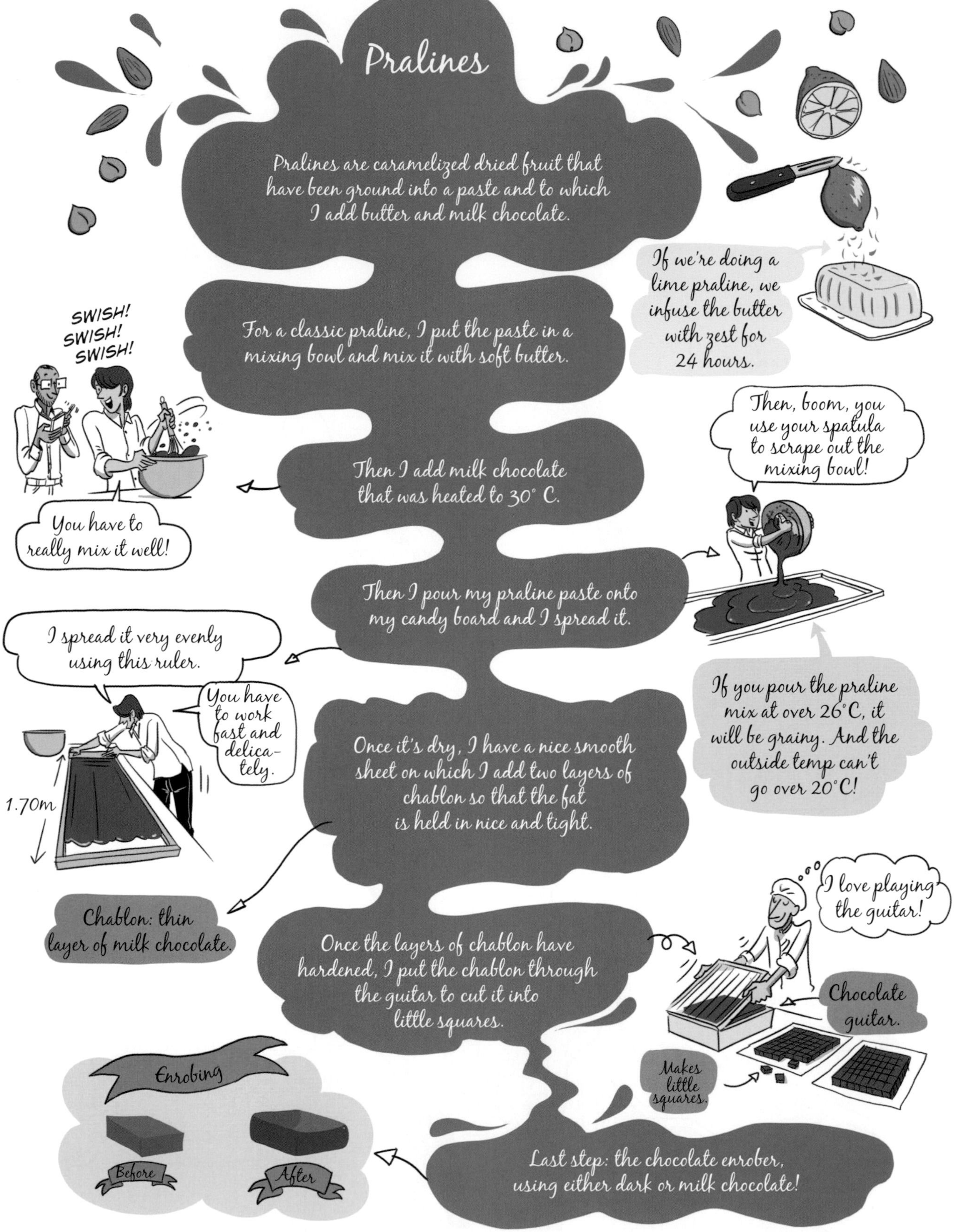
Pralines are caramelized dried fruit that have been ground into a paste and to which I add butter and milk chocolate.
If we're doing a lime praline, we infuse the butter with zest for 24 hours.
For a classic praline, I put the paste in a mixing bowl and mix it with soft butter.
SWISH! SWISH! SWISH!
Then I add milk chocolate that was heated to 30° C.
You have to really mix it well!
Then, boom, you use your spatula to scrape out the mixing bowl!
Then I pour my praline paste onto my candy board and I spread it.
I spread it very evenly using this ruler.
You have to work fast and delica-tely.
1.70m
If you pour the praline mix at over 26°C, it will be grainy. And the outside temp can't go over 20°C!
Once it's dry, I have a nice smooth sheet on which I add two layers of chablon so that the fat is held in nice and tight.
Chablon: thin layer of milk chocolate.
I love playing the guitar!
Once the layers of chablon have hardened, I put the chablon through the guitar to cut it into little squares.
Chocolate guitar.
Makes little squares.
Last step: the chocolate enrober, using either dark or milk chocolate!
Enrobing
Before
After

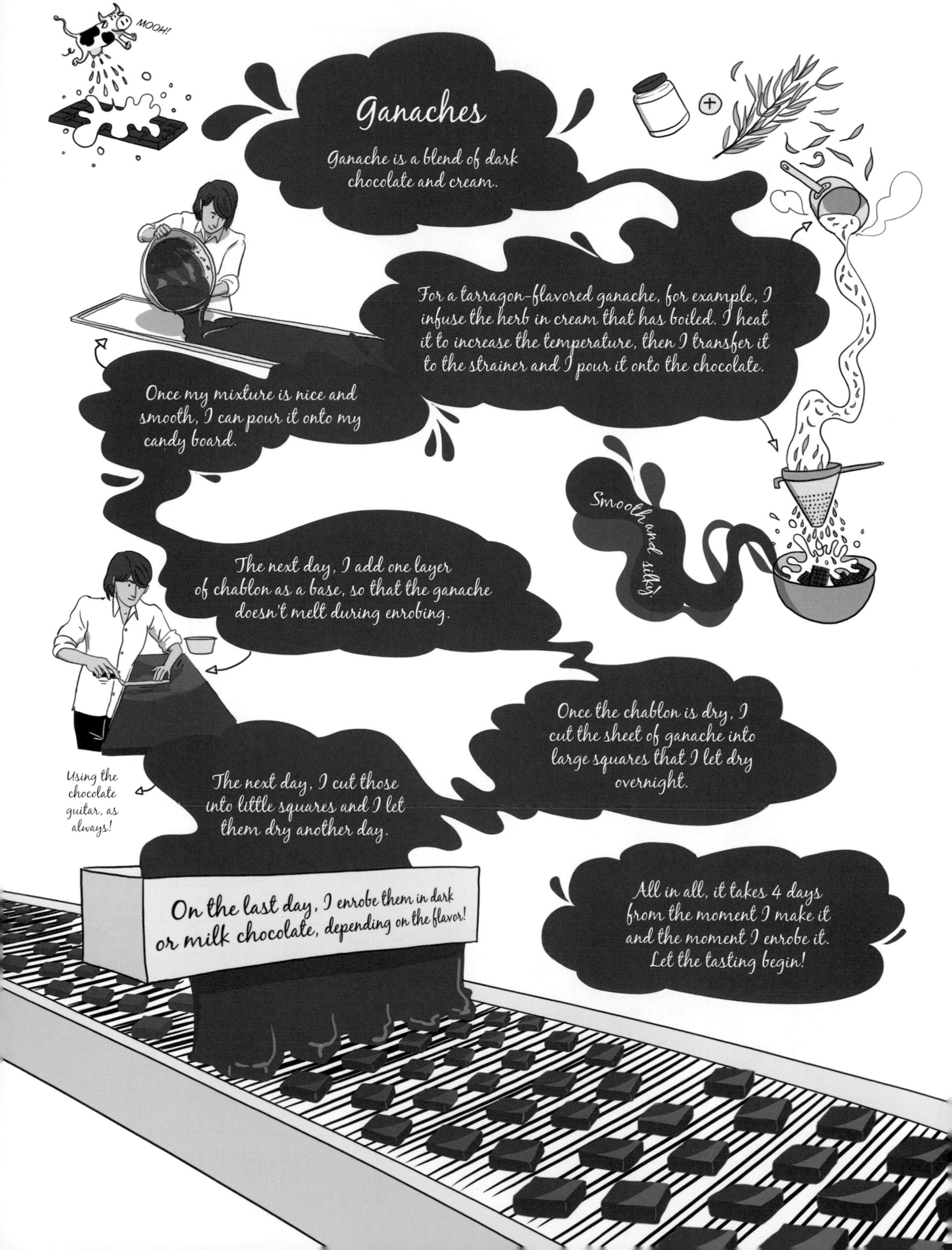
MOOH!
Ganaches
Ganache is a blend of dark chocolate and cream.
For a tarragon-flavored ganache, for example, I infuse the herb in cream that has boiled. I heat it to increase the temperature, then I transfer it to the strainer and I pour it onto the chocolate.
Smooth and silky!
Once my mixture is nice and smooth, I can pour it onto my candy board.
The next day, I add one layer of chablon as a base, so that the ganache doesn't melt during enrobing.
Once the chablon is dry, I cut the sheet of ganache into large squares that I let dry overnight.
Using the chocolate guitar, as always!
The next day, I cut those into little squares and I let them dry another day.
On the last day, I enrobe them in dark or milk chocolate, depending on the flavor!
All in all, it takes 4 days from the moment I make it and the moment I enrobe it. Let the tasting begin!

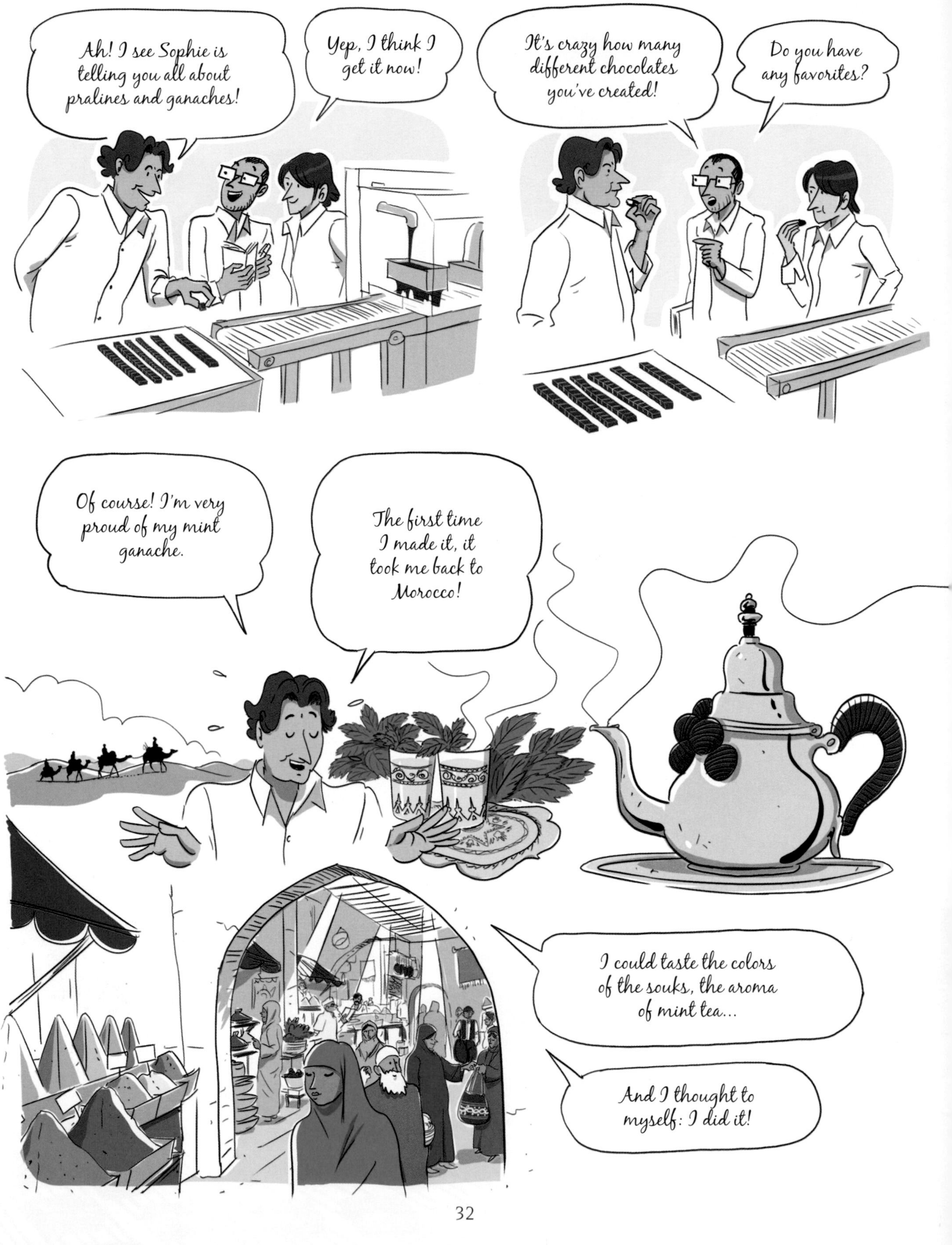
Ah! I see Sophie is telling you all about pralines and ganaches!
Yep, I think I get it now!
It's crazy how many different chocolates you've created!
Do you have any favorites?
Of course! I'm very proud of my mint ganache.
The first time I made it, it took me back to Morocco!
I could taste the colors of the souks, the aroma of mint tea...
And I thought to myself: I did it!

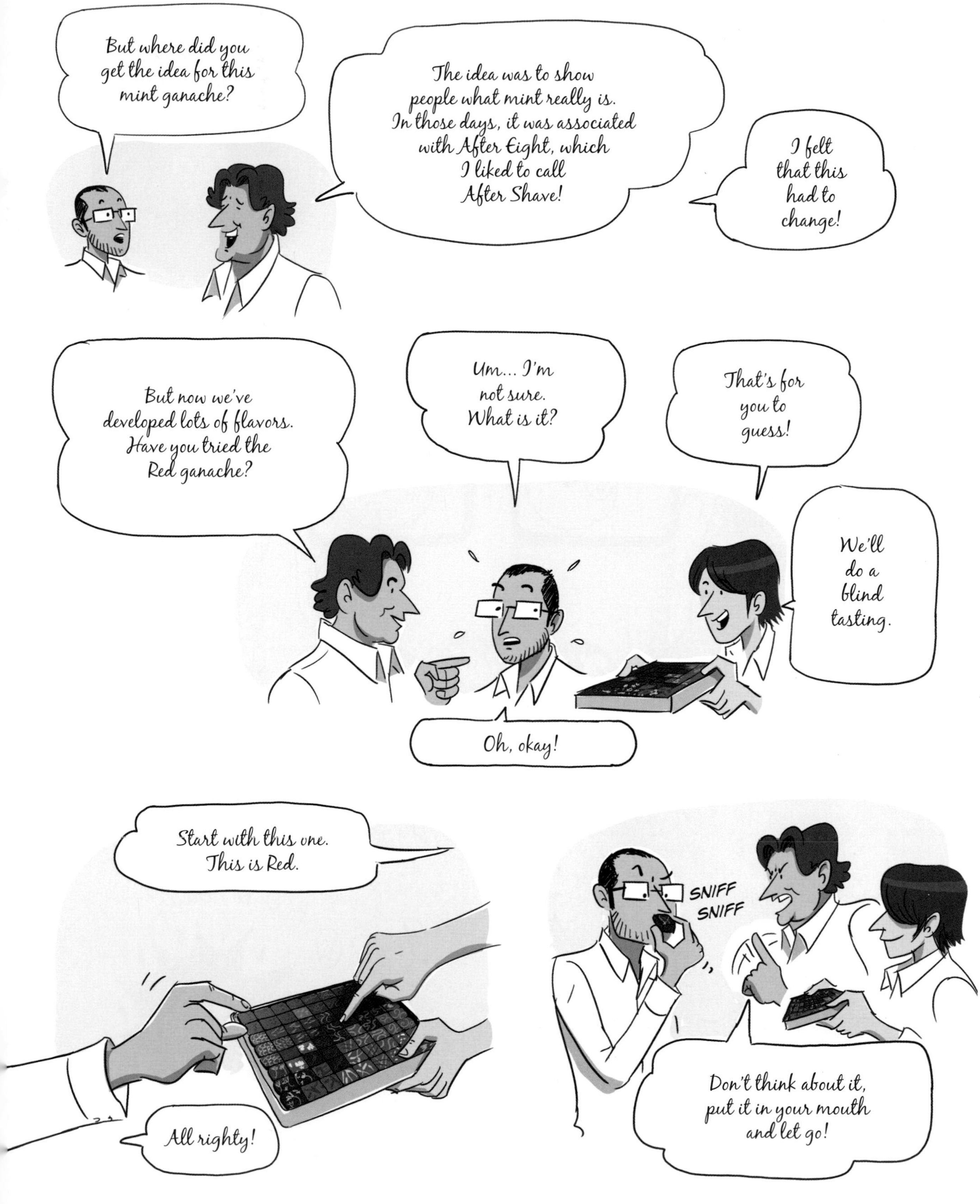
But where did you get the idea for this mint ganache?
The idea was to show people what mint really is. In those days, it was associated with After Eight, which I liked to call After Shave!
I felt that this had to change!
But now we've developed lots of flavors. Have you tried the Red ganache?
Um... I'm not sure. What is it?
That's for you to guess!
We'll do a blind tasting.
Oh, okay!
Start with this one. This is Red.
All righty!
SNIFF SNIFF
Don't think about it, put it in your mouth and let go!

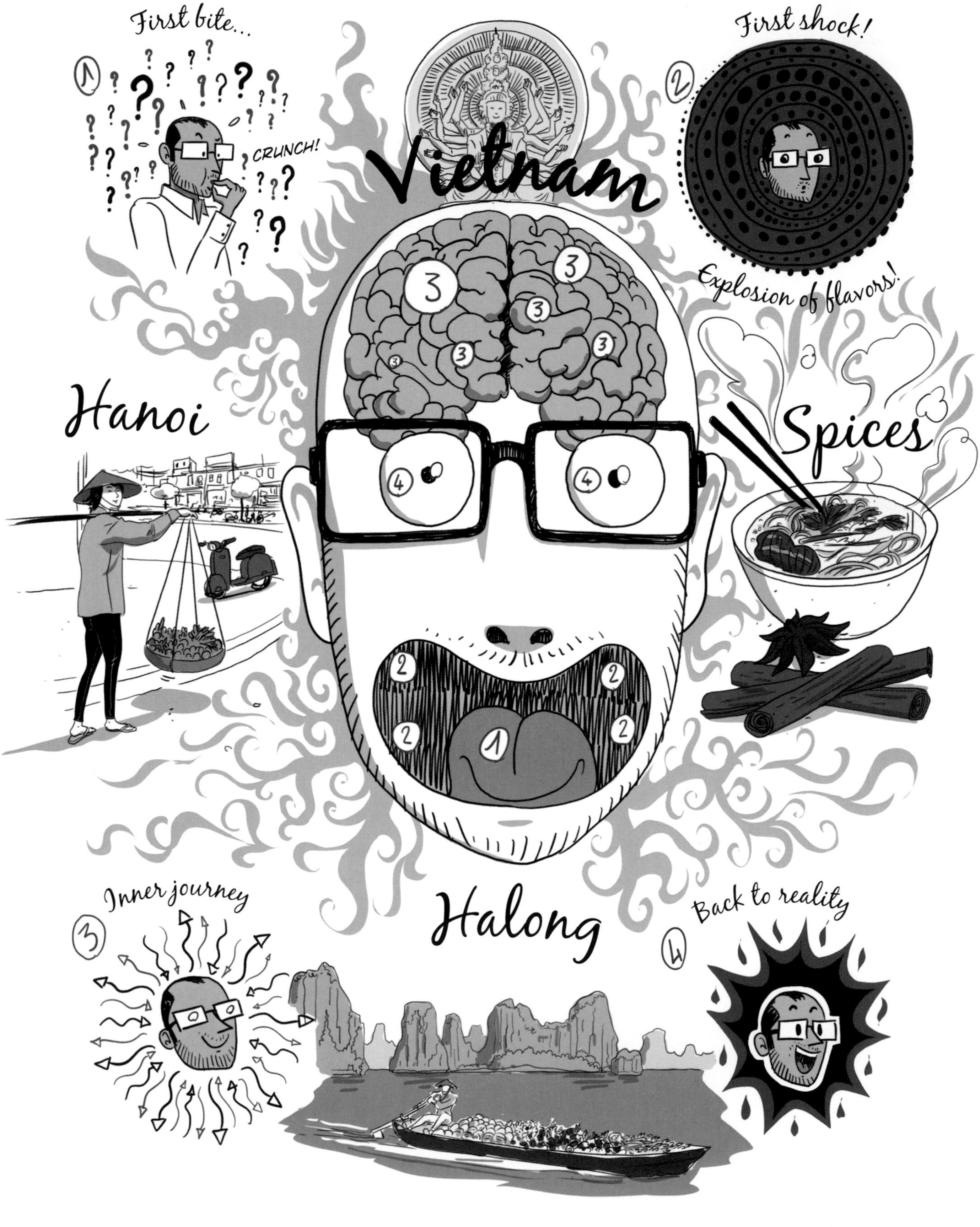

First bite...
1
CRUNCH!
First shock!
2
Explosion of flavors!
Vietnam
Hanoi
Spices
Inner journey
3
Halong
Back to reality
4

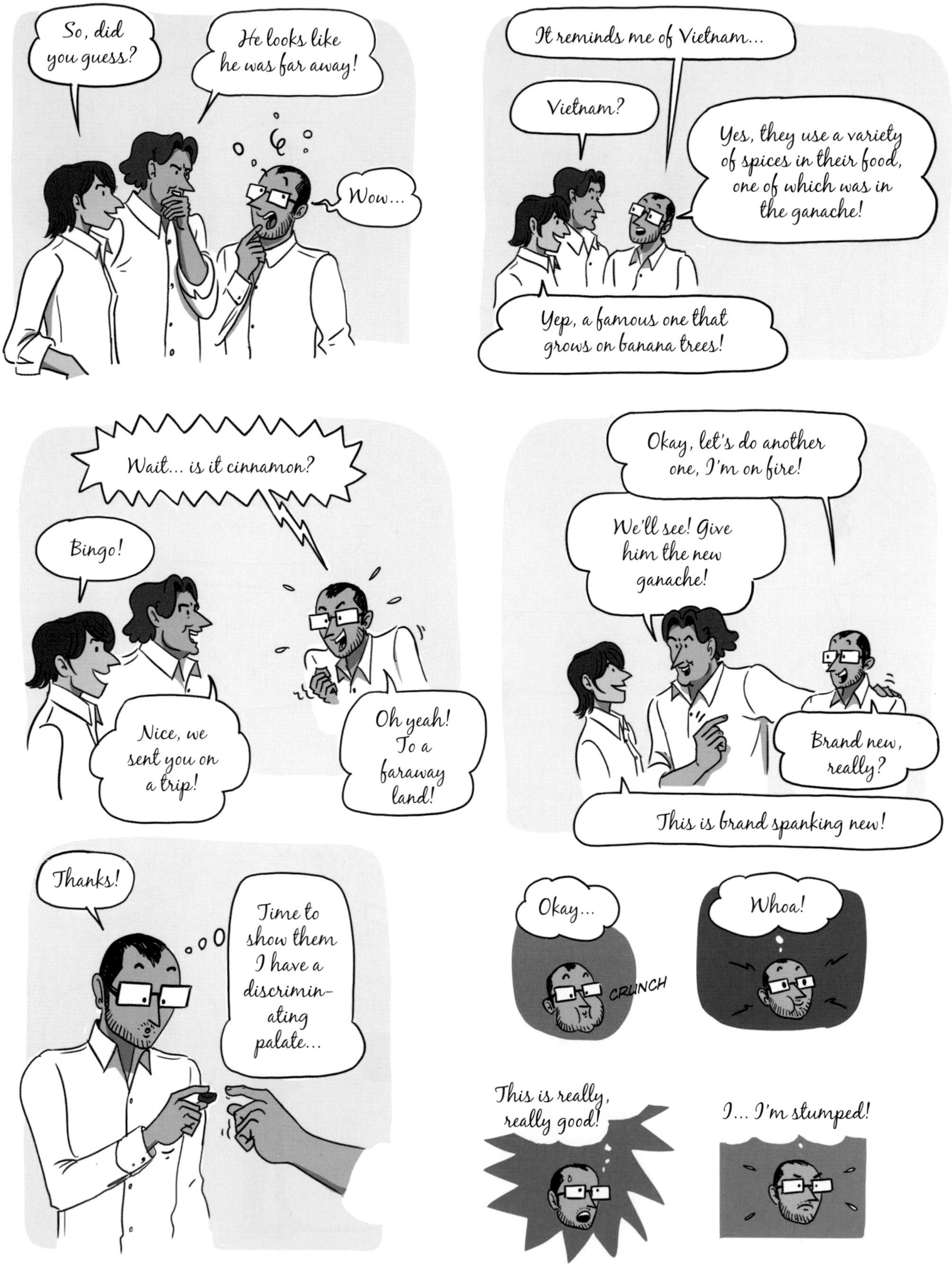
So, did you guess?
He looks like he was far away!
Wow...
It reminds me of Vietnam...
Vietnam?
Yes, they use a variety of spices in their food, one of which was in the ganache!
Yep, a famous one that grows on banana trees!
Wait... is it cinnamon?
Bingo!
Nice, we sent you on a trip!
Oh yeah! To a faraway land!
Okay, let's do another one, I'm on fire!
We'll see! Give him the new ganache!
Brand new, really?
This is brand spanking new!
Thanks!
Time to show them I have a discriminating palate...
Okay...
CRUNCH
Whoa!
This is really, really good!
I... I'm stumped!

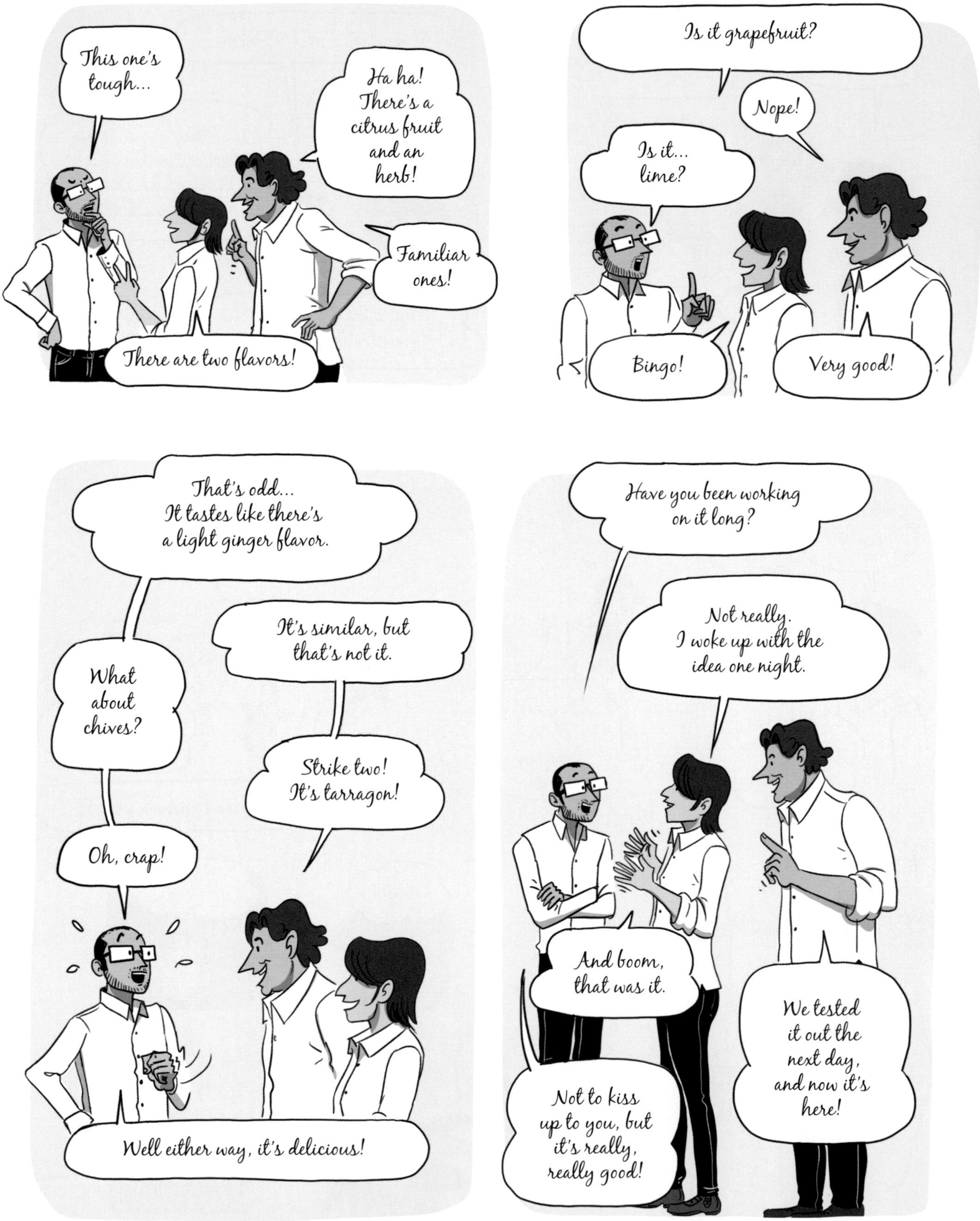
This one's tough...
Ha ha! There's a citrus fruit and an herb!
Familiar ones!
There are two flavors!
Is it grapefruit?
Nope!
Is it... lime?
Bingo!
Very good!
That's odd... It tastes like there's a light ginger flavor.
It's similar, but that's not it.
What about chives?
Strike two! It's tarragon!
Oh, crap!
Well either way, it's delicious!
Have you been working on it long?
Not really. I woke up with the idea one night.
And boom, that was it.
We tested it out the next day, and now it's here!
Not to kiss up to you, but it's really, really good!

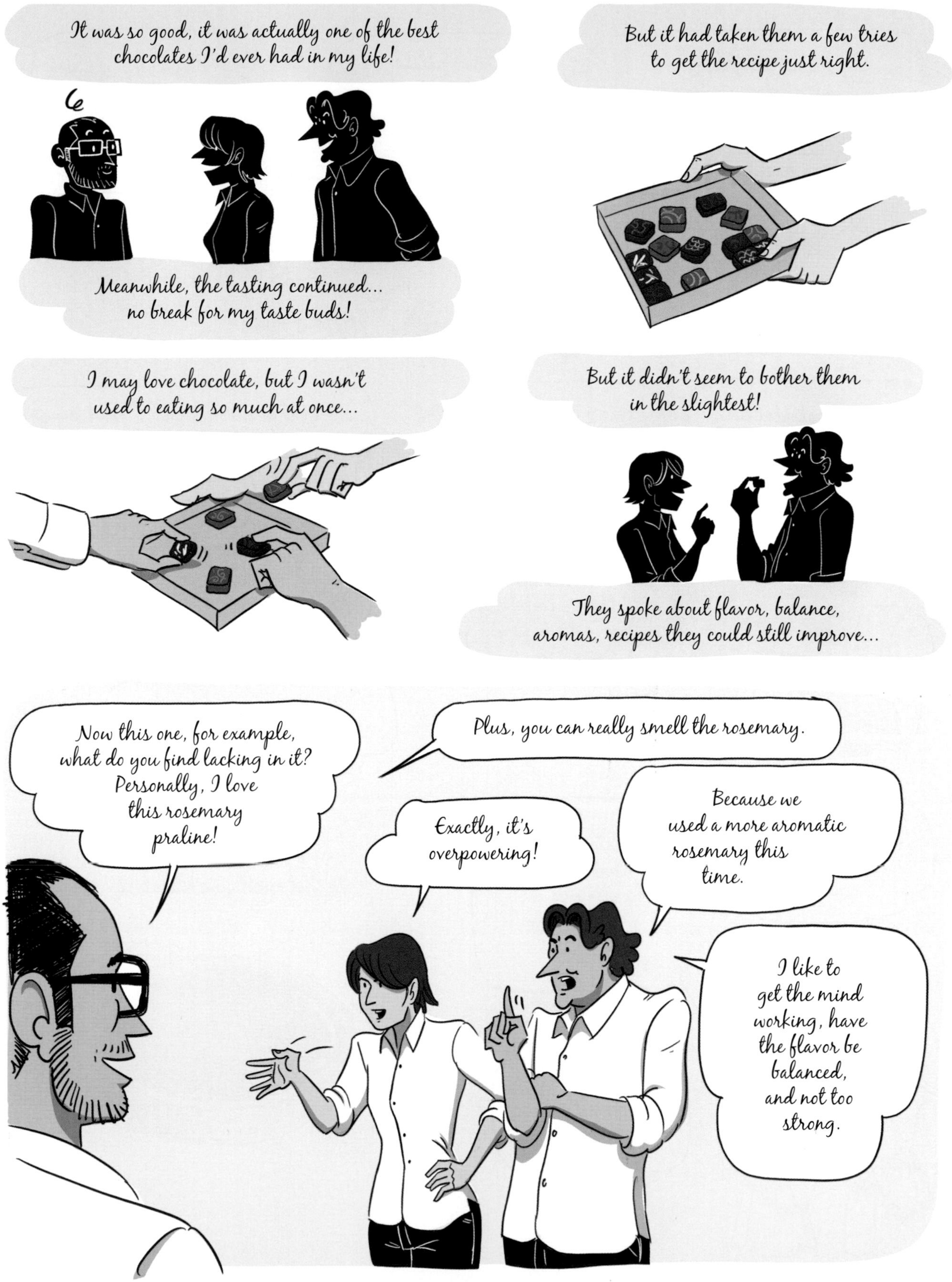

It was so good, it was actually one of the best chocolates I'd ever had in my life!
Meanwhile, the tasting continued... no break for my taste buds!
But it had taken them a few tries to get the recipe just right.
I may love chocolate, but I wasn't used to eating so much at once...
But it didn't seem to bother them in the slightest!
They spoke about flavor, balance, aromas, recipes they could still improve...
Now this one, for example, what do you find lacking in it? Personally, I love this rosemary praline!
Plus, you can really smell the rosemary.
Exactly, it's overpowering!
Because we used a more aromatic rosemary this time.
I like to get the mind working, have the flavor be balanced, and not too strong.

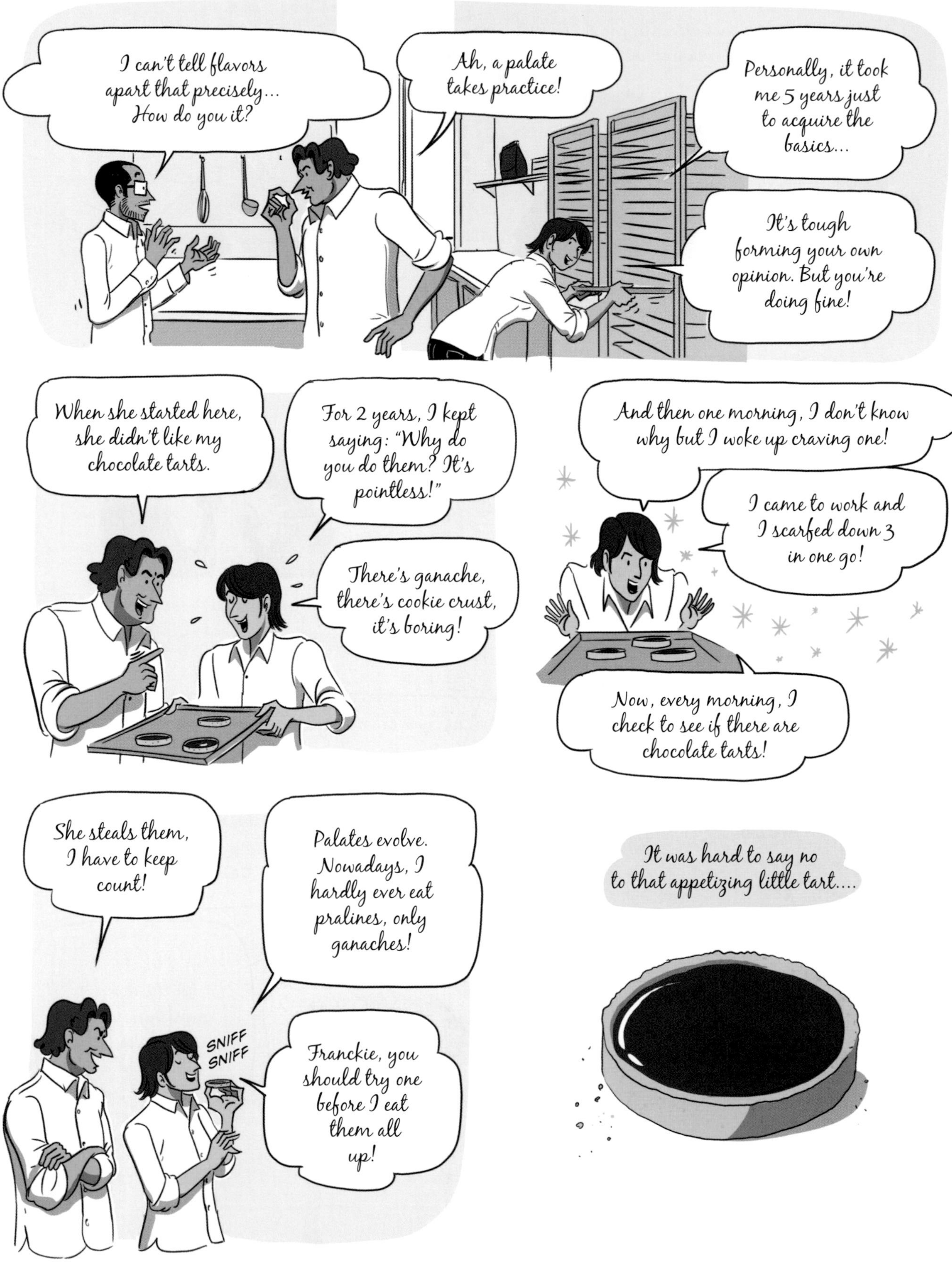
I can't tell flavors apart that precisely... How do you it?
Ah, a palate takes practice!
Personally, it took me 5 years just to acquire the basics...
It's tough forming your own opinion. But you're doing fine!
When she started here, she didn't like my chocolate tarts.
For 2 years, I kept saying: "Why do you do them? It's pointless!"
There's ganache, there's cookie crust, it's boring!
And then one morning, I don't know why but I woke up craving one!
I came to work and I scarfed down 3 in one go!
Now, every morning, I check to see if there are chocolate tarts!
She steals them, I have to keep count!
Palates evolve. Nowadays, I hardly ever eat pralines, only ganaches!
SNIFF SNIFF
Franckie, you should try one before I eat them all up!
It was hard to say no to that appetizing little tart....

A recipe in 2 parts: first the crust, then the ganache fondant!

Chocolate Tart

Plan on 25 min to prepare the crust, 90 min to let it set in the fridge, and 20 min bake time.

The sweet crust

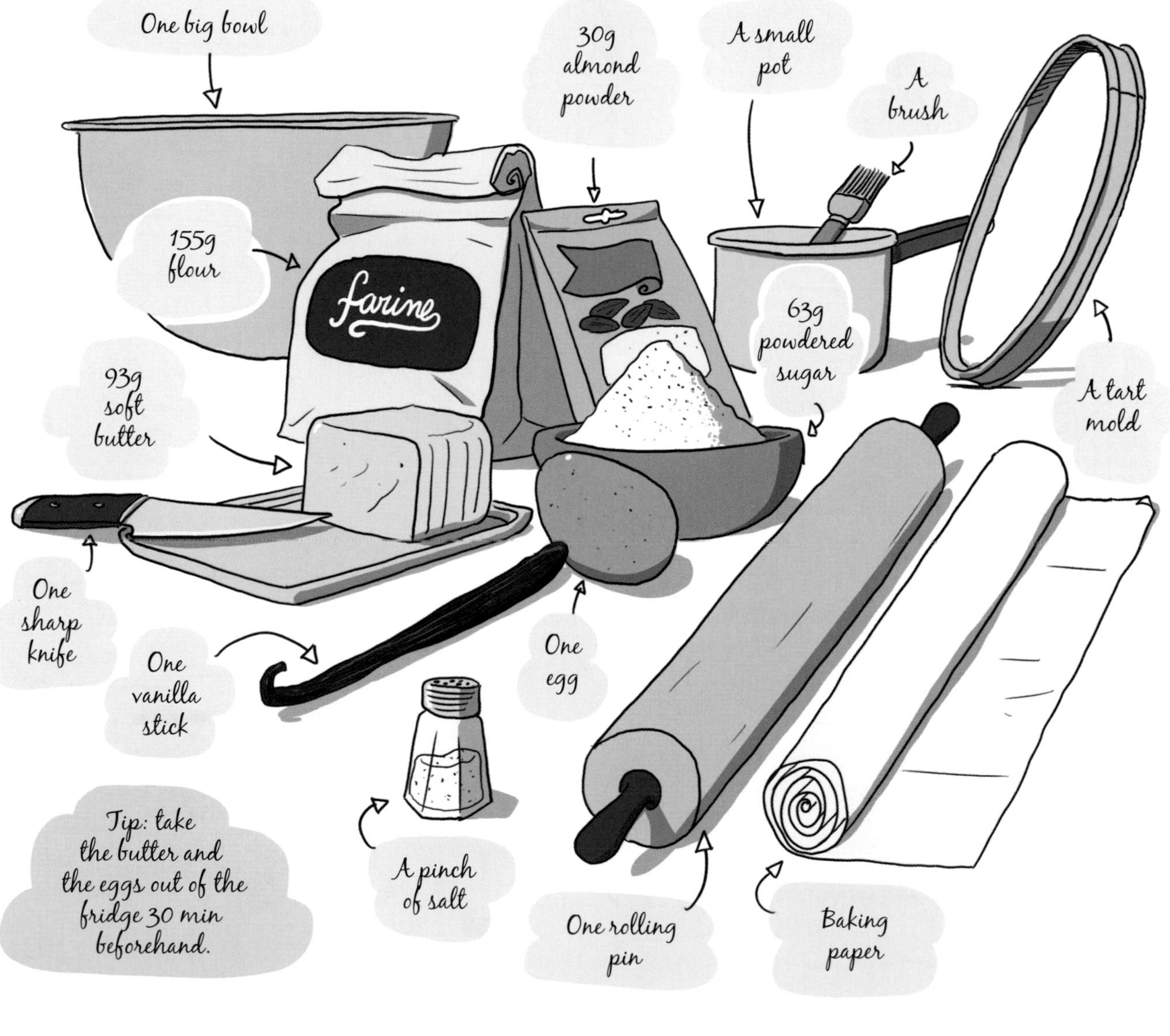

One big bowl
30g almond powder
A small pot
A brush
155g flour
farine
63g powdered sugar
93g soft butter
A tart mold
One sharp knife
One vanilla stick
One egg
Tip: take the butter and the eggs out of the fridge 30 min beforehand.
A pinch of salt
One rolling pin
Baking paper

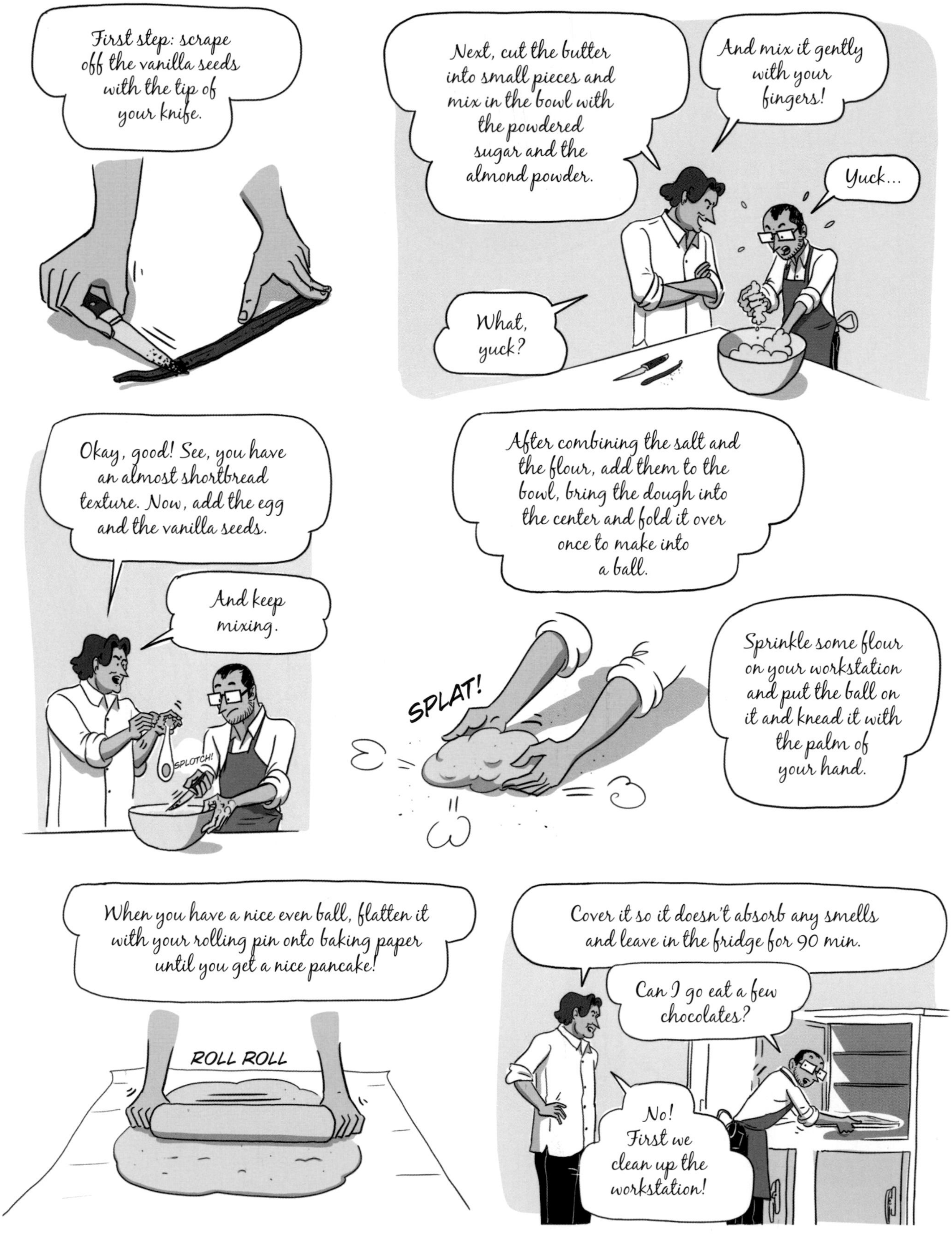
First step: scrape off the vanilla seeds with the tip of your knife.
Next, cut the butter into small pieces and mix in the bowl with the powdered sugar and the almond powder.
And mix it gently with your fingers!
Yuck...
What, yuck?
Okay, good! See, you have an almost shortbread texture. Now, add the egg and the vanilla seeds.
And keep mixing.
SPLOTCH!
After combining the salt and the flour, add them to the bowl, bring the dough into the center and fold it over once to make into a ball.
SPLAT!
Sprinkle some flour on your workstation and put the ball on it and knead it with the palm of your hand.
When you have a nice even ball, flatten it with your rolling pin onto baking paper until you get a nice pancake!
ROLL ROLL
Cover it so it doesn't absorb any smells and leave in the fridge for 90 min.
Can I go eat a few chocolates?
No! First we clean up the workstation!

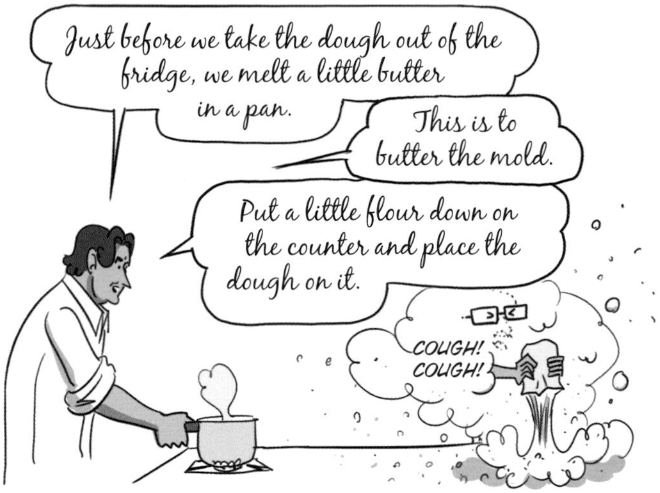
Just before we take the dough out of the fridge, we melt a little butter in a pan.
This is to butter the mold.
Put a little flour down on the counter and place the dough on it.
COUGH! COUGH!

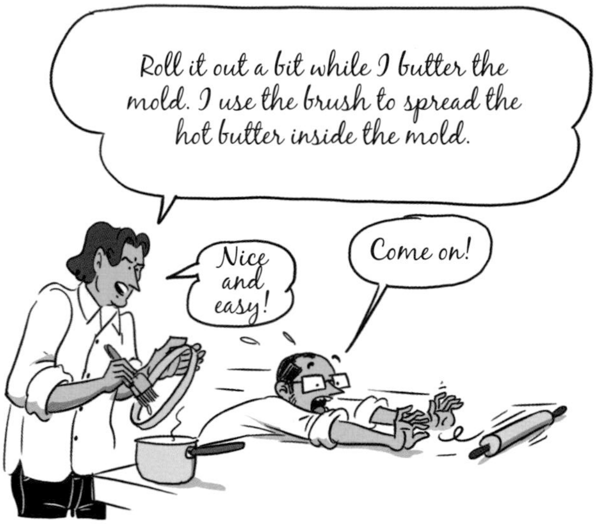
Roll it out a bit while I butter the mold. I use the brush to spread the hot butter inside the mold.
Nice and easy!
Come on!

Last step before baking: look closely at what I'm doing, ok?
Preheat the oven at 170° C.

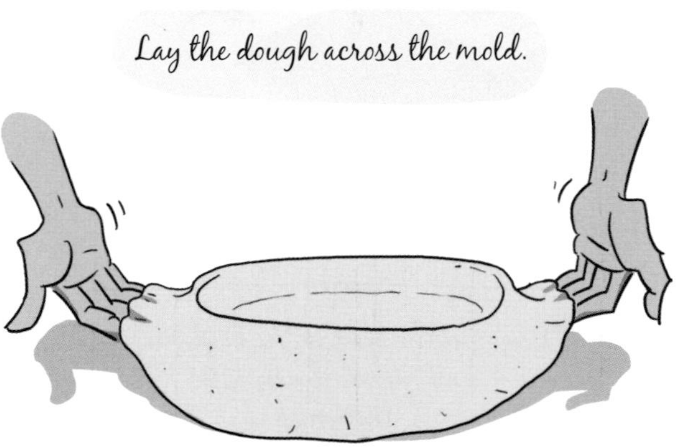
Lay the dough across the mold.

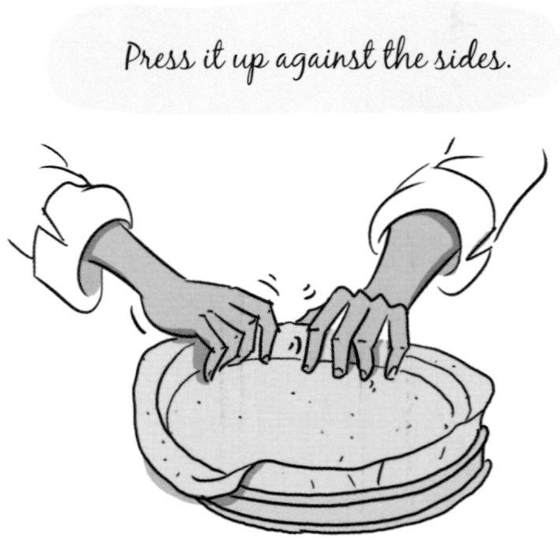
Press it up against the sides.

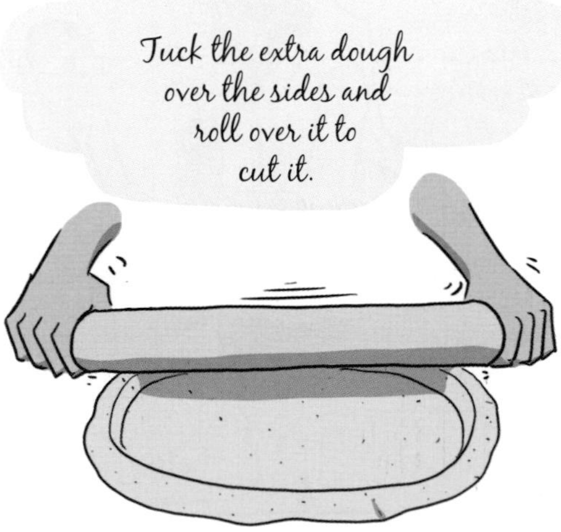
Tuck the extra dough over the sides and roll over it to cut it.

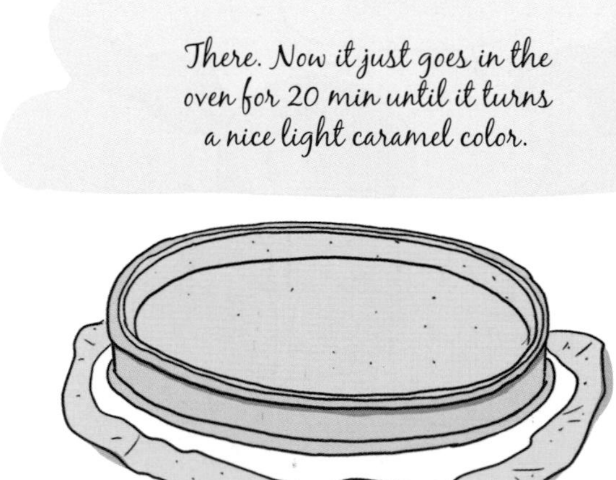
There. Now it just goes in the oven for 20 min until it turns a nice light caramel color.

The ganache

Get a pot of boiling water ready so as to make a bain-marie for the mixing bowl.

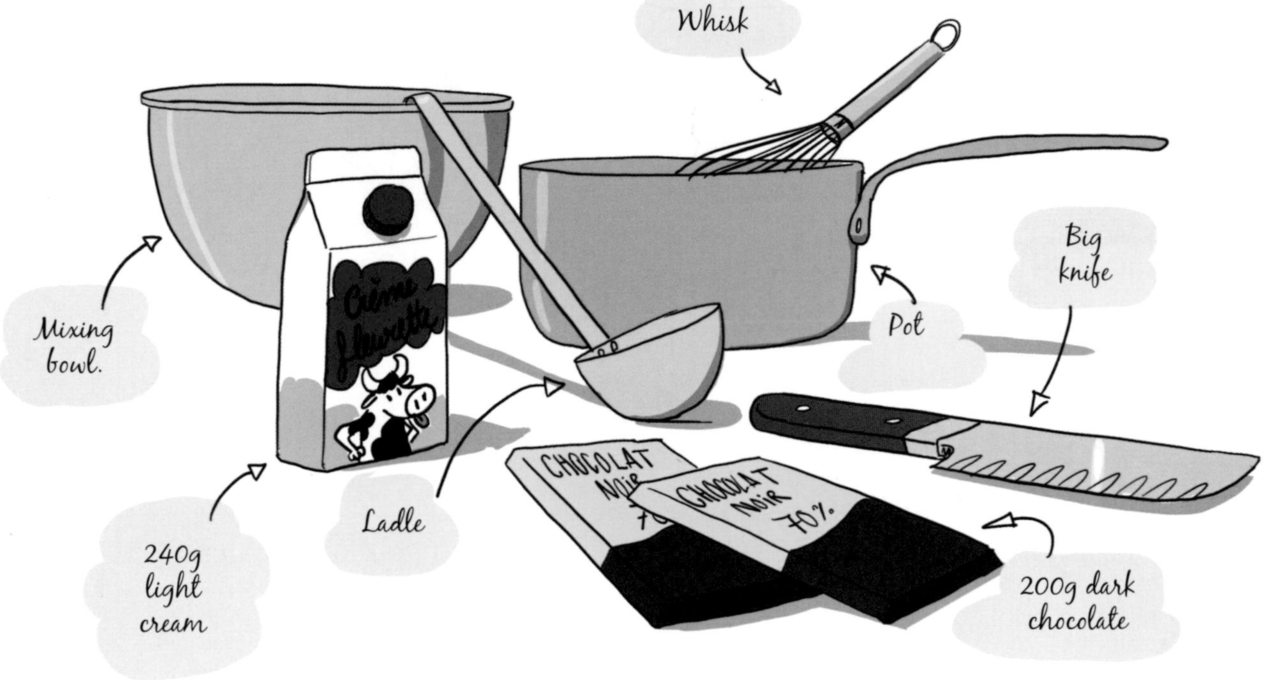
Whisk
Big knife
Pot
Mixing bowl.
Crème fleurette
CHOCOLAT NOIR 70%
Ladle
240g light cream
200g dark chocolate

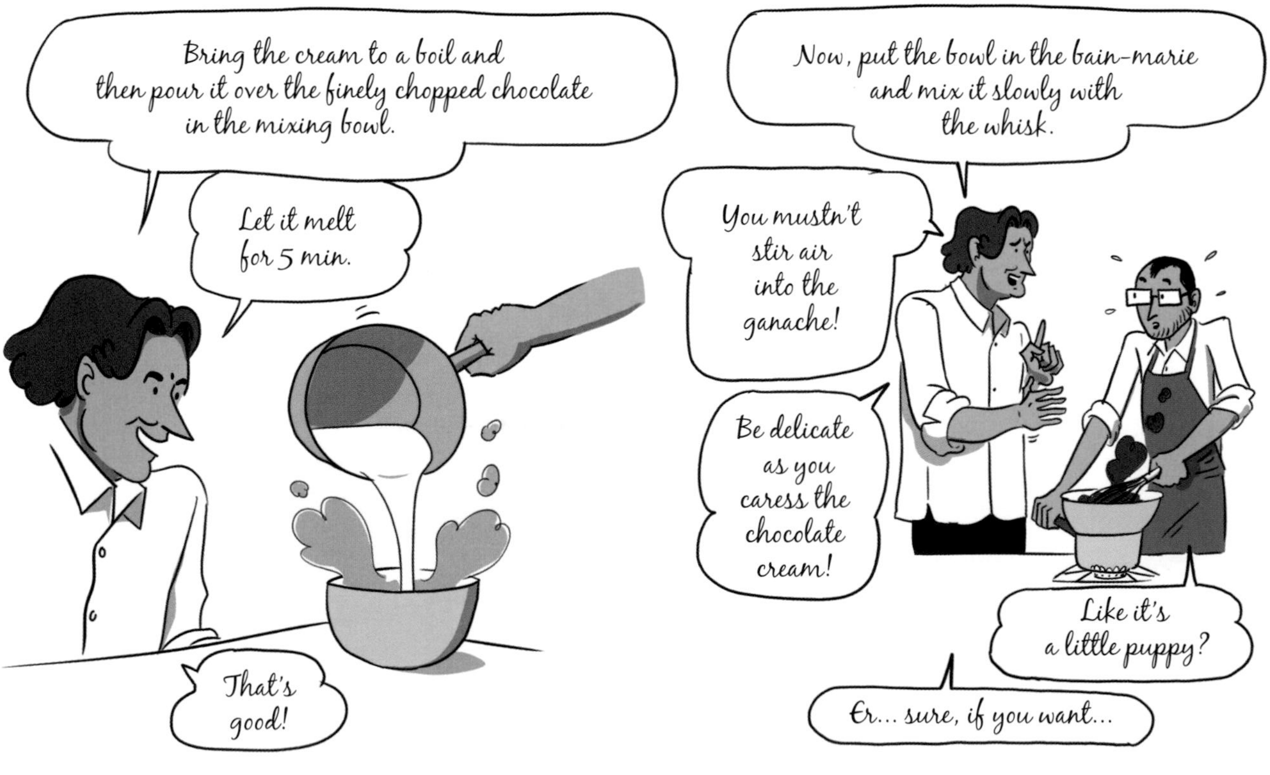
Bring the cream to a boil and then pour it over the finely chopped chocolate in the mixing bowl.
Let it melt for 5 min.
That's good!
Now, put the bowl in the bain-marie and mix it slowly with the whisk.
You mustn't stir air into the ganache!
Be delicate as you caress the chocolate cream!
Like it's a little puppy?
Er... sure, if you want...

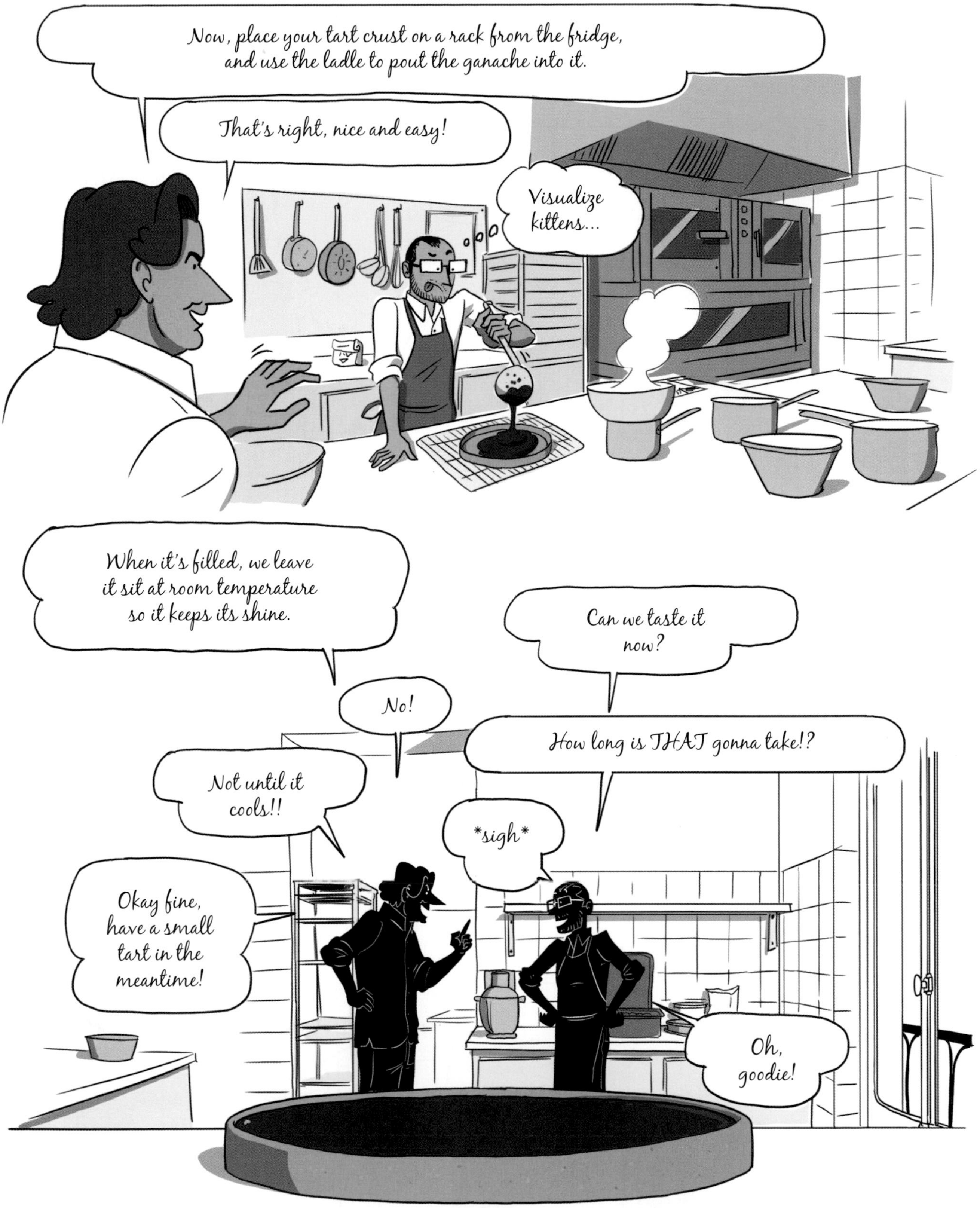
Now, place your tart crust on a rack from the fridge, and use the ladle to pout the ganache into it.
That's right, nice and easy!
Visualize kittens...
When it's filled, we leave it sit at room temperature so it keeps its shine.
Can we taste it now?
No!
How long is THAT gonna take!?
Not until it cools!!
sigh
Okay fine, have a small tart in the meantime!
Oh, goodie!

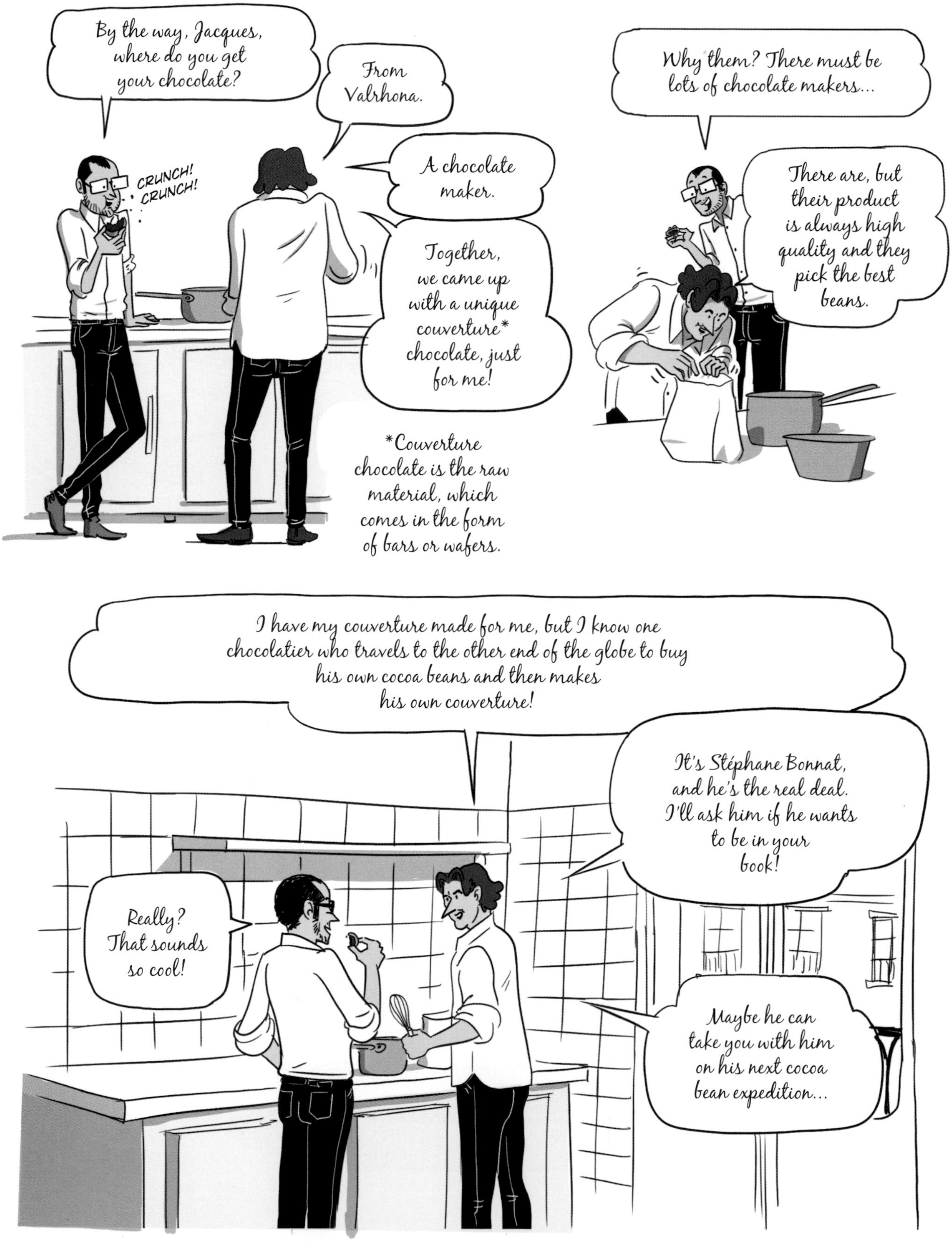

By the way, Jacques, where do you get your chocolate?
CRUNCH! CRUNCH!
From Valrhona.
A chocolate maker.
Together, we came up with a unique couverture* chocolate, just for me!
*Couverture chocolate is the raw material, which comes in the form of bars or wafers.
Why them? There must be lots of chocolate makers...
There are, but their product is always high quality and they pick the best beans.
I have my couverture made for me, but I know one chocolatier who travels to the other end of the globe to buy his own cocoa beans and then makes his own couverture!
It's Stéphane Bonnat, and he's the real deal. I'll ask him if he wants to be in your book!
Really? That sounds so cool!
Maybe he can take you with him on his next cocoa bean expedition...

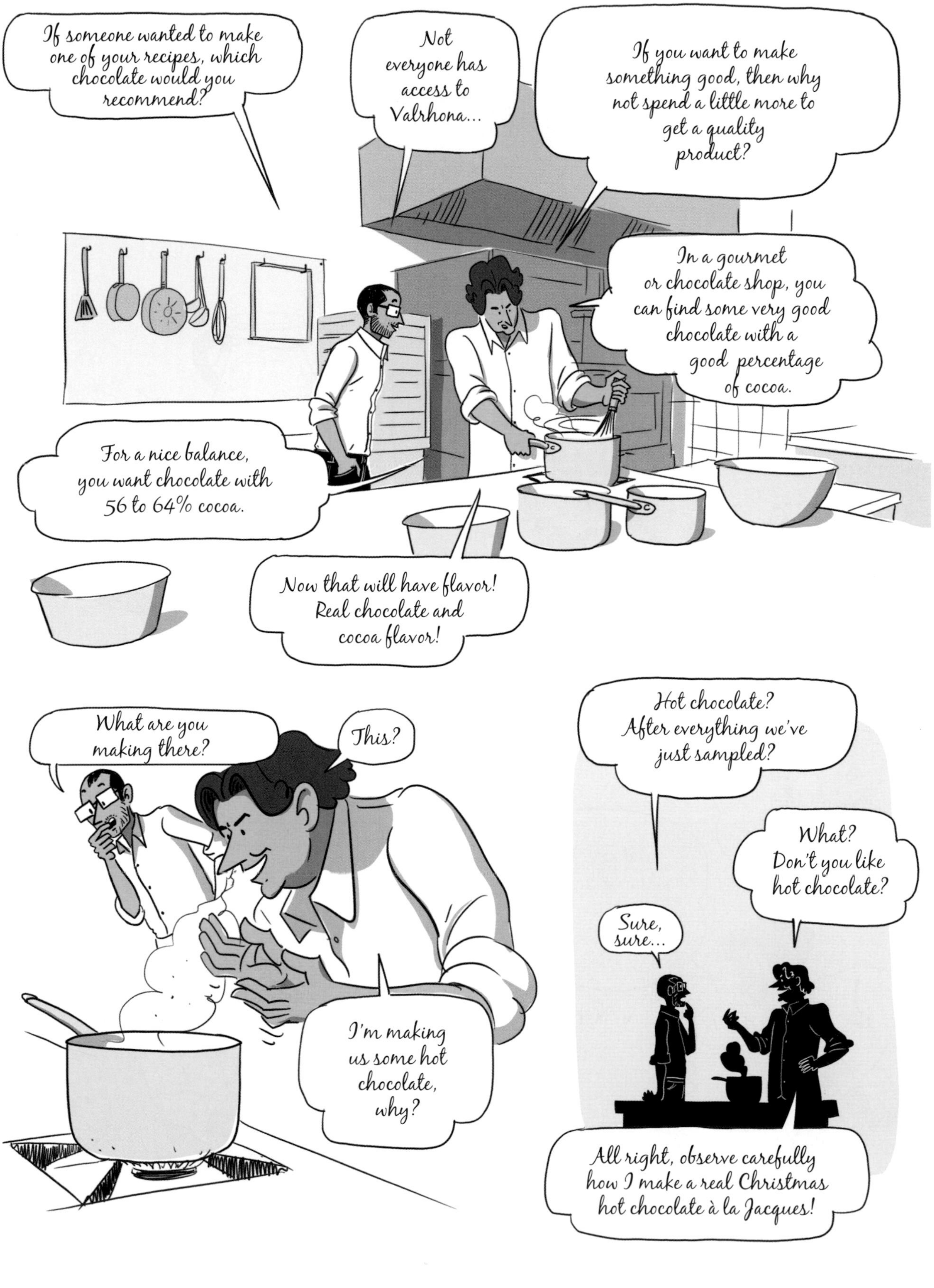
If someone wanted to make one of your recipes, which chocolate would you recommend?
Not everyone has access to Valrhona...
If you want to make something good, then why not spend a little more to get a quality product?
In a gourmet or chocolate shop, you can find some very good chocolate with a good percentage of cocoa.
For a nice balance, you want chocolate with 56 to 64% cocoa.
Now that will have flavor! Real chocolate and cocoa flavor!
What are you making there?
This?
I'm making us some hot chocolate, why?
Hot chocolate? After everything we've just sampled?
What? Don't you like hot chocolate?
Sure, sure...
All right, observe carefully how I make a real Christmas hot chocolate à la Jacques!

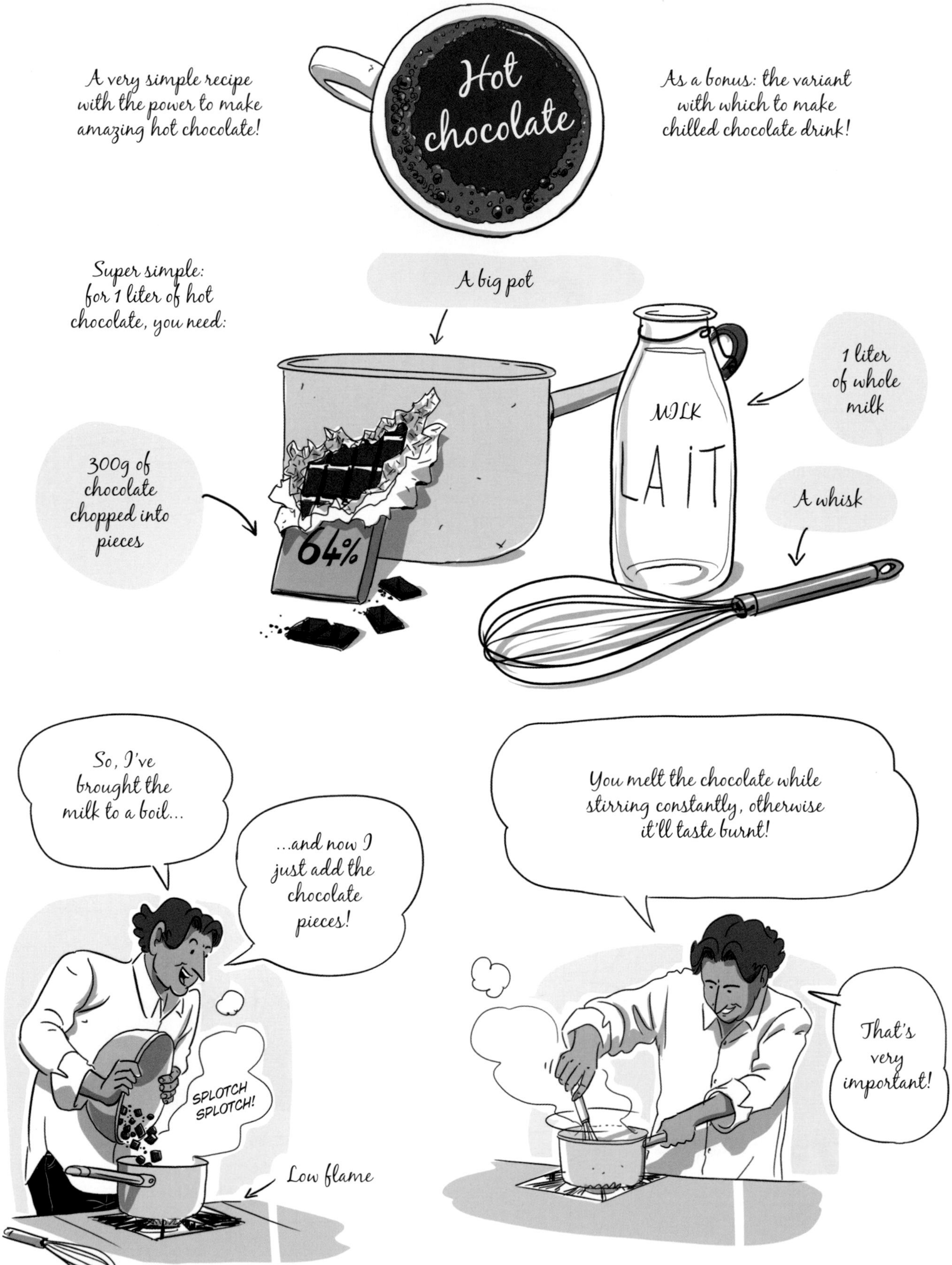
Hot chocolate
A very simple recipe with the power to make amazing hot chocolate!
As a bonus: the variant with which to make chilled chocolate drink!
Super simple: for 1 liter of hot chocolate, you need:
A big pot
1 liter of whole milk
MILK
LAIT
300g of chocolate chopped into pieces
64%
A whisk
So, I've brought the milk to a boil...
...and now I just add the chocolate pieces!
SPLOTCH SPLOTCH!
Low flame
You melt the chocolate while stirring constantly, otherwise it'll taste burnt!
That's very important!

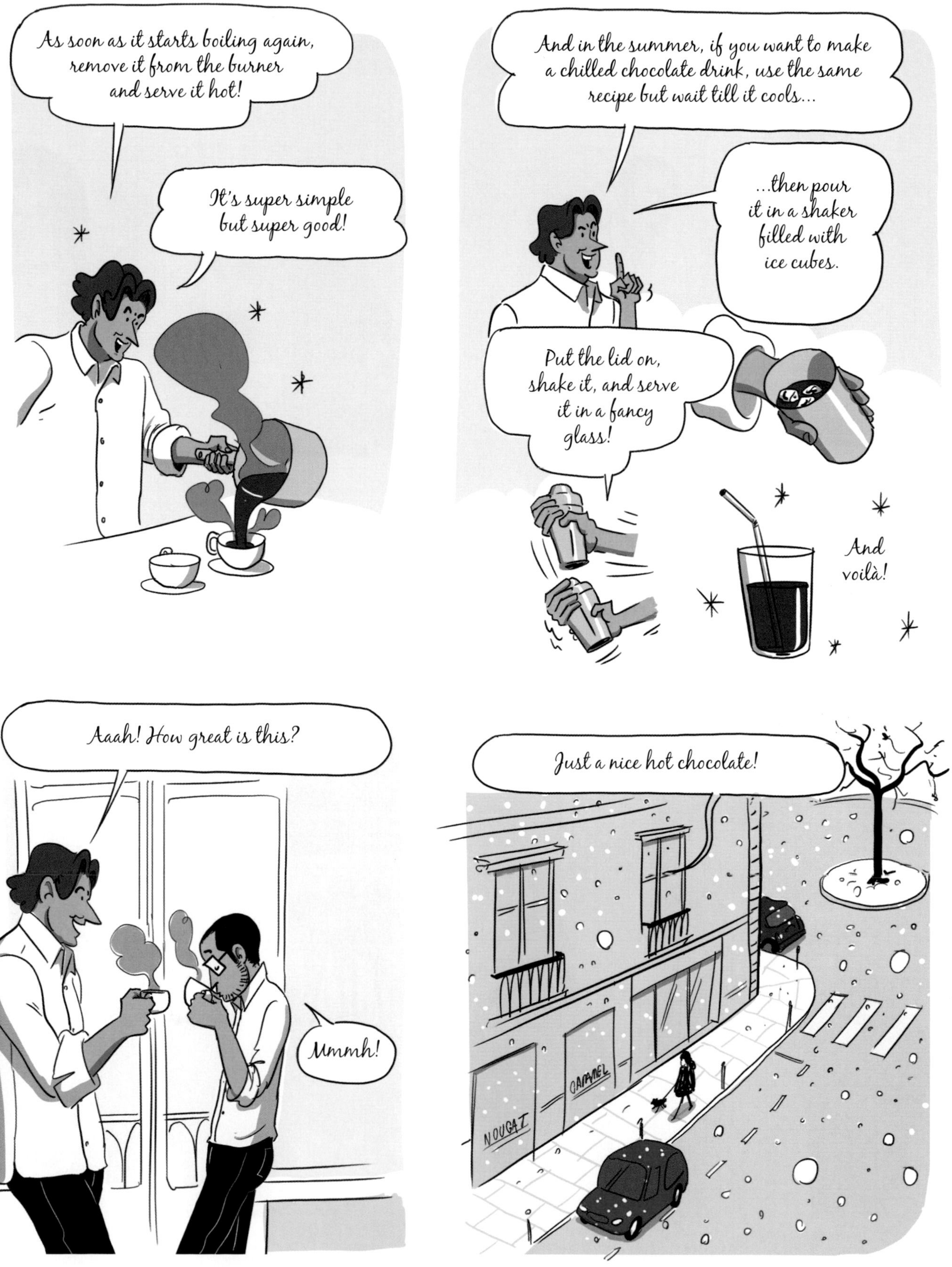
As soon as it starts boiling again, remove it from the burner and serve it hot!
It's super simple but super good!
And in the summer, if you want to make a chilled chocolate drink, use the same recipe but wait till it cools...
...then pour it in a shaker filled with ice cubes.
Put the lid on, shake it, and serve it in a fancy glass!
And voilà!
Aaah! How great is this?
Mmmh!
Just a nice hot chocolate!
CARAMEL
NOUGAT

I went home with a little box of cinnamon chocolates.

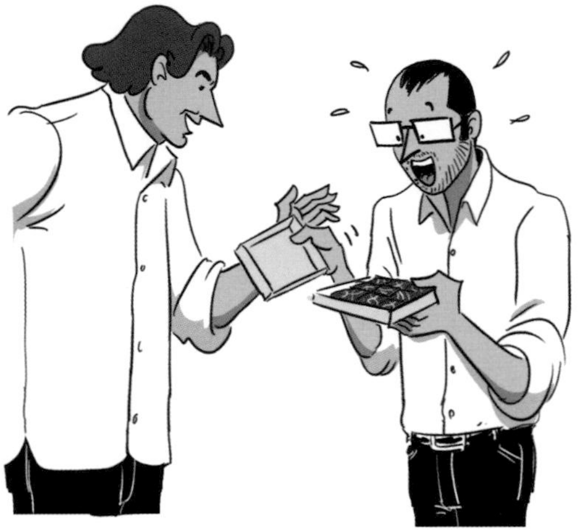

I couldn't wait to have my girlfriend try them. Maybe it would remind her of our trip to Vietnam...

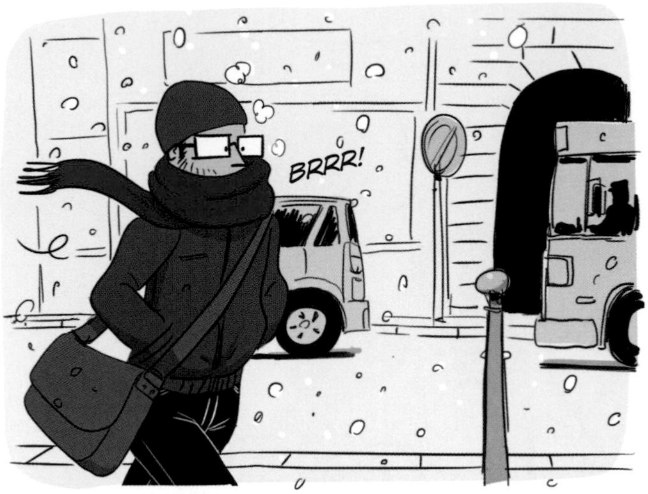
BRRR!

Or maybe not...

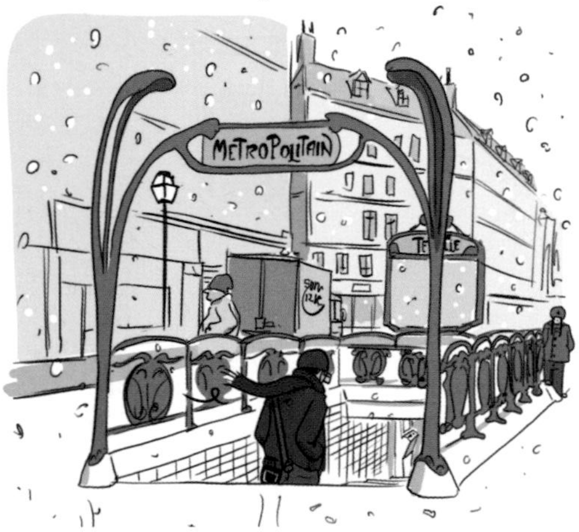
METROPOLITAIN

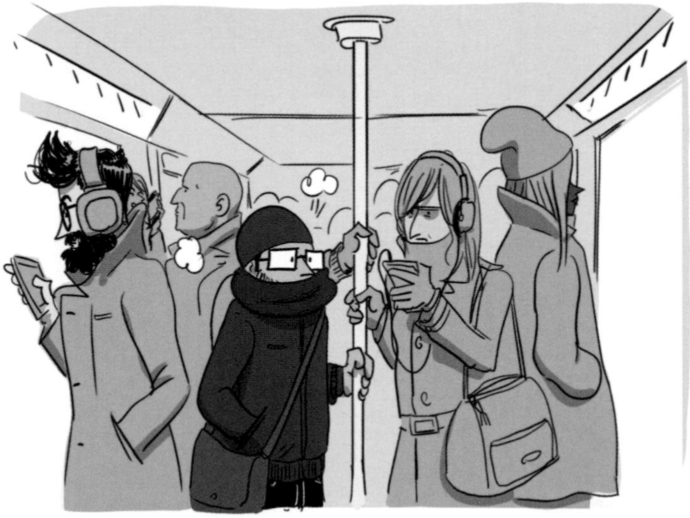

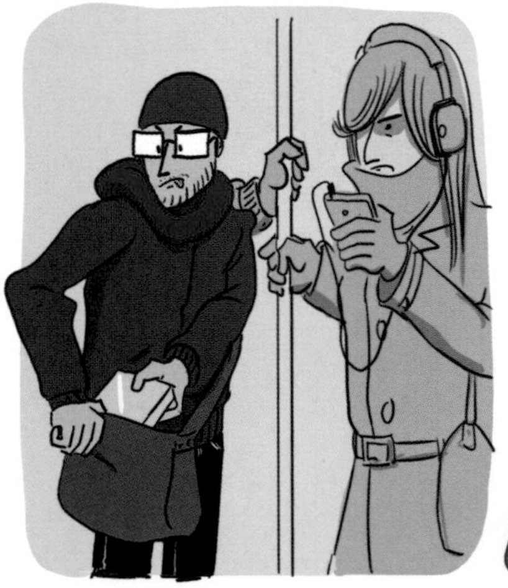

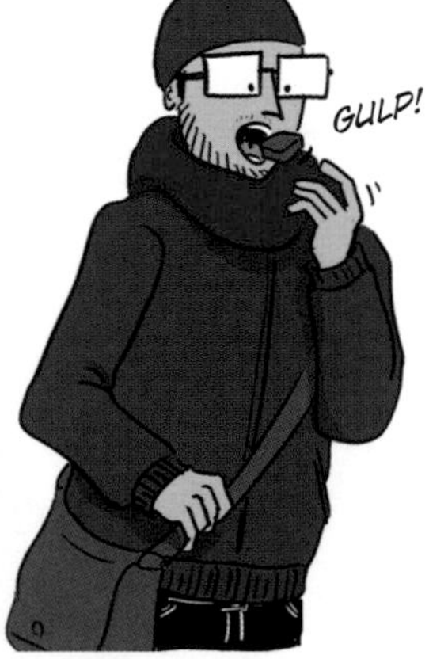
GULP!

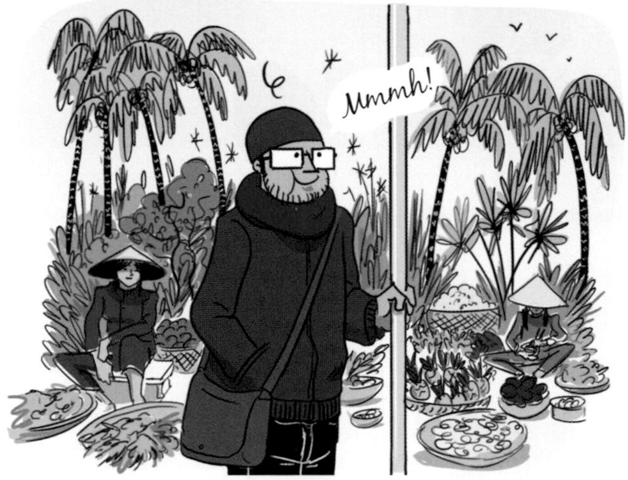
Mmmh!

Thanks to Jacques, I had found the quickest and easiest way to travel to a distant land!

STEPHANE BONNAT

FROM BEAN TO BAR

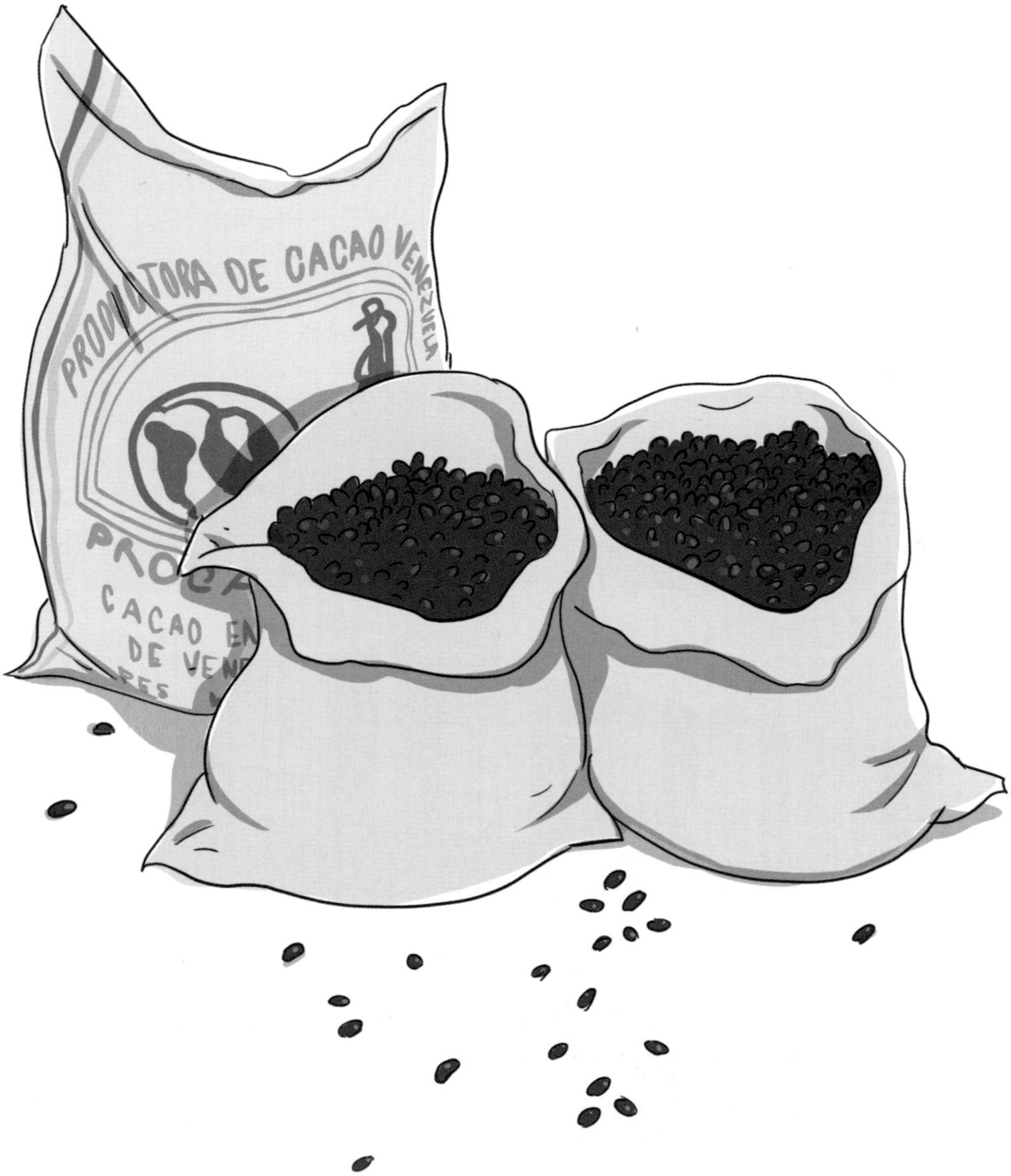
DE CACAO VENEZUELA

January 28, 2014. Jacques gave me Stéphane Bonnat's number.

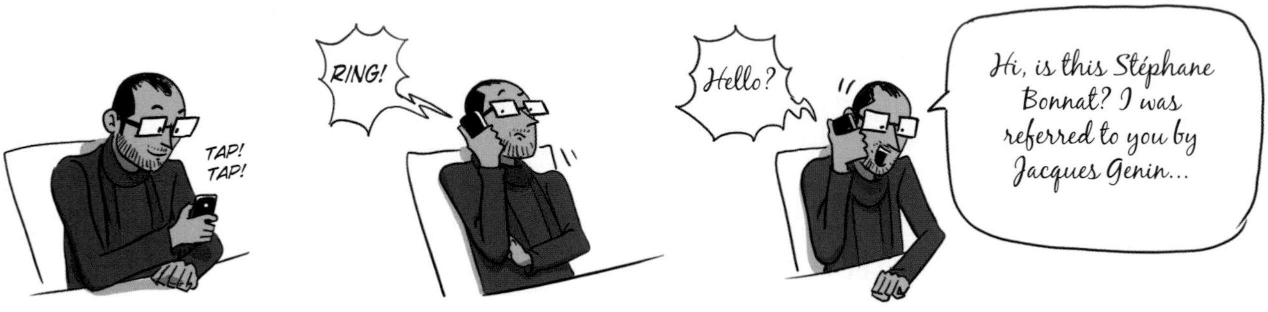
TAP! TAP!
RING!
Hello?
Hi, is this Stéphane Bonnat? I was referred to you by Jacques Genin...

I explained the graphic novel project to him. He was excited from the get-go, so we arranged for me to visit him in his chocolate factory in Voiron!

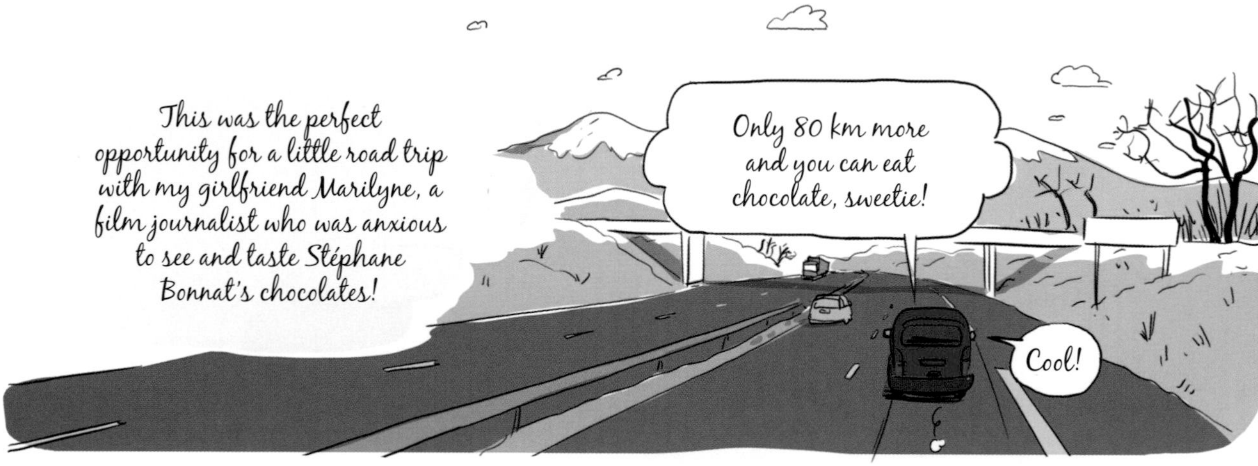
This was the perfect opportunity for a little road trip with my girlfriend Marilyne, a film journalist who was anxious to see and taste Stéphane Bonnat's chocolates!
Only 80 km more and you can eat chocolate, sweetie!
Cool!

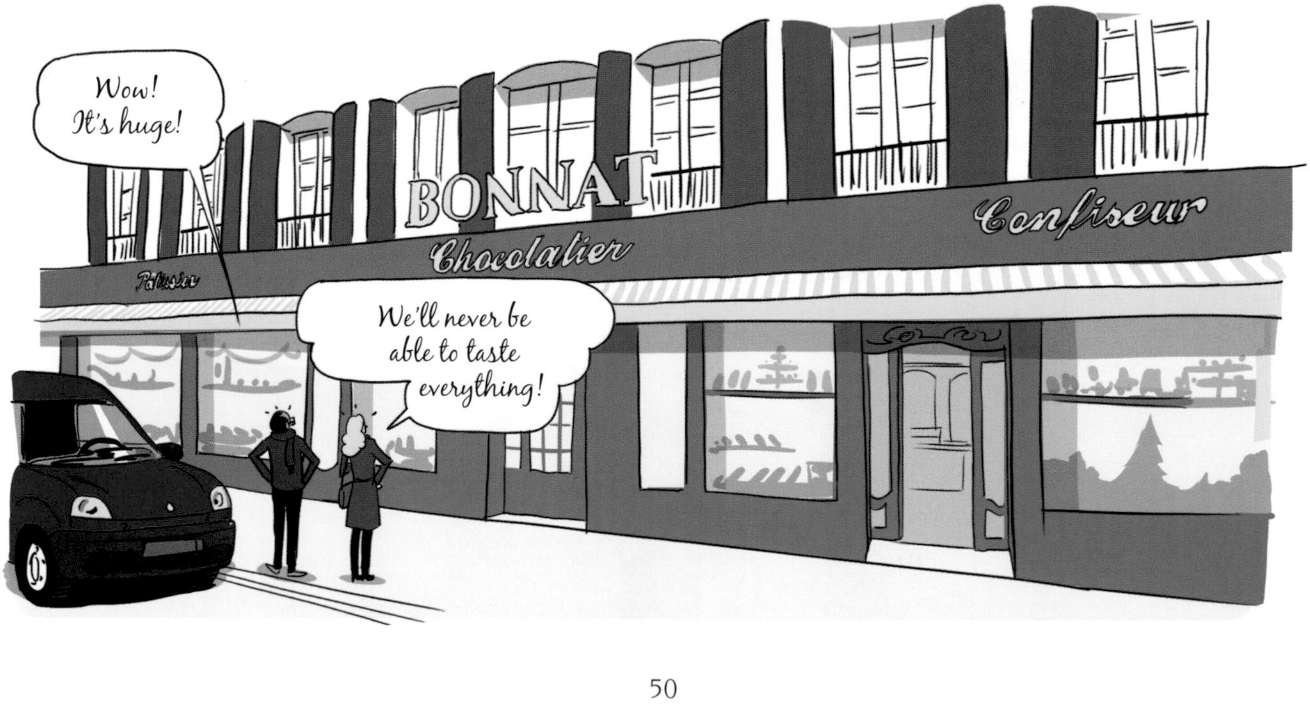
Wow! It's huge!
BONNAT
Chocolatier
Confiseur
We'll never be able to taste everything!

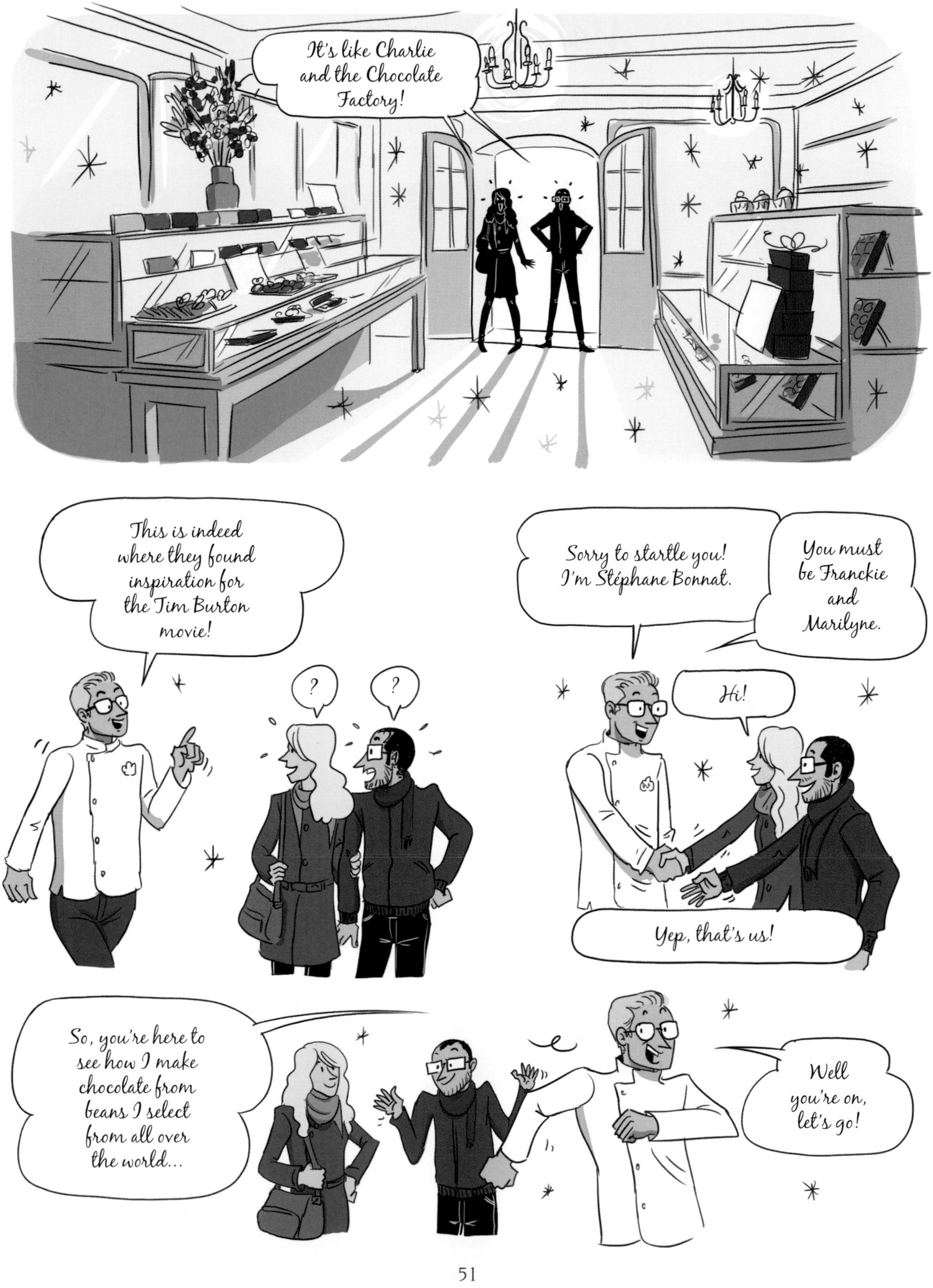
It's like Charlie and the Chocolate Factory!
This is indeed where they found inspiration for the Tim Burton movie!
?
?
Sorry to startle you! I'm Stéphane Bonnat.
You must be Franckie and Marilyne.
Hi!
Yep, that's us!
So, you're here to see how I make chocolate from beans I select from all over the world...
Well you're on, let's go!

Making chocolate

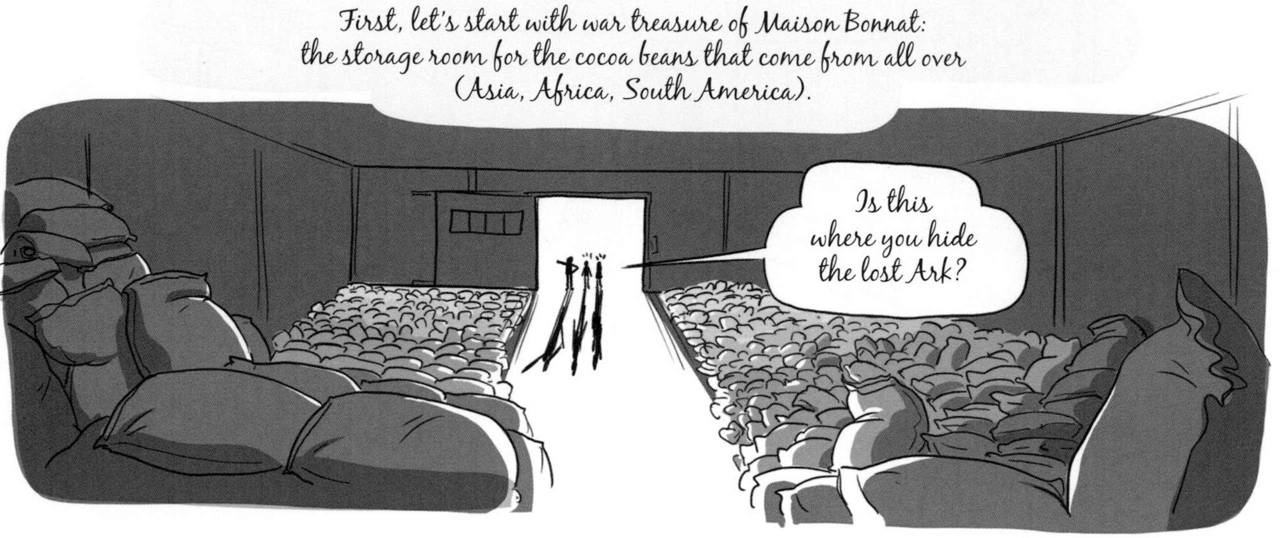
First, let's start with war treasure of Maison Bonnat: the storage room for the cocoa beans that come from all over (Asia, Africa, South America).
Is this where you hide the lost Ark?

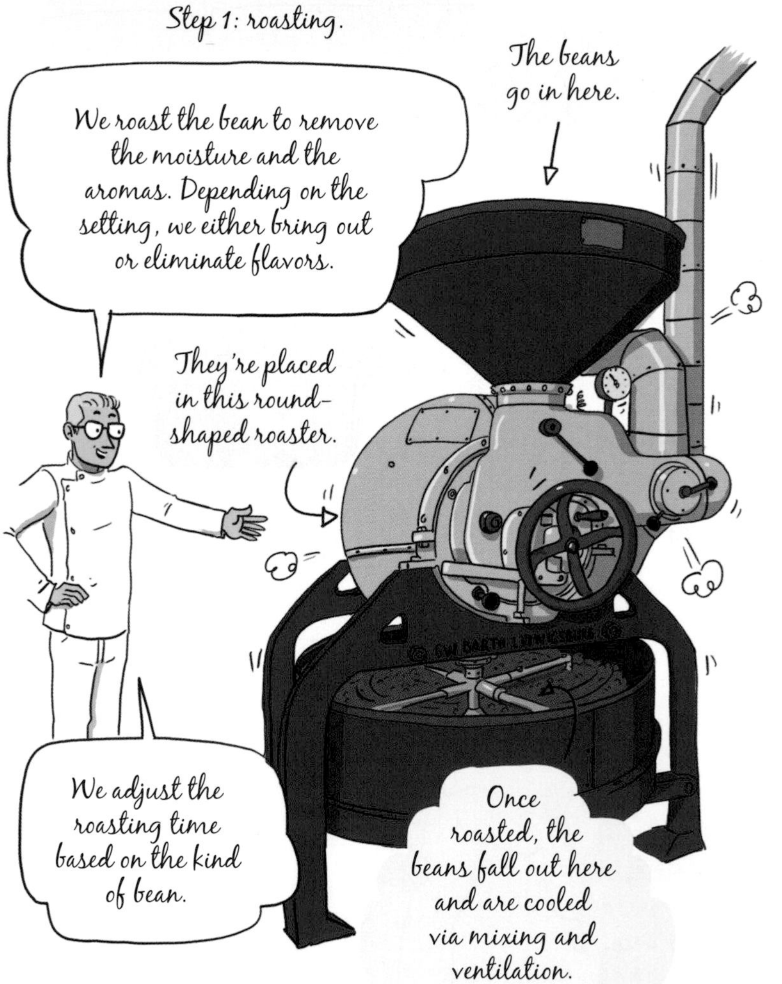
Step 1: roasting.
We roast the bean to remove the moisture and the aromas. Depending on the setting, we either bring out or eliminate flavors.
The beans go in here.
They're placed in this round-shaped roaster.
We adjust the roasting time based on the kind of bean.
Once roasted, the beans fall out here and are cooled via mixing and ventilation.

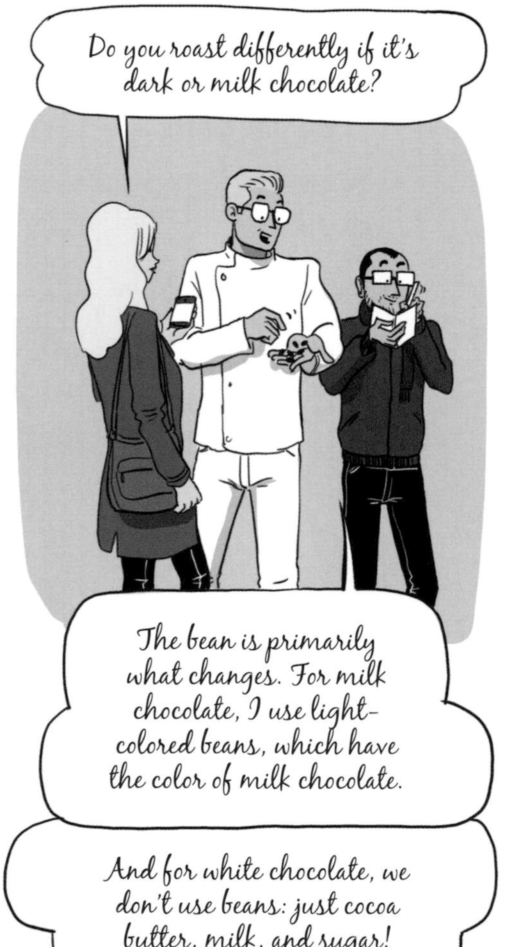
Do you roast differently if it's dark or milk chocolate?
The bean is primarily what changes. For milk chocolate, I use light-colored beans, which have the color of milk chocolate.
And for white chocolate, we don't use beans: just cocoa butter, milk, and sugar!

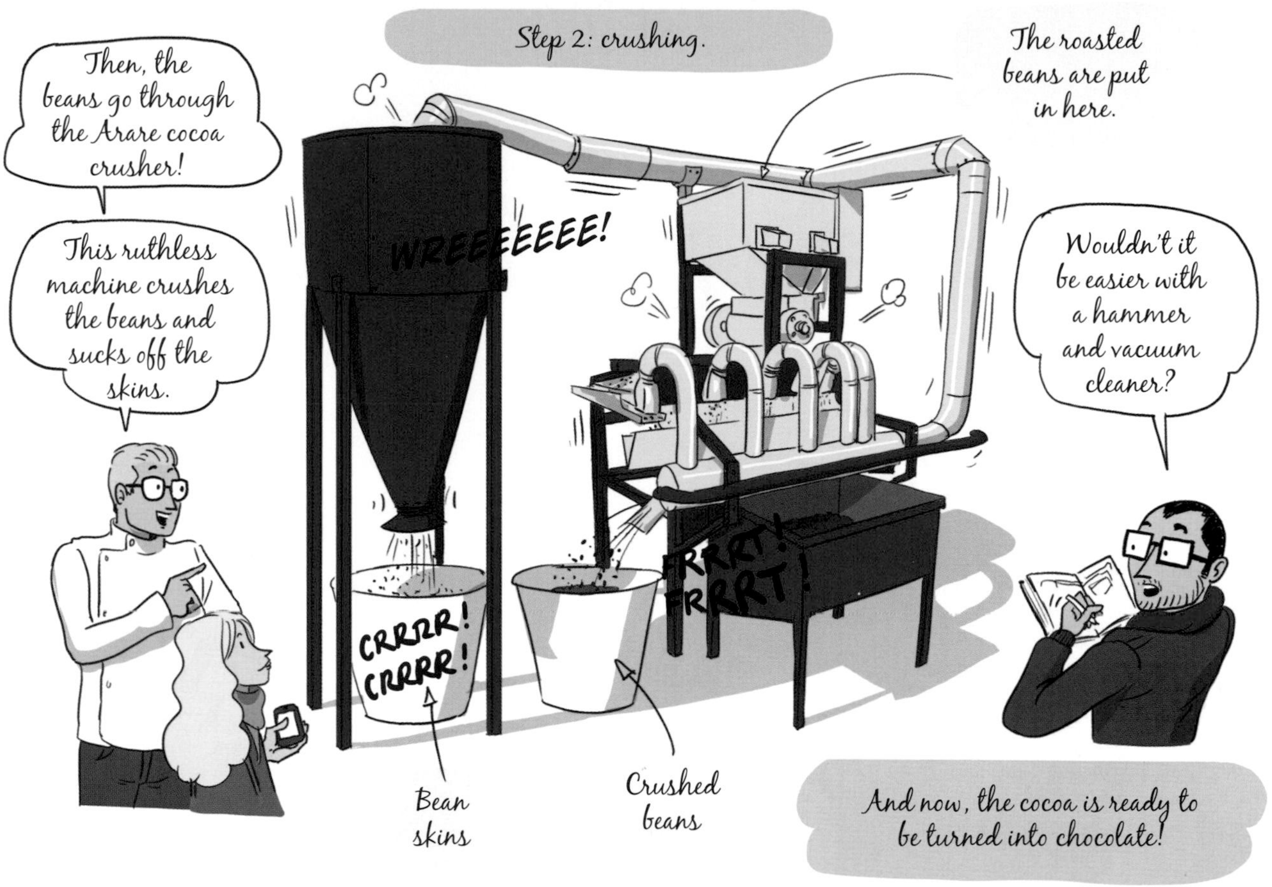
Step 2: crushing.
Then, the beans go through the Arare cocoa crusher!
This ruthless machine crushes the beans and sucks off the skins.
WREEEEEEE!
The roasted beans are put in here.
Wouldn't it be easier with a hammer and vacuum cleaner?
CRRRR! CRRRR!
FRRRT! FRRRT!
Bean skins
Crushed beans
And now, the cocoa is ready to be turned into chocolate!

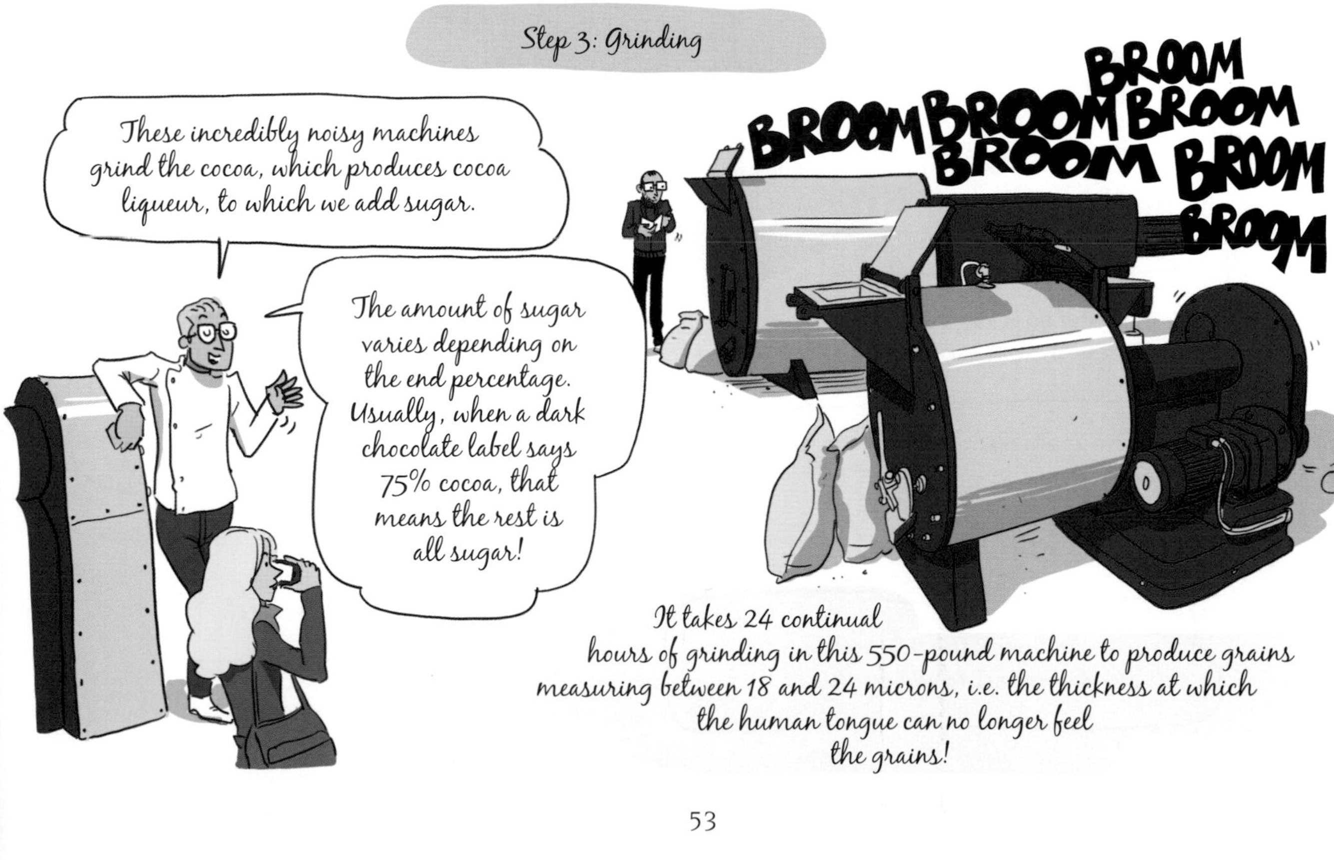
Step 3: Grinding
These incredibly noisy machines grind the cocoa, which produces cocoa liqueur, to which we add sugar.
The amount of sugar varies depending on the end percentage. Usually, when a dark chocolate label says 75% cocoa, that means the rest is all sugar!
BROOM BROOM BROOM BROOM BROOM BROOM BROOM
It takes 24 continual hours of grinding in this 550-pound machine to produce grains measuring between 18 and 24 microns, i.e. the thickness at which the human tongue can no longer feel the grains!

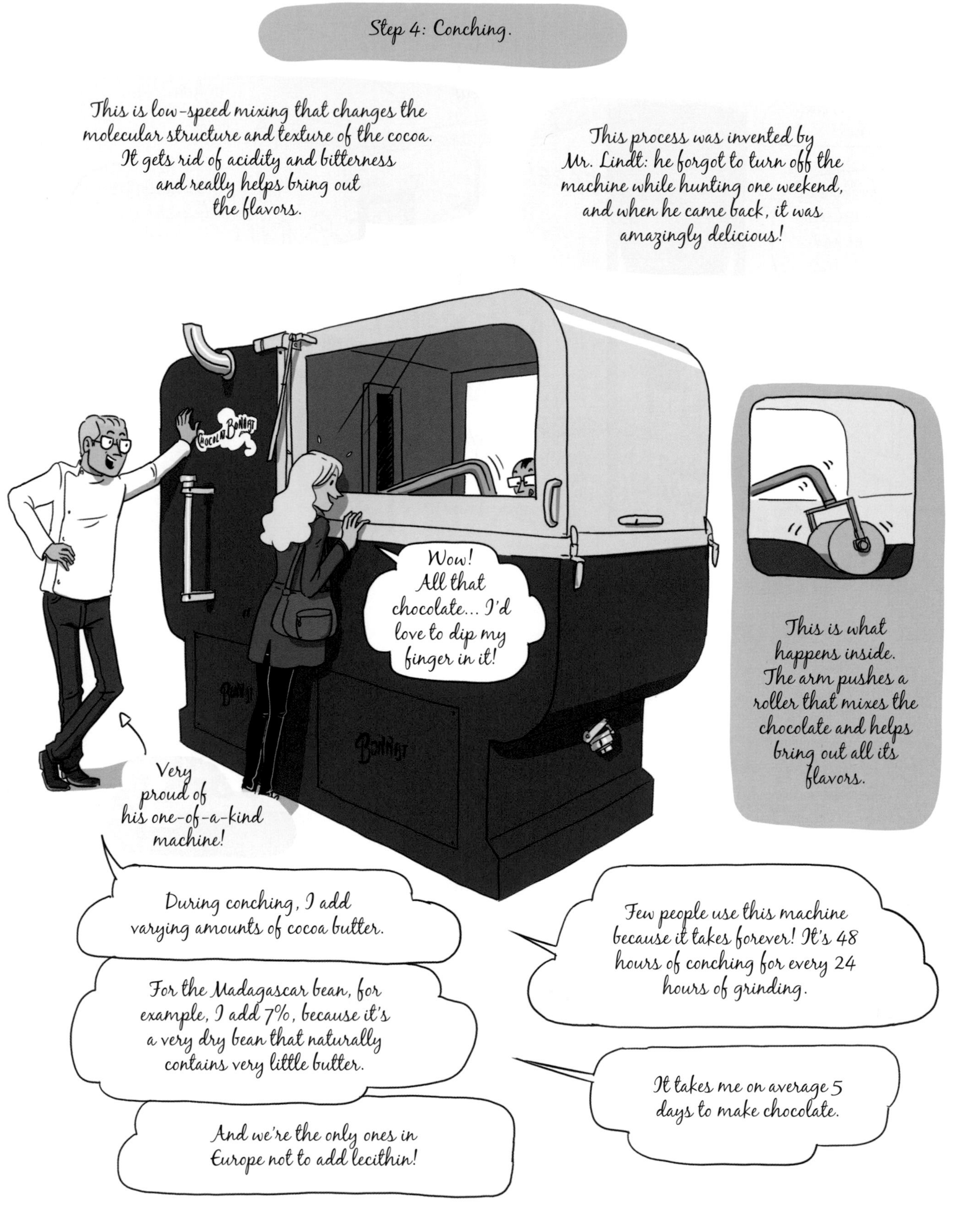
Step 4: Conching.
This is low-speed mixing that changes the molecular structure and texture of the cocoa. It gets rid of acidity and bitterness and really helps bring out the flavors.
This process was invented by Mr. Lindt: he forgot to turn off the machine while hunting one weekend, and when he came back, it was amazingly delicious!
Wow! All that chocolate... I'd love to dip my finger in it!
This is what happens inside. The arm pushes a roller that mixes the chocolate and helps bring out all its flavors.
Very proud of his one-of-a-kind machine!
During conching, I add varying amounts of cocoa butter.
For the Madagascar bean, for example, I add 7%, because it's a very dry bean that naturally contains very little butter.
And we're the only ones in Europe not to add lecithin!
Few people use this machine because it takes forever! It's 48 hours of conching for every 24 hours of grinding.
It takes me on average 5 days to make chocolate.

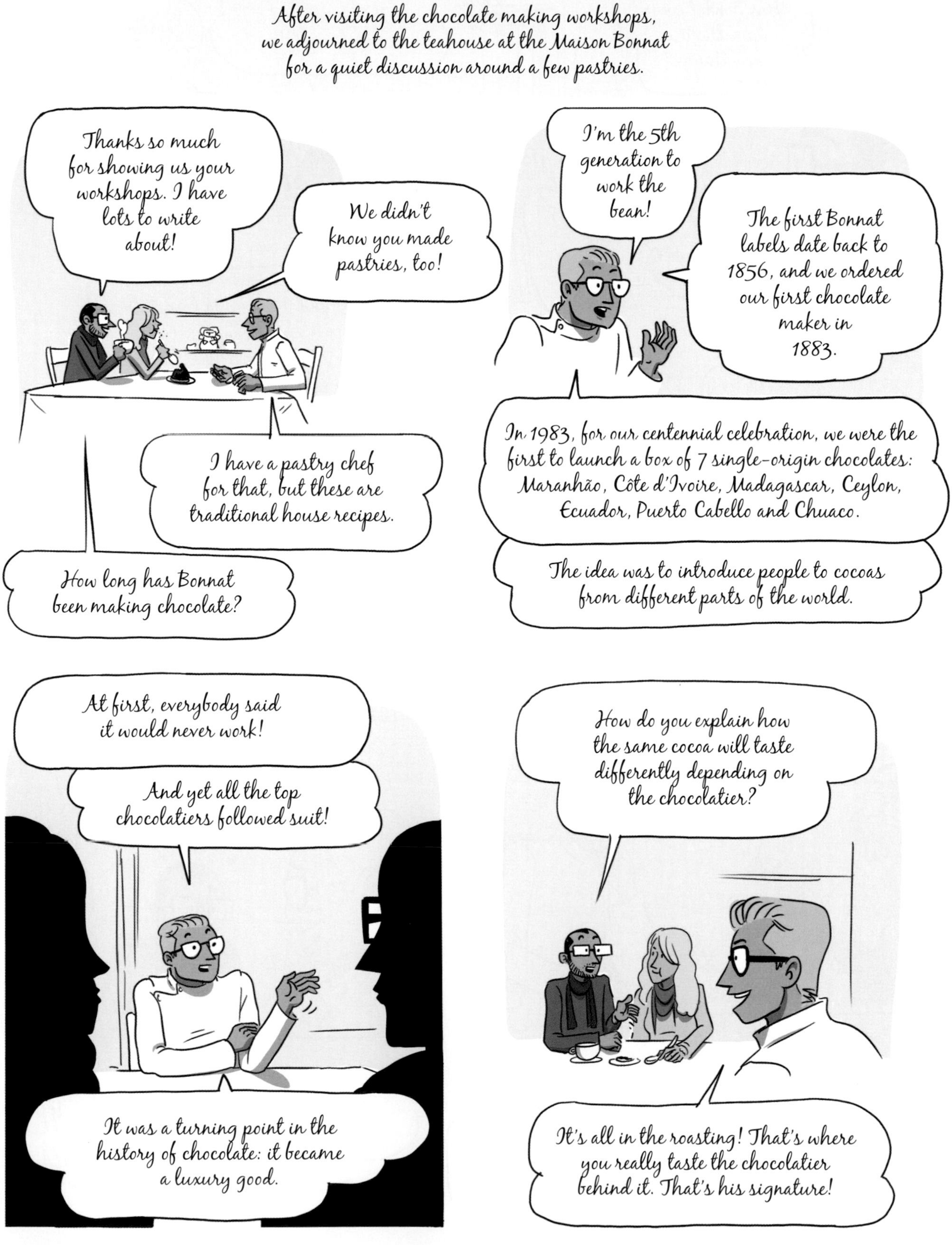

After visiting the chocolate making workshops, we adjourned to the teahouse at the Maison Bonnat for a quiet discussion around a few pastries.
Thanks so much for showing us your workshops. I have lots to write about!
We didn't know you made pastries, too!
I have a pastry chef for that, but these are traditional house recipes.
How long has Bonnat been making chocolate?
I'm the 5th generation to work the bean!
The first Bonnat labels date back to 1856, and we ordered our first chocolate maker in 1883.
In 1983, for our centennial celebration, we were the first to launch a box of 7 single-origin chocolates: Maranhão, Côte d'Ivoire, Madagascar, Ceylon, Ecuador, Puerto Cabello and Chuaco.
The idea was to introduce people to cocoas from different parts of the world.
At first, everybody said it would never work!
And yet all the top chocolatiers followed suit!
It was a turning point in the history of chocolate: it became a luxury good.
How do you explain how the same cocoa will taste differently depending on the chocolatier?
It's all in the roasting! That's where you really taste the chocolatier behind it. That's his signature!

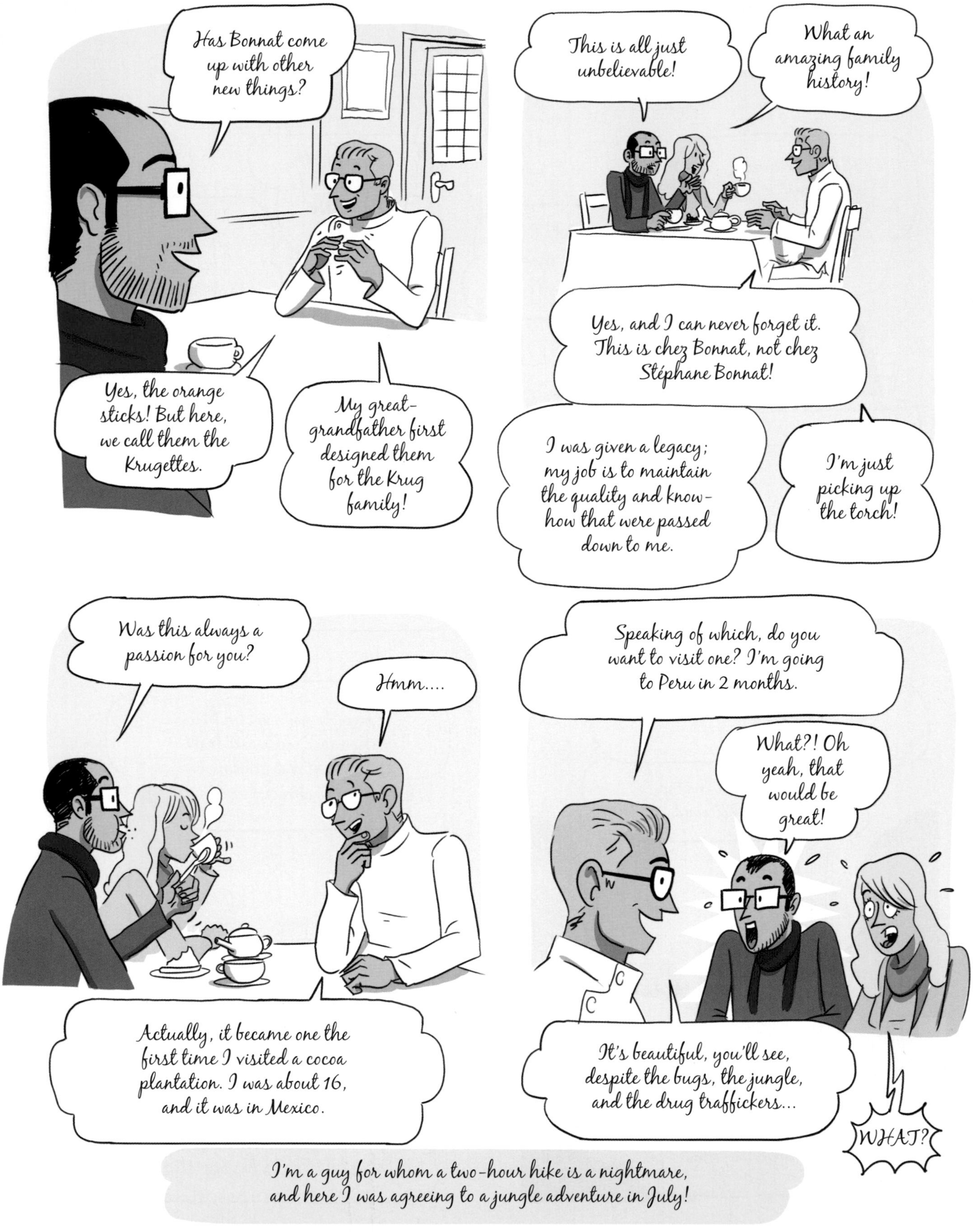
Has Bonnat come up with other new things?
Yes, the orange sticks! But here, we call them the Krugettes.
My great-grandfather first designed them for the Krug family!
This is all just unbelievable!
What an amazing family history!
Yes, and I can never forget it. This is chez Bonnat, not chez Stéphane Bonnat!
I was given a legacy; my job is to maintain the quality and know-how that were passed down to me.
I'm just picking up the torch!
Was this always a passion for you?
Hmm....
Actually, it became one the first time I visited a cocoa plantation. I was about 16, and it was in Mexico.
Speaking of which, do you want to visit one? I'm going to Peru in 2 months.
What?! Oh yeah, that would be great!
It's beautiful, you'll see, despite the bugs, the jungle, and the drug traffickers...
WHAT?
I'm a guy for whom a two-hour hike is a nightmare, and here I was agreeing to a jungle adventure in July!

VALENTINE'S DAY
LOVE IN THE FORM OF CHOCOLATE

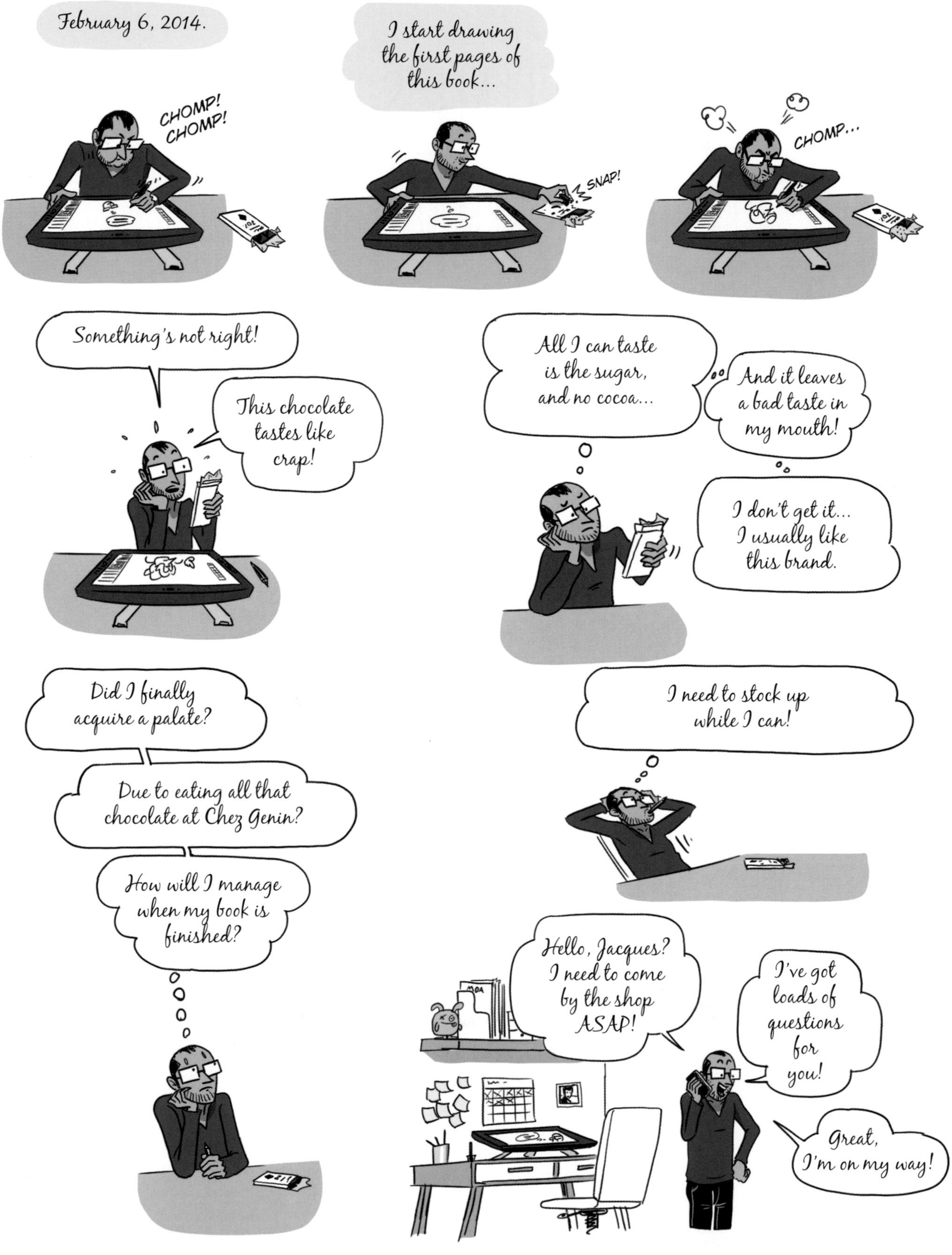
February 6, 2014.
I start drawing the first pages of this book...
CHOMP! CHOMP!
SNAP!
CHOMP...
Something's not right!
This chocolate tastes like crap!
All I can taste is the sugar, and no cocoa...
And it leaves a bad taste in my mouth!
I don't get it... I usually like this brand.
Did I finally acquire a palate?
Due to eating all that chocolate at Chez Genin?
How will I manage when my book is finished?
I need to stock up while I can!
Hello, Jacques? I need to come by the shop ASAP!
I've got loads of questions for you!
Great, I'm on my way!

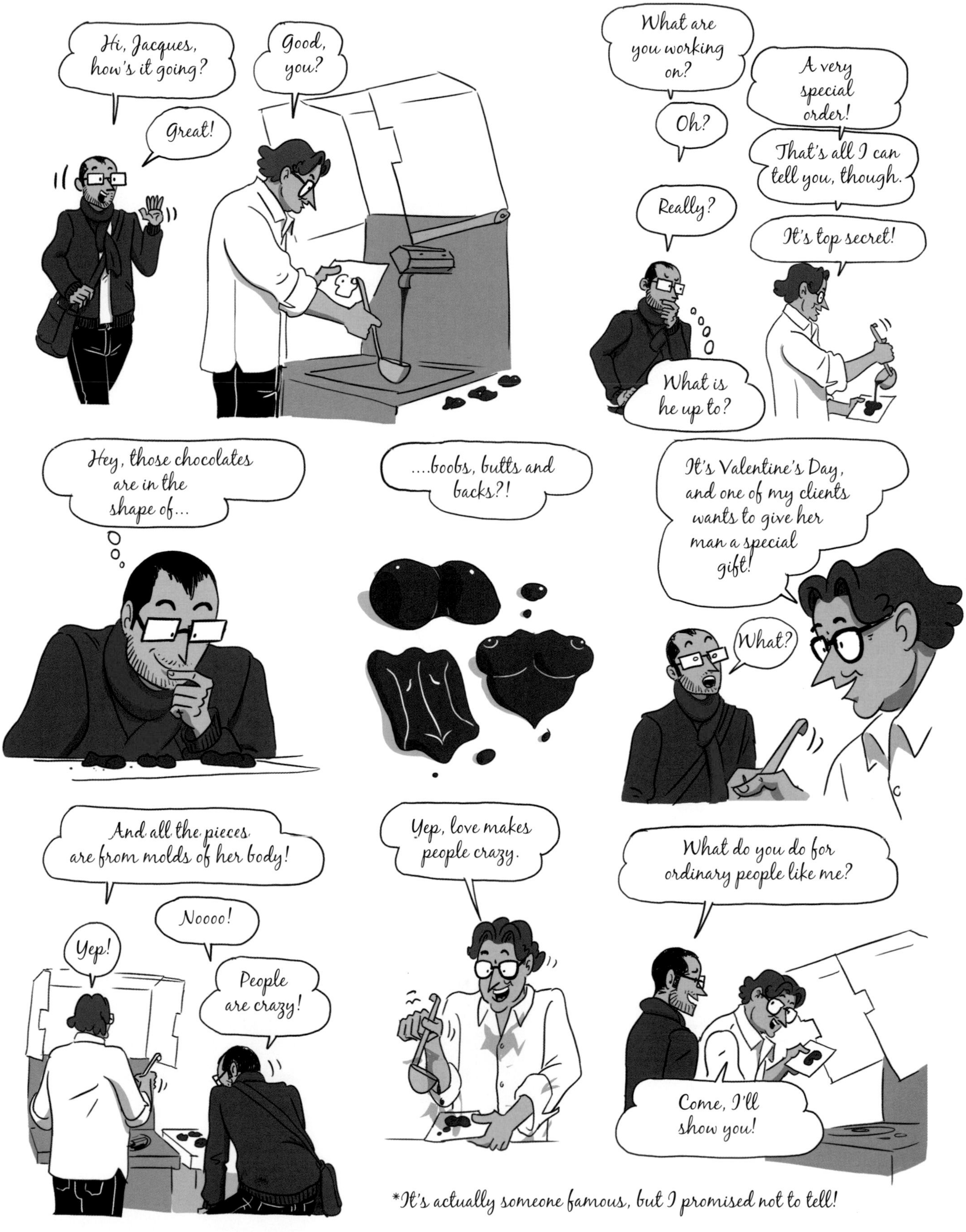

Hi, Jacques, how's it going?
Good, you?
Great!
What are you working on?
Oh?
A very special order!
That's all I can tell you, though.
Really?
It's top secret!
What is he up to?
Hey, those chocolates are in the shape of...
....boobs, butts and backs?!
It's Valentine's Day, and one of my clients wants to give her man a special gift!
What?
And all the pieces are from molds of her body!
Noooo!
Yep!
People are crazy!
Yep, love makes people crazy.
What do you do for ordinary people like me?
Come, I'll show you!

*It's actually someone famous, but I promised not to tell!

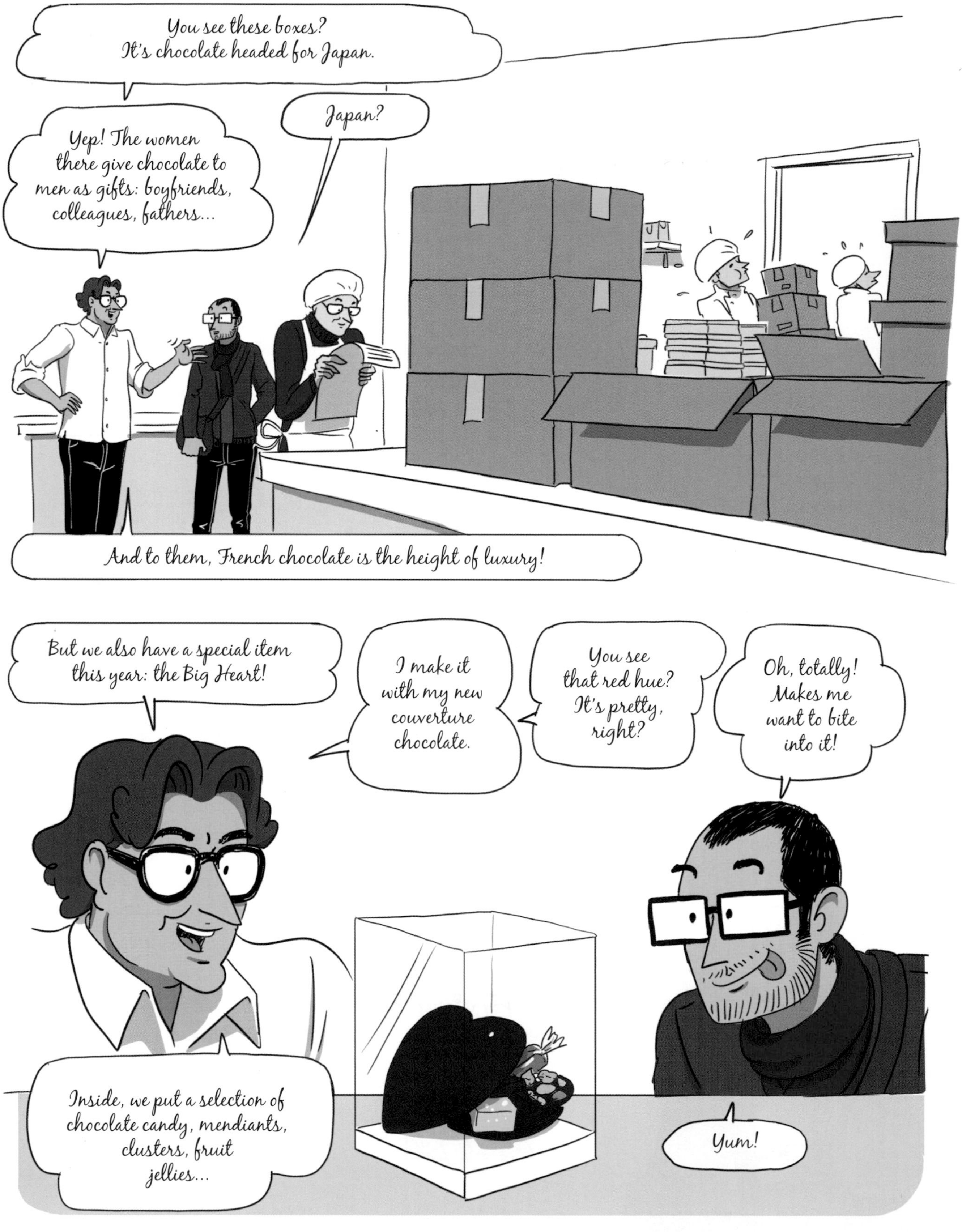
You see these boxes? It's chocolate headed for Japan.
Yep! The women there give chocolate to men as gifts: boyfriends, colleagues, fathers...
Japan?
And to them, French chocolate is the height of luxury!
But we also have a special item this year: the Big Heart!
I make it with my new couverture chocolate.
You see that red hue? It's pretty, right?
Oh, totally! Makes me want to bite into it!
Inside, we put a selection of chocolate candy, mendiants, clusters, fruit jellies...
Yum!

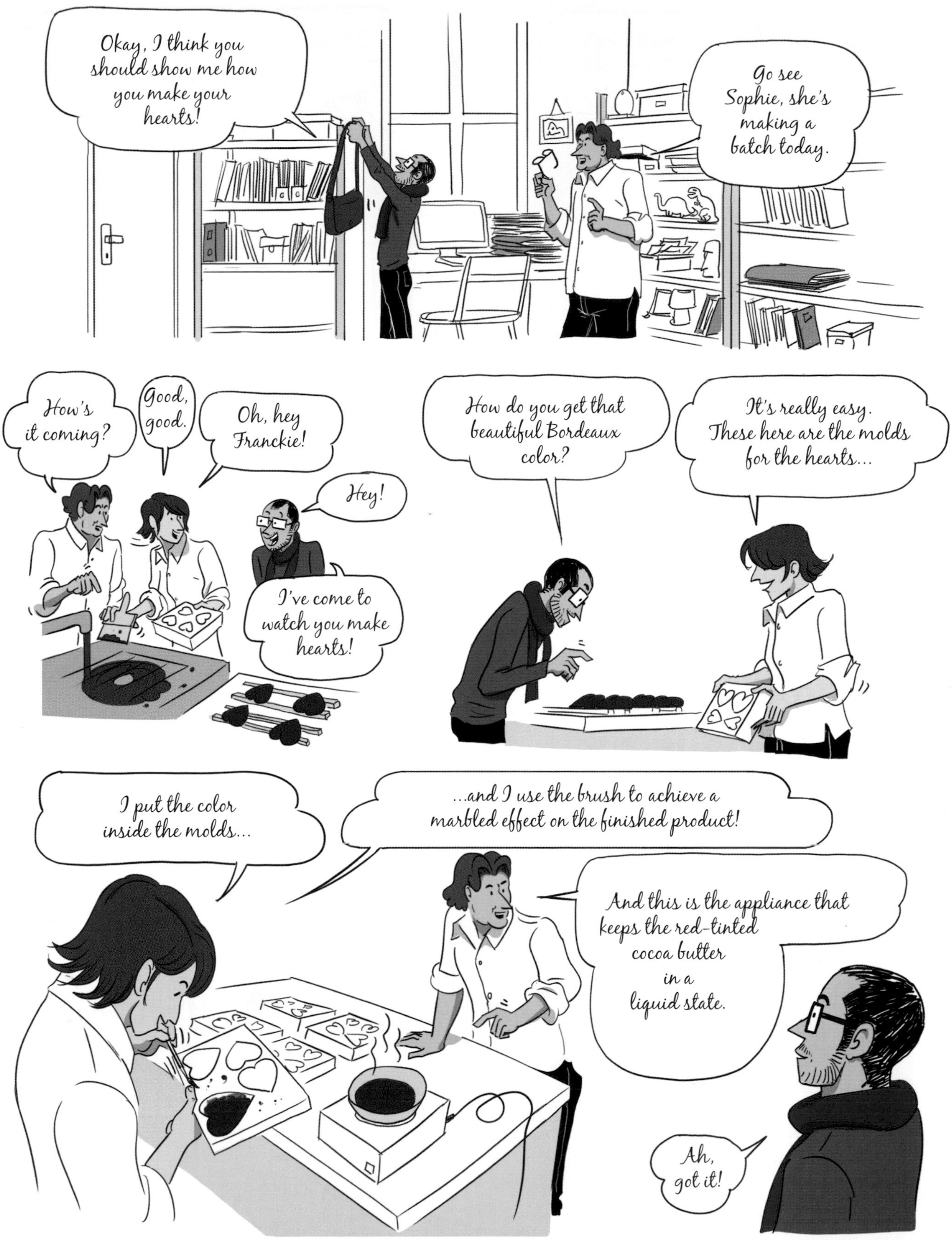
Okay, I think you should show me how you make your hearts!
Go see Sophie, she's making a batch today.
How's it coming?
Good, good.
Oh, hey Franckie!
Hey!
I've come to watch you make hearts!
How do you get that beautiful Bordeaux color?
It's really easy. These here are the molds for the hearts...
I put the color inside the molds...
...and I use the brush to achieve a marbled effect on the finished product!
And this is the appliance that keeps the red-tinted cocoa butter in a liquid state.
Ah, got it!

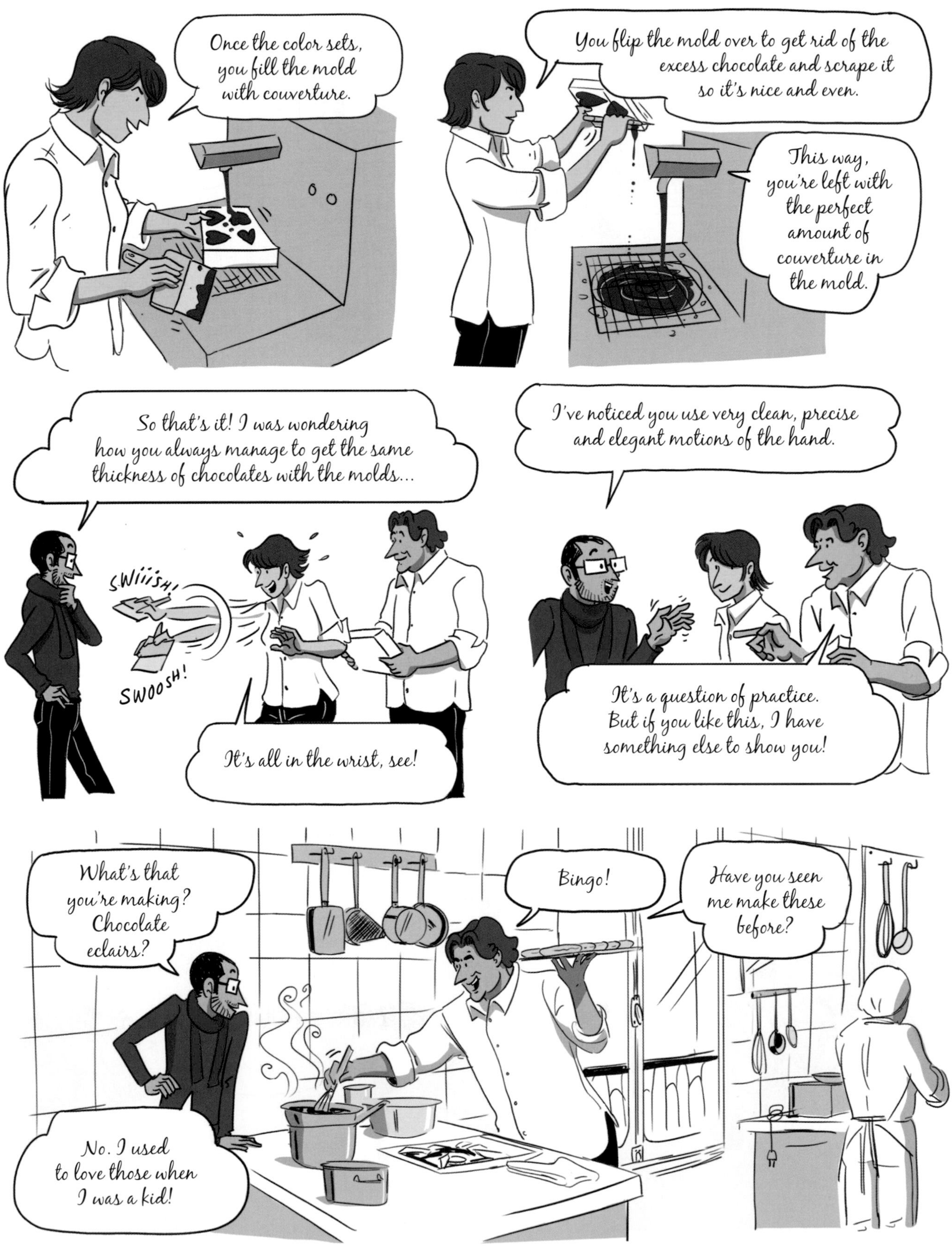
Once the color sets, you fill the mold with couverture.
You flip the mold over to get rid of the excess chocolate and scrape it so it's nice and even.
This way, you're left with the perfect amount of couverture in the mold.
So that's it! I was wondering how you always manage to get the same thickness of chocolates with the molds...
SWIIISH!
SWOOSH!
It's all in the wrist, see!
I've noticed you use very clean, precise and elegant motions of the hand.
It's a question of practice. But if you like this, I have something else to show you!
What's that you're making? Chocolate eclairs?
Bingo!
Have you seen me make these before?
No. I used to love those when I was a kid!

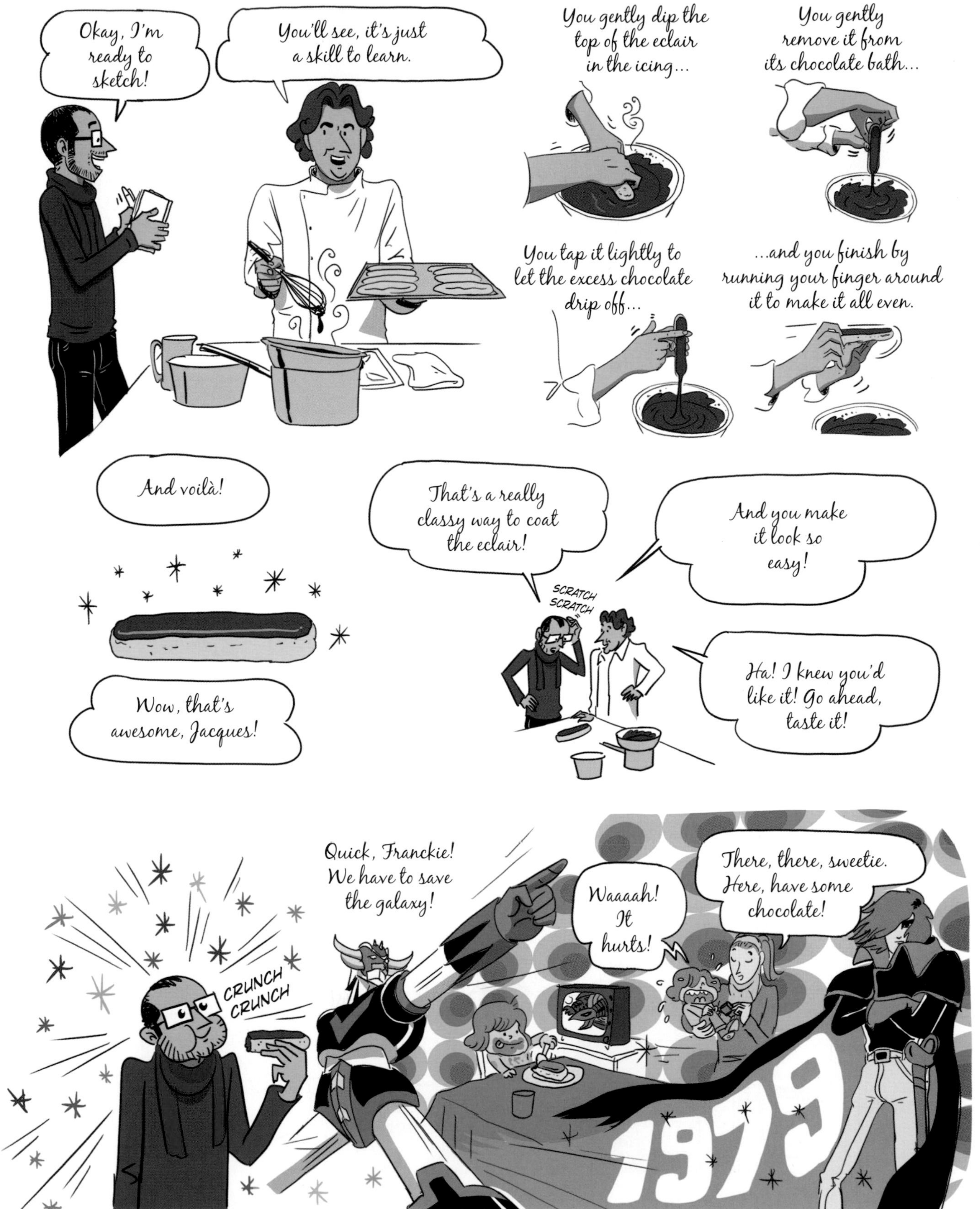
Okay, I'm ready to sketch!
You'll see, it's just a skill to learn.
You gently dip the top of the eclair in the icing...
You gently remove it from its chocolate bath...
You tap it lightly to let the excess chocolate drip off...
...and you finish by running your finger around it to make it all even.
And voilà!
Wow, that's awesome, Jacques!
That's a really classy way to coat the eclair!
And you make it look so easy!
SCRATCH SCRATCH
Ha! I knew you'd like it! Go ahead, taste it!
CRUNCH CRUNCH
Quick, Franckie! We have to save the galaxy!
Waaaah! It hurts!
There, there, sweetie. Here, have some chocolate!
1979

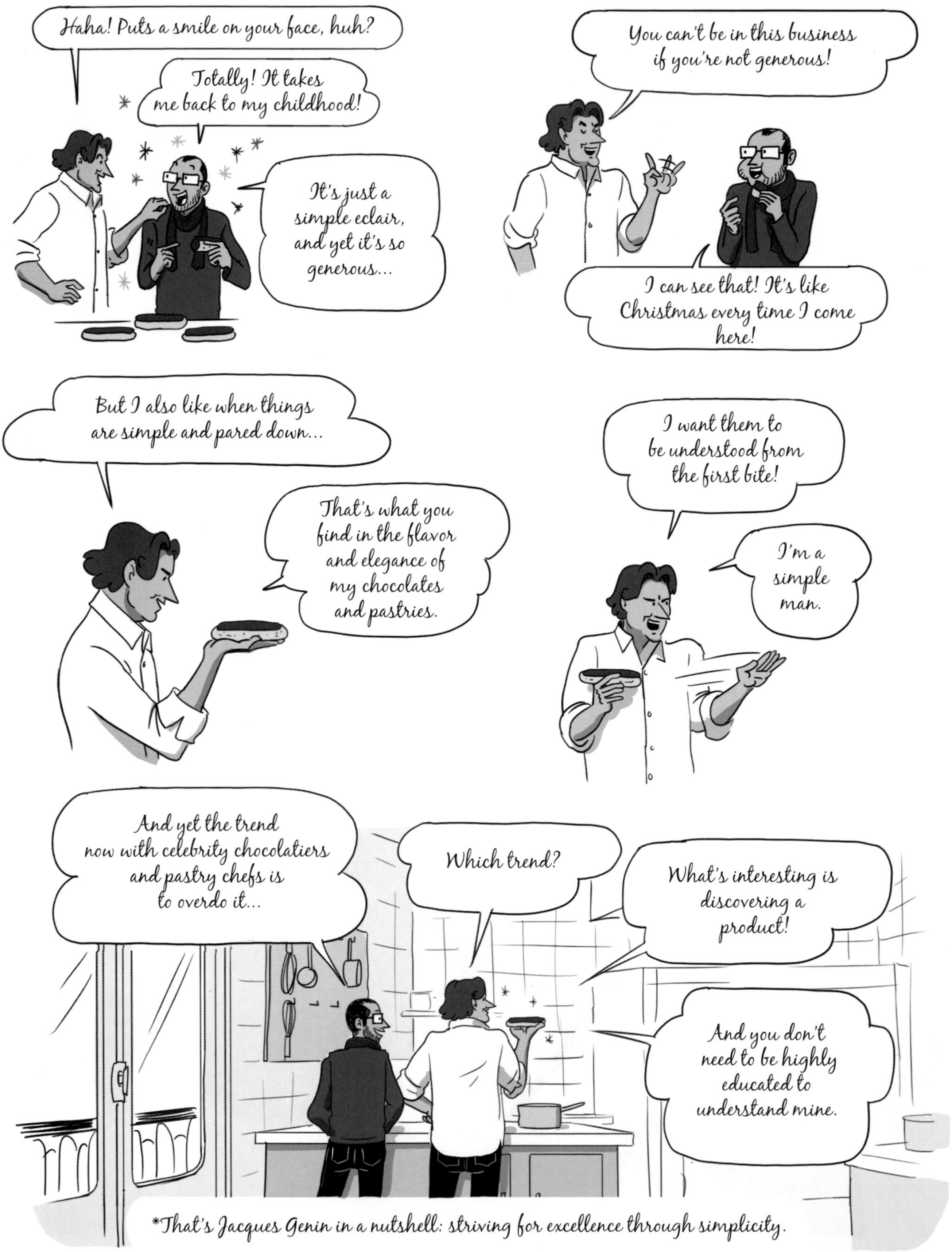
Haha! Puts a smile on your face, huh?
Totally! It takes me back to my childhood!
It's just a simple eclair, and yet it's so generous...
You can't be in this business if you're not generous!
I can see that! It's like Christmas every time I come here!
But I also like when things are simple and pared down...
That's what you find in the flavor and elegance of my chocolates and pastries.
I want them to be understood from the first bite!
I'm a simple man.
And yet the trend now with celebrity chocolatiers and pastry chefs is to overdo it...
Which trend?
What's interesting is discovering a product!
And you don't need to be highly educated to understand mine.
*That's Jacques Genin in a nutshell: striving for excellence through simplicity.

EASTER

ART ON CHOCOLATE

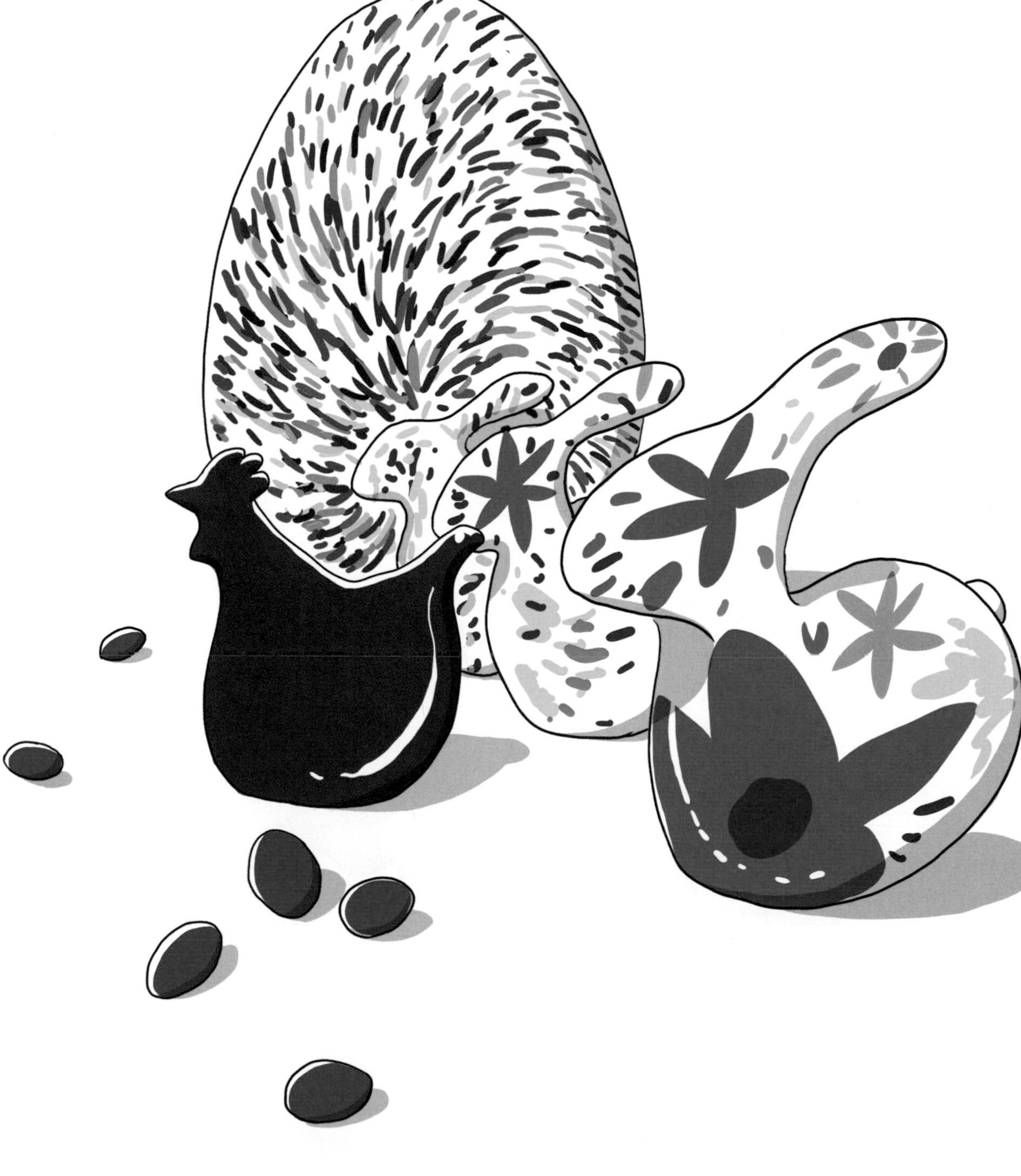

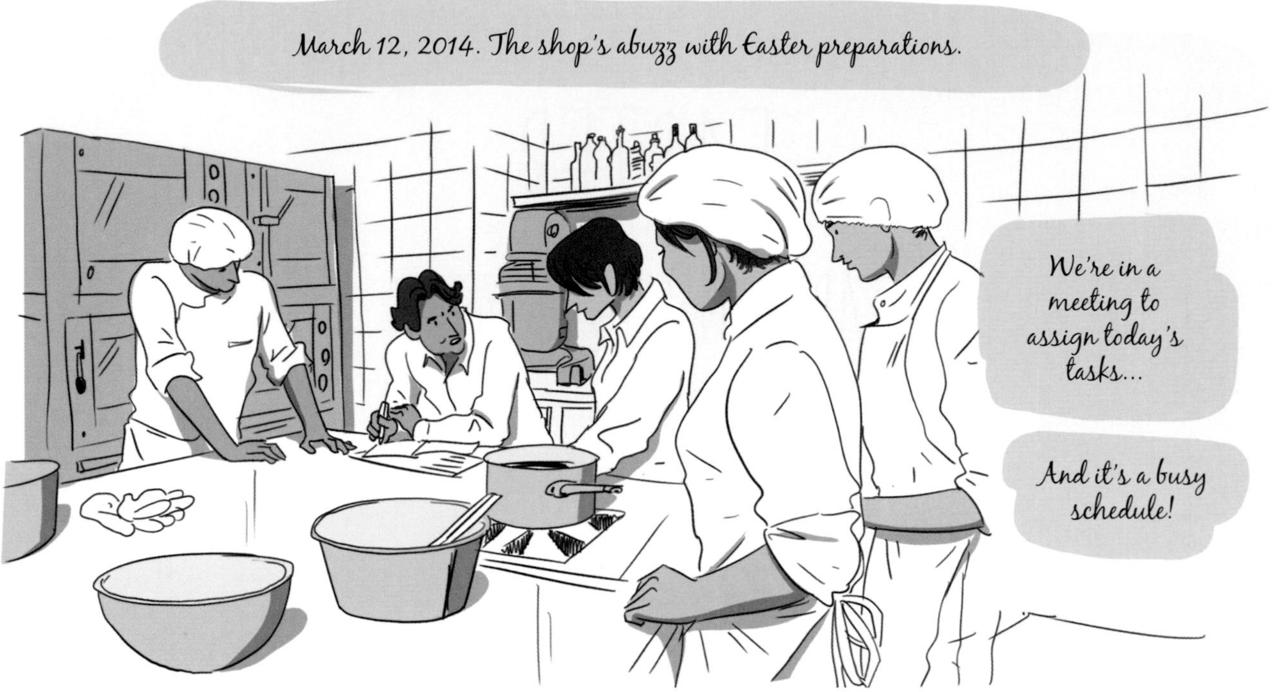
March 12, 2014. The shop's abuzz with Easter preparations.
We're in a meeting to assign today's tasks...
And it's a busy schedule!

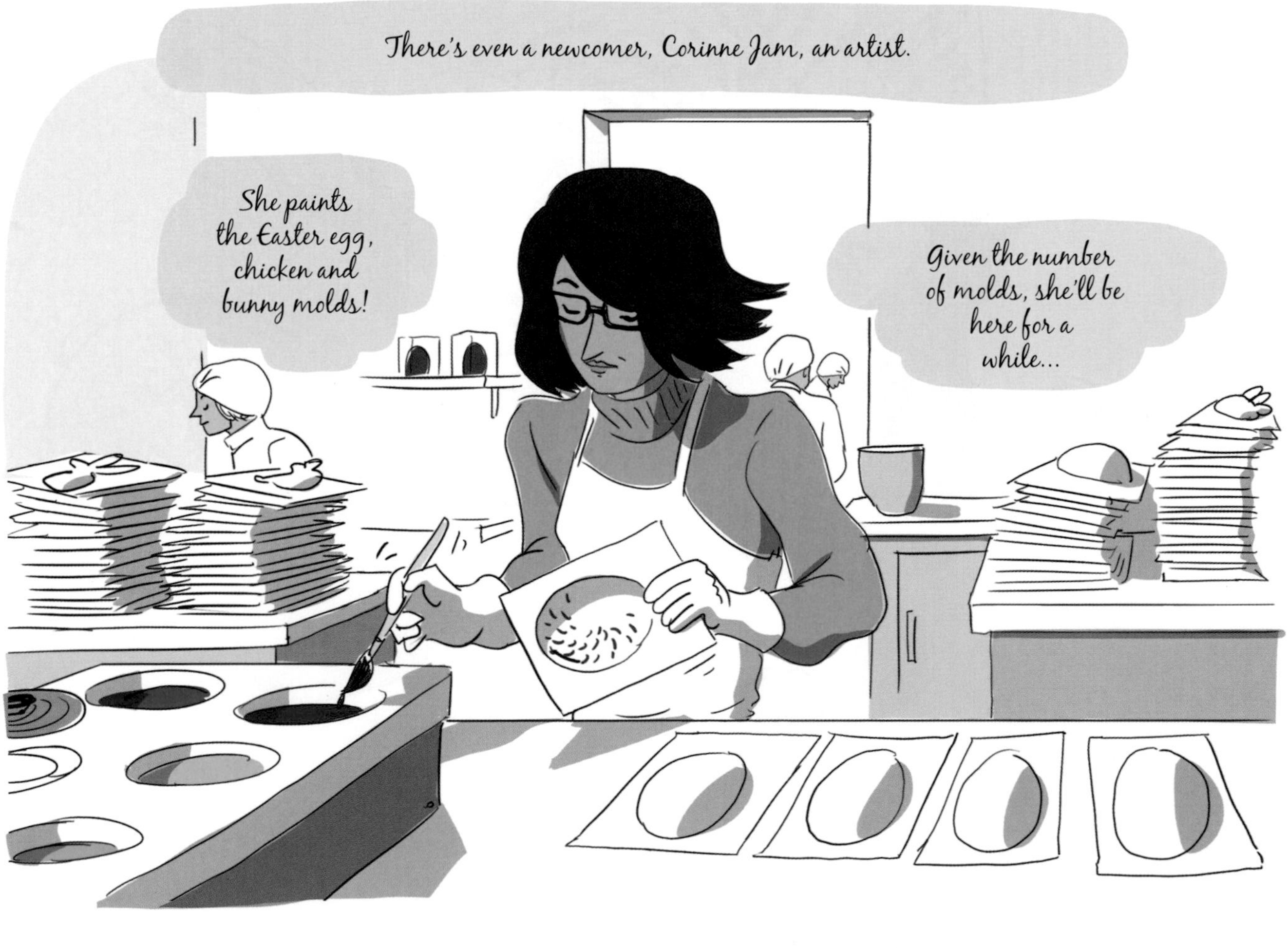
There's even a newcomer, Corinne Jam, an artist.
She paints the Easter egg, chicken and bunny molds!
Given the number of molds, she'll be here for a while...

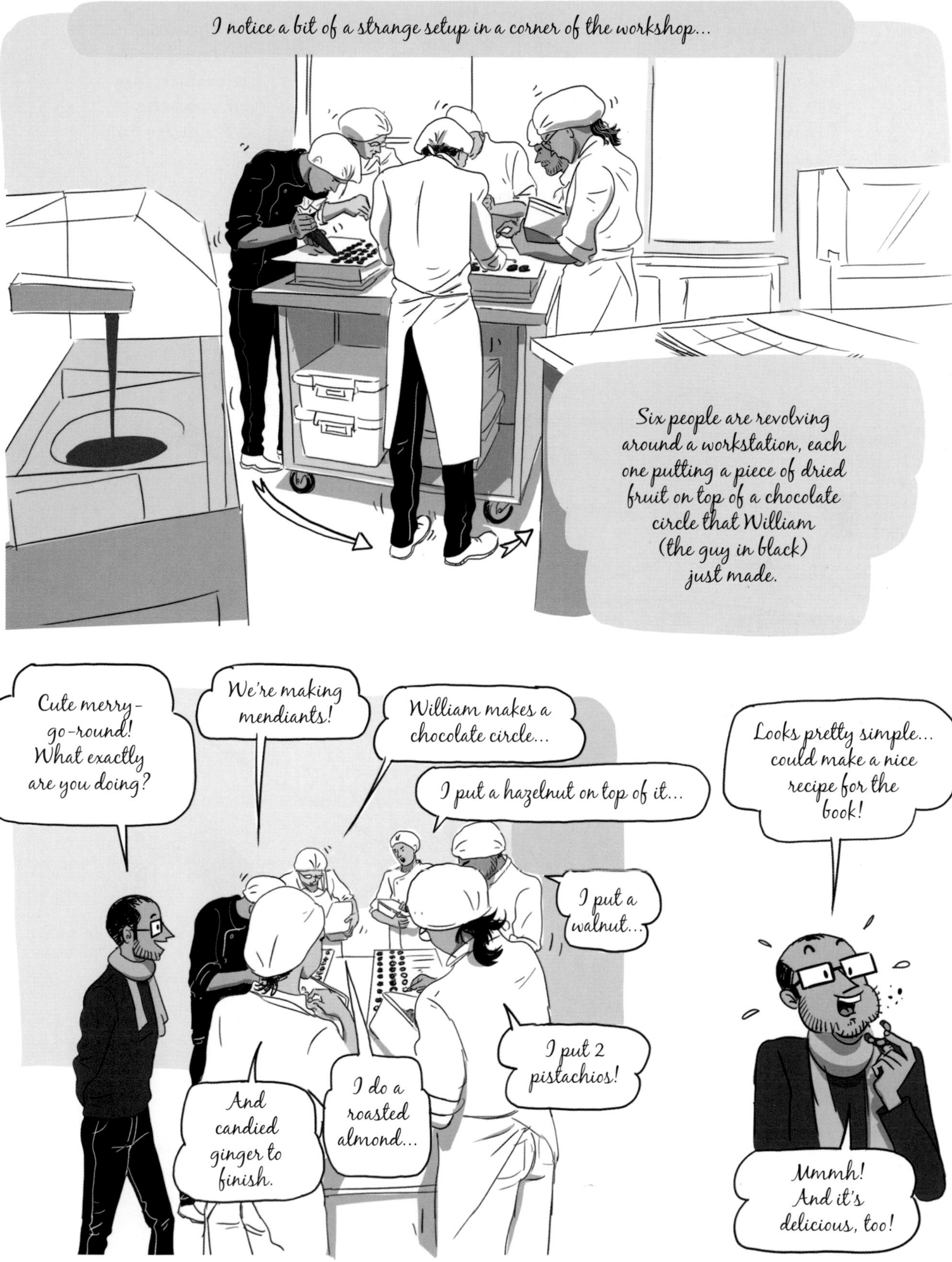
I notice a bit of a strange setup in a corner of the workshop...
Six people are revolving around a workstation, each one putting a piece of dried fruit on top of a chocolate circle that William (the guy in black) just made.
Cute merry-go-round! What exactly are you doing?
We're making mendiants!
William makes a chocolate circle...
I put a hazelnut on top of it...
I put a walnut...
I put 2 pistachios!
I do a roasted almond...
And candied ginger to finish.
Looks pretty simple... could make a nice recipe for the book!
Mmmh! And it's delicious, too!

For this recipe, I asked the mendiant team to demonstrate: William, Rami, Richard, Marie and Sasha.

Chocolate Mendiants

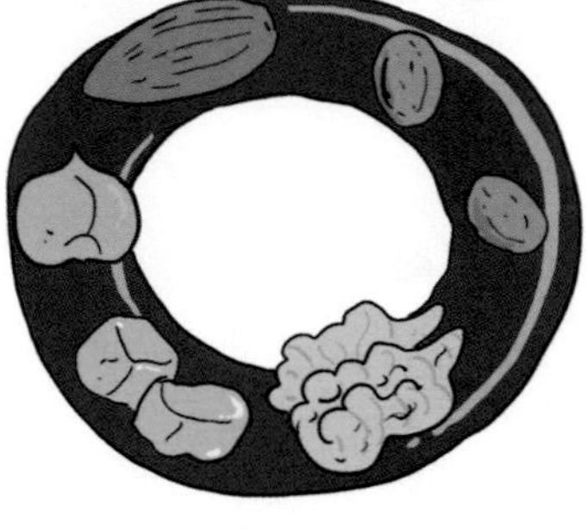

There are 2 steps to this recipe. First, making the couverture, then the confection, with a pastry bag.

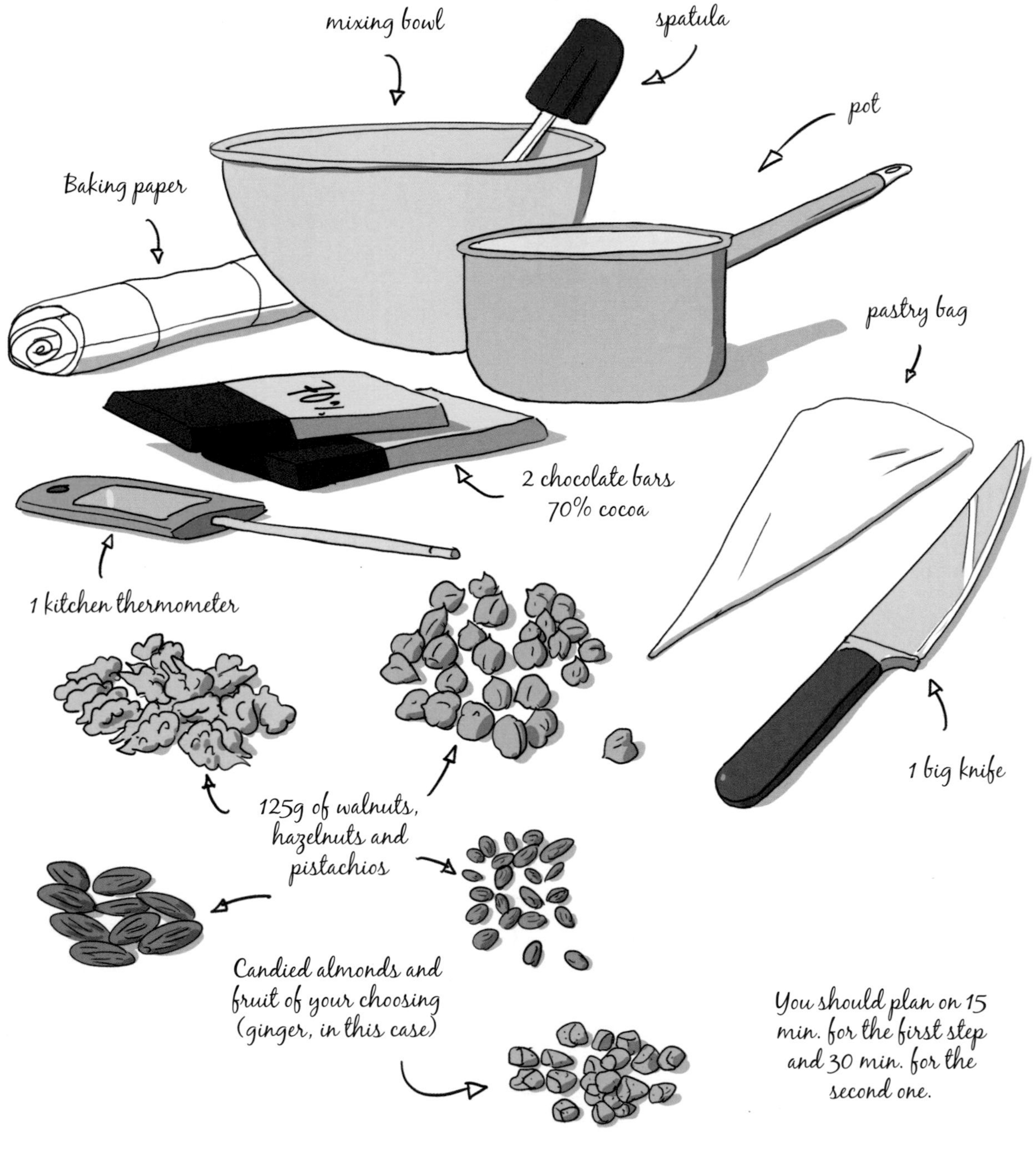
mixing bowl
spatula
pot
Baking paper
pastry bag
70%
2 chocolate bars 70% cocoa
1 kitchen thermometer
1 big knife
125g of walnuts, hazelnuts and pistachios
Candied almonds and fruit of your choosing (ginger, in this case)

You should plan on 15 min. for the first step and 30 min. for the second one.

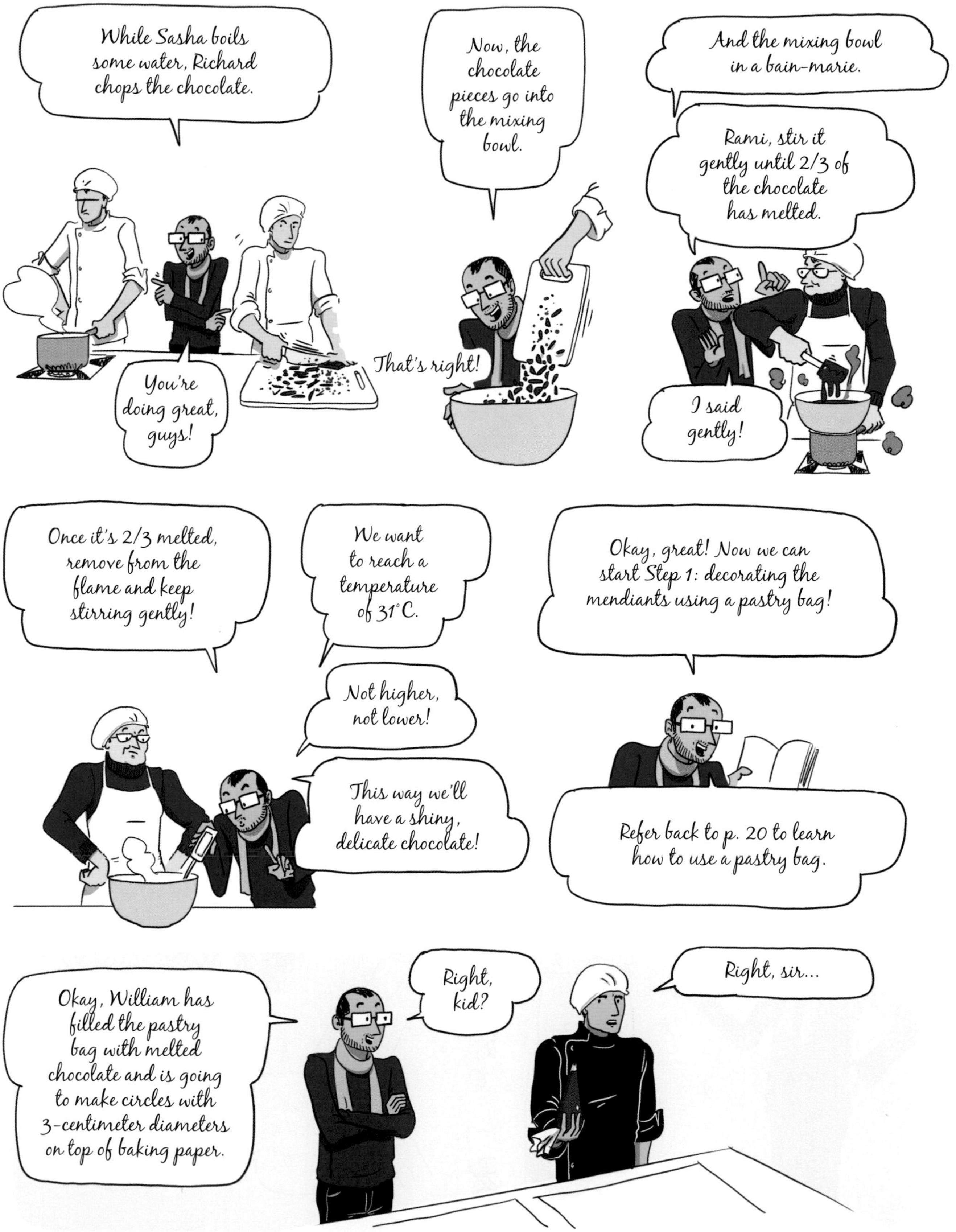
While Sasha boils some water, Richard chops the chocolate.
You're doing great, guys!
That's right!
Now, the chocolate pieces go into the mixing bowl.
And the mixing bowl in a bain-marie.
Rami, stir it gently until 2/3 of the chocolate has melted.
I said gently!
Once it's 2/3 melted, remove from the flame and keep stirring gently!
We want to reach a temperature of 31°C.
Not higher, not lower!
This way we'll have a shiny, delicate chocolate!
Okay, great! Now we can start Step 1: decorating the mendiants using a pastry bag!
Refer back to p. 20 to learn how to use a pastry bag.
Okay, William has filled the pastry bag with melted chocolate and is going to make circles with 3-centimeter diameters on top of baking paper.
Right, kid?
Right, sir...

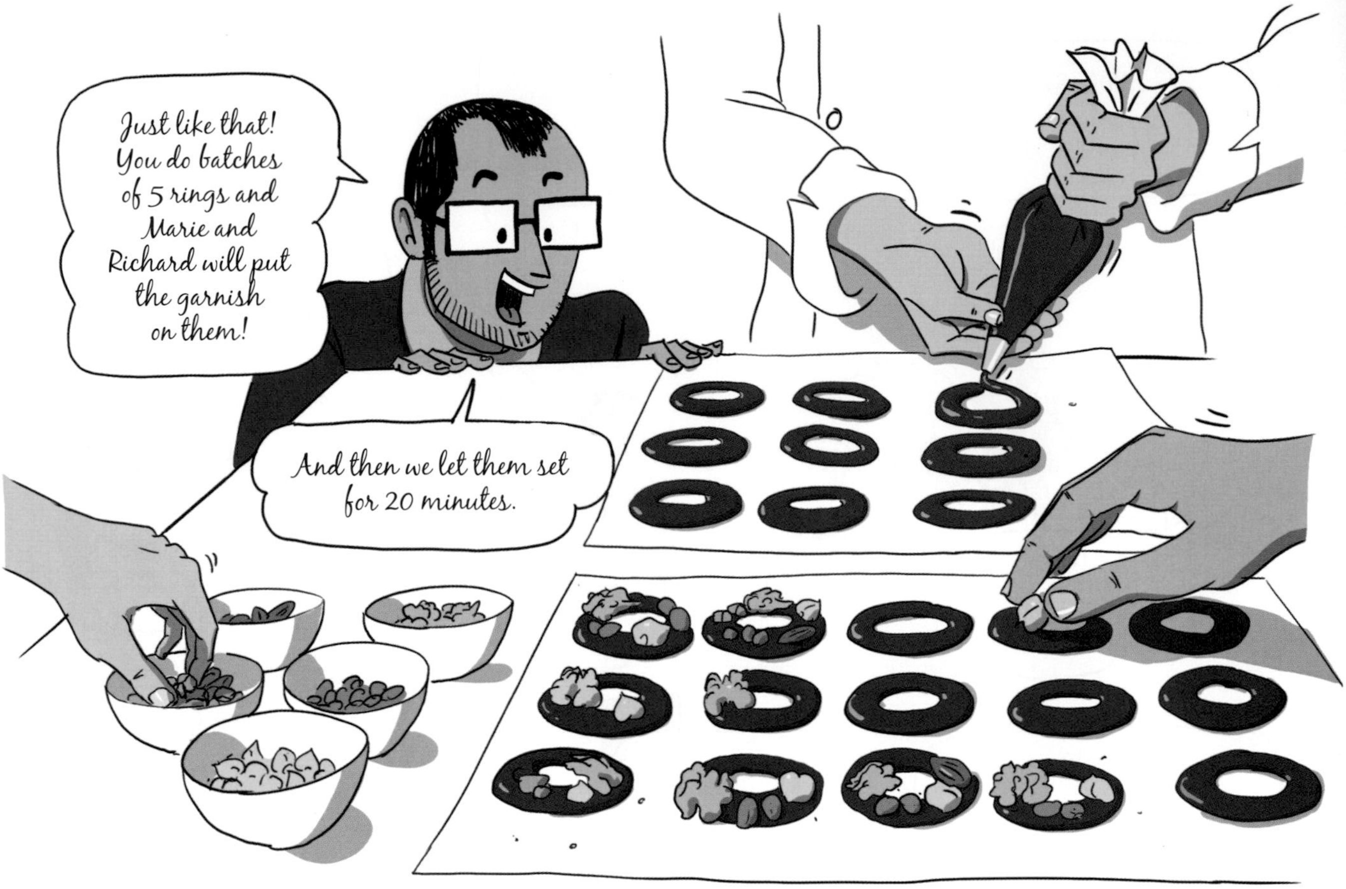
Just like that! You do batches of 5 rings and Marie and Richard will put the garnish on them!
And then we let them set for 20 minutes.

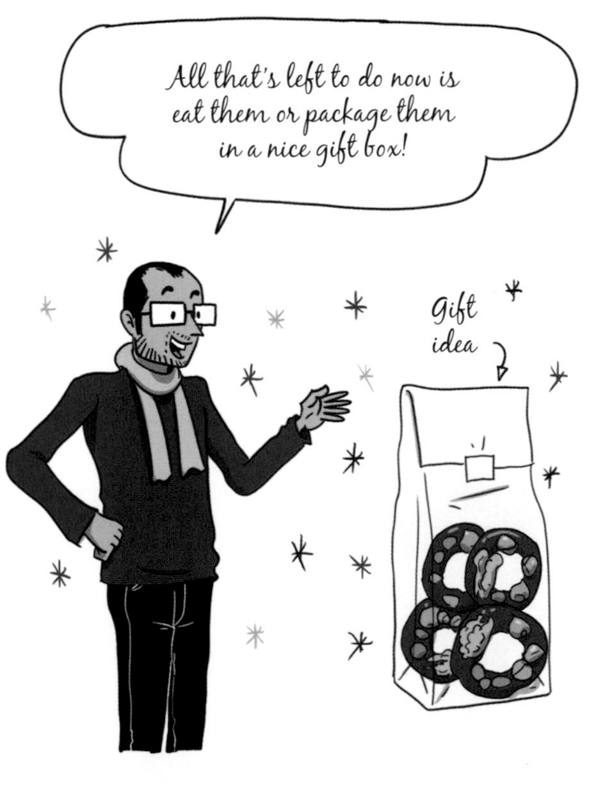
All that's left to do now is eat them or package them in a nice gift box!
Gift idea

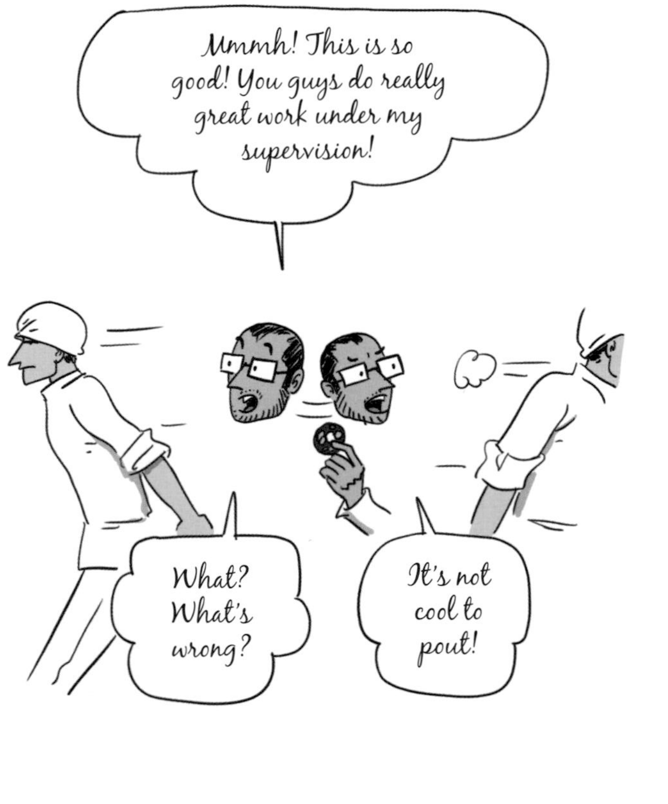
Mmmh! This is so good! You guys do really great work under my supervision!
What? What's wrong?
It's not cool to pout!

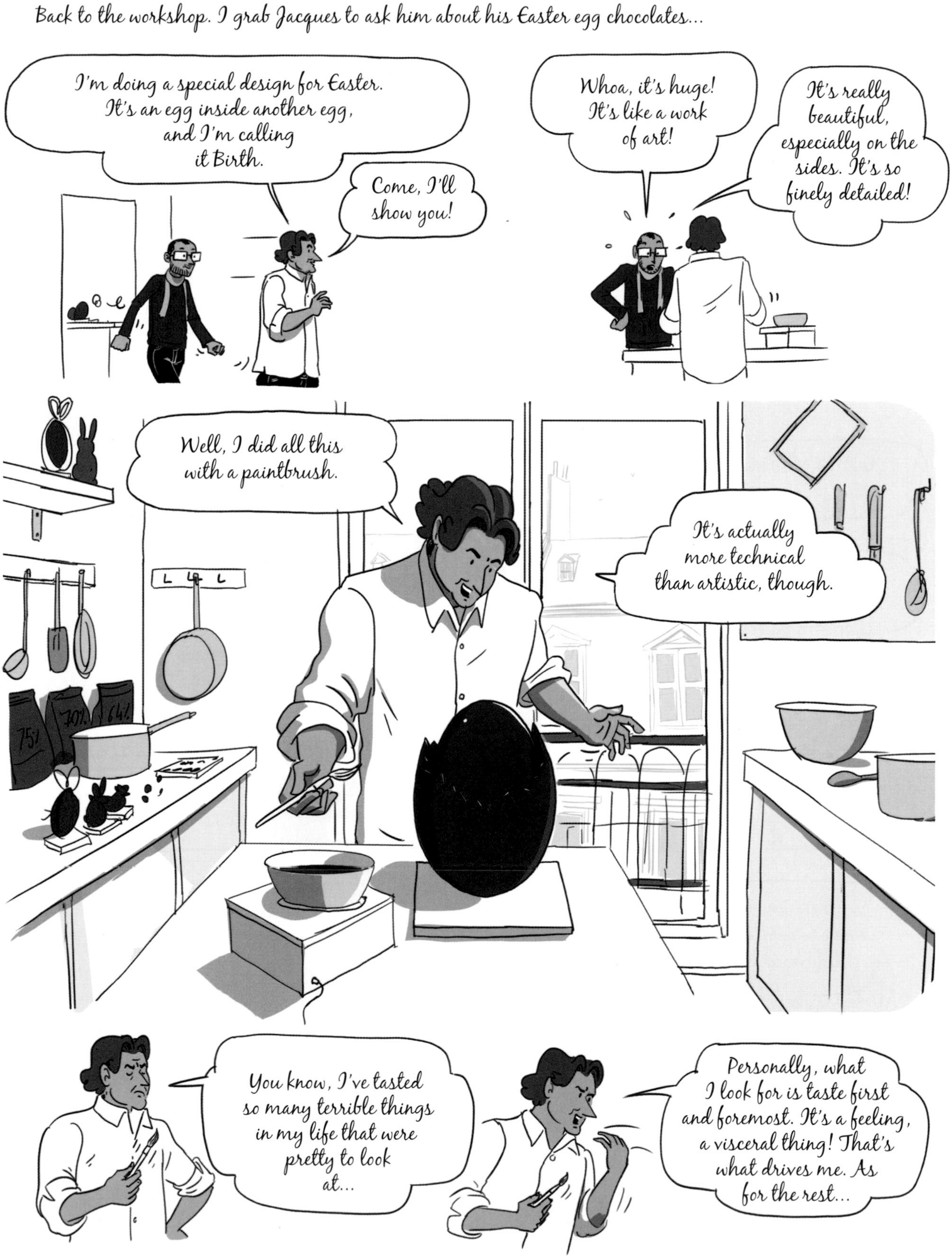
Back to the workshop. I grab Jacques to ask him about his Easter egg chocolates...
I'm doing a special design for Easter. It's an egg inside another egg, and I'm calling it Birth.
Come, I'll show you!
Whoa, it's huge! It's like a work of art!
It's really beautiful, especially on the sides. It's so finely detailed!
Well, I did all this with a paintbrush.
It's actually more technical than artistic, though.
You know, I've tasted so many terrible things in my life that were pretty to look at...
Personally, what I look for is taste first and foremost. It's a feeling, a visceral thing! That's what drives me. As for the rest...

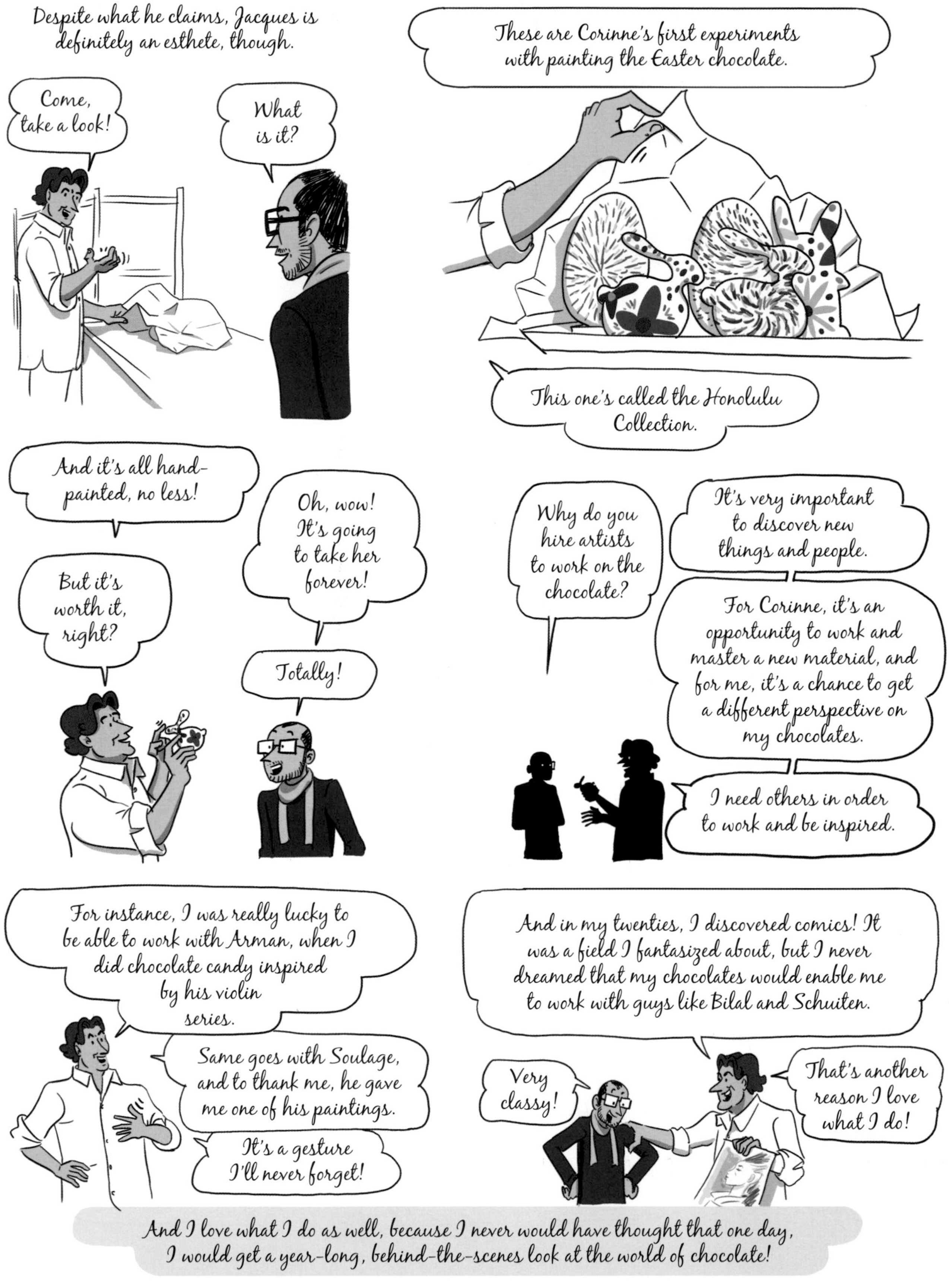

Despite what he claims, Jacques is definitely an esthete, though.
Come, take a look!
What is it?
These are Corinne's first experiments with painting the Easter chocolate.
This one's called the Honolulu Collection.
And it's all hand-painted, no less!
But it's worth it, right?
Oh, wow! It's going to take her forever!
Totally!
Why do you hire artists to work on the chocolate?
It's very important to discover new things and people.
For Corinne, it's an opportunity to work and master a new material, and for me, it's a chance to get a different perspective on my chocolates.
I need others in order to work and be inspired.
For instance, I was really lucky to be able to work with Arman, when I did chocolate candy inspired by his violin series.
Same goes with Soulage, and to thank me, he gave me one of his paintings.
It's a gesture I'll never forget!
And in my twenties, I discovered comics! It was a field I fantasized about, but I never dreamed that my chocolates would enable me to work with guys like Bilal and Schuiten.
Very classy!
That's another reason I love what I do!
And I love what I do as well, because I never would have thought that one day, I would get a year-long, behind-the-scenes look at the world of chocolate!

INTERN

A DIFFICULT LEARNING EXPERIENCE

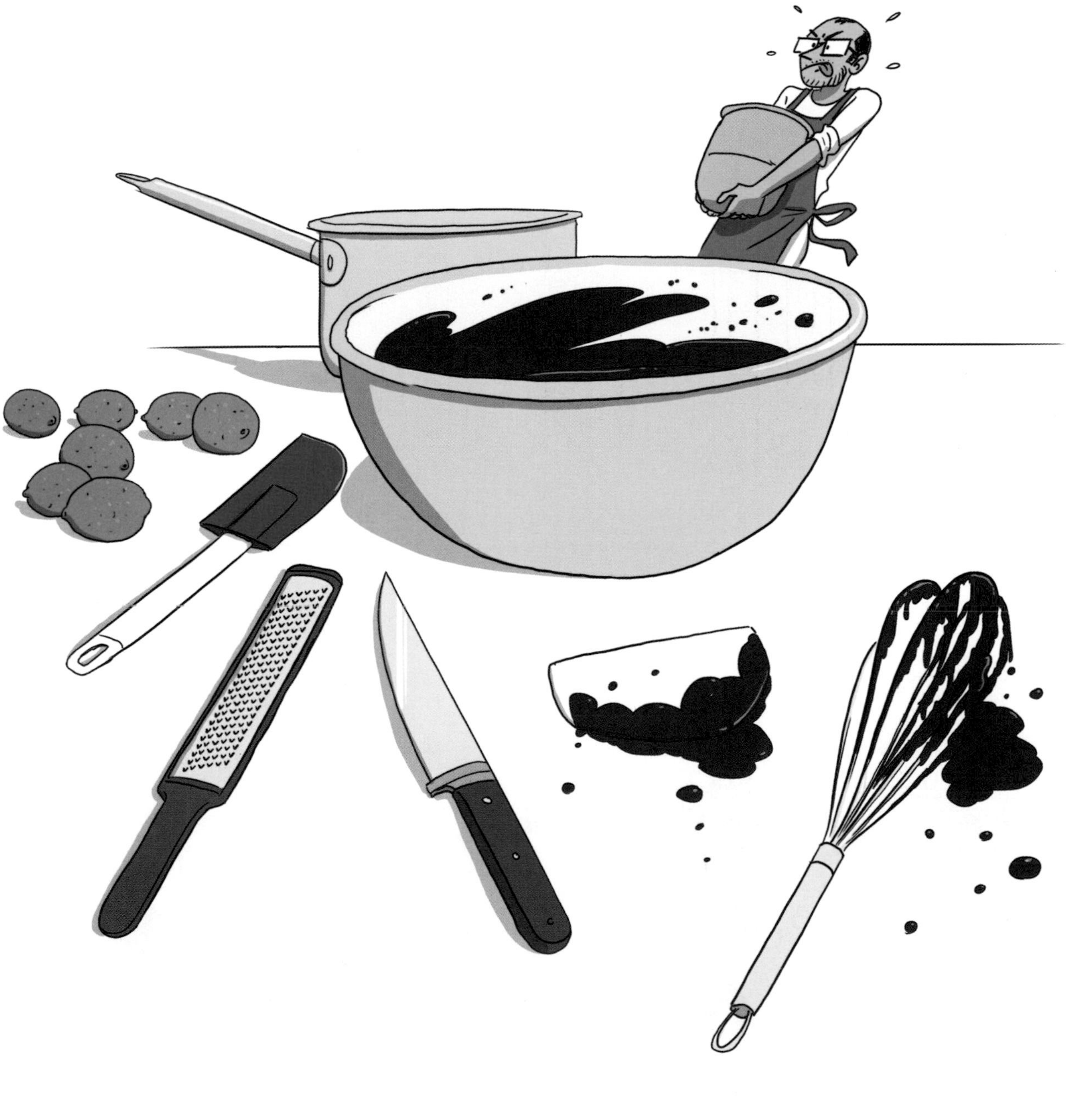

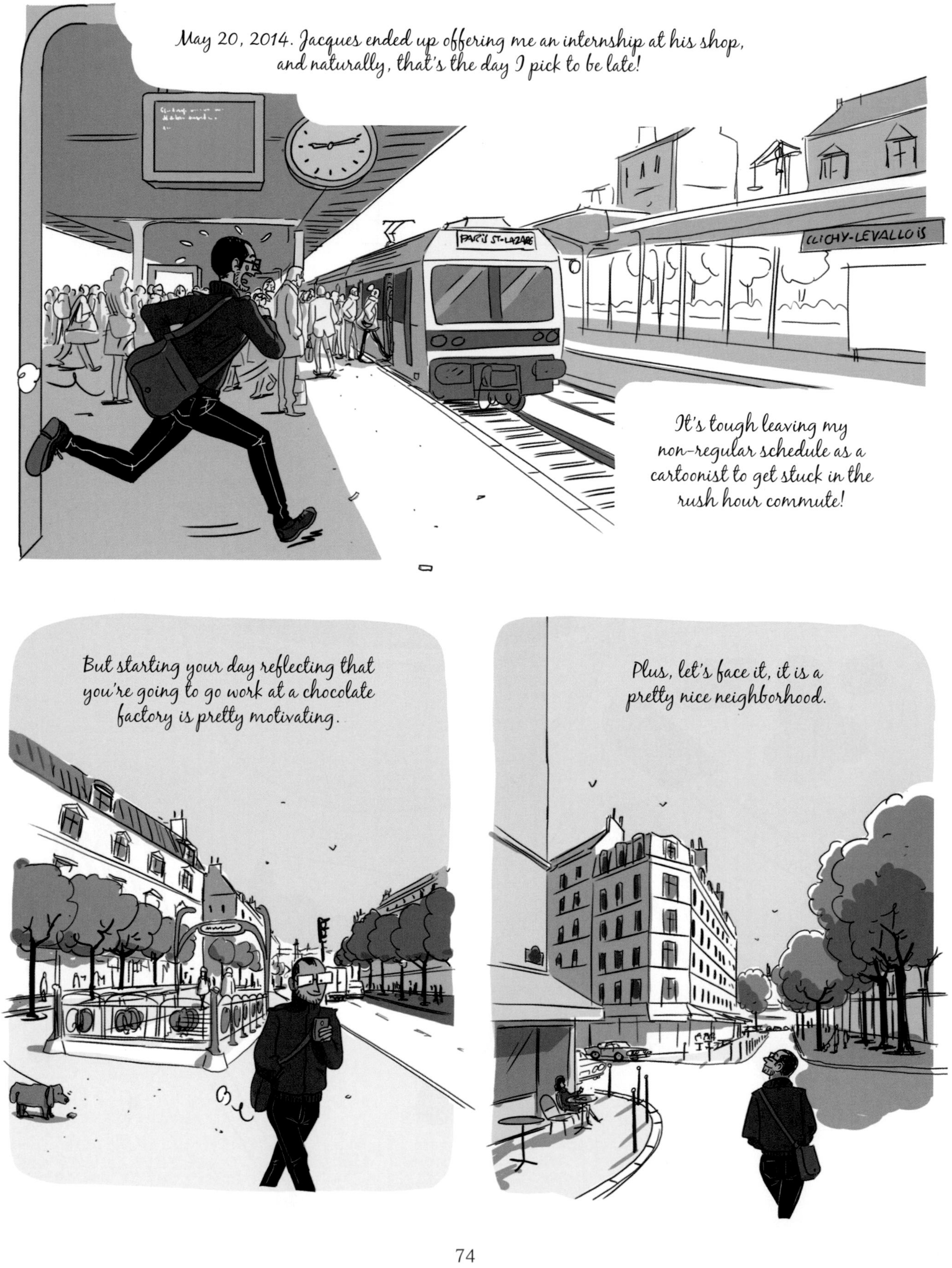
May 20, 2014. Jacques ended up offering me an internship at his shop, and naturally, that's the day I pick to be late!
PARIS ST-LAZARE
CLICHY-LEVALLOIS
It's tough leaving my non-regular schedule as a cartoonist to get stuck in the rush hour commute!
But starting your day reflecting that you're going to go work at a chocolate factory is pretty motivating.
Plus, let's face it, it is a pretty nice neighborhood.

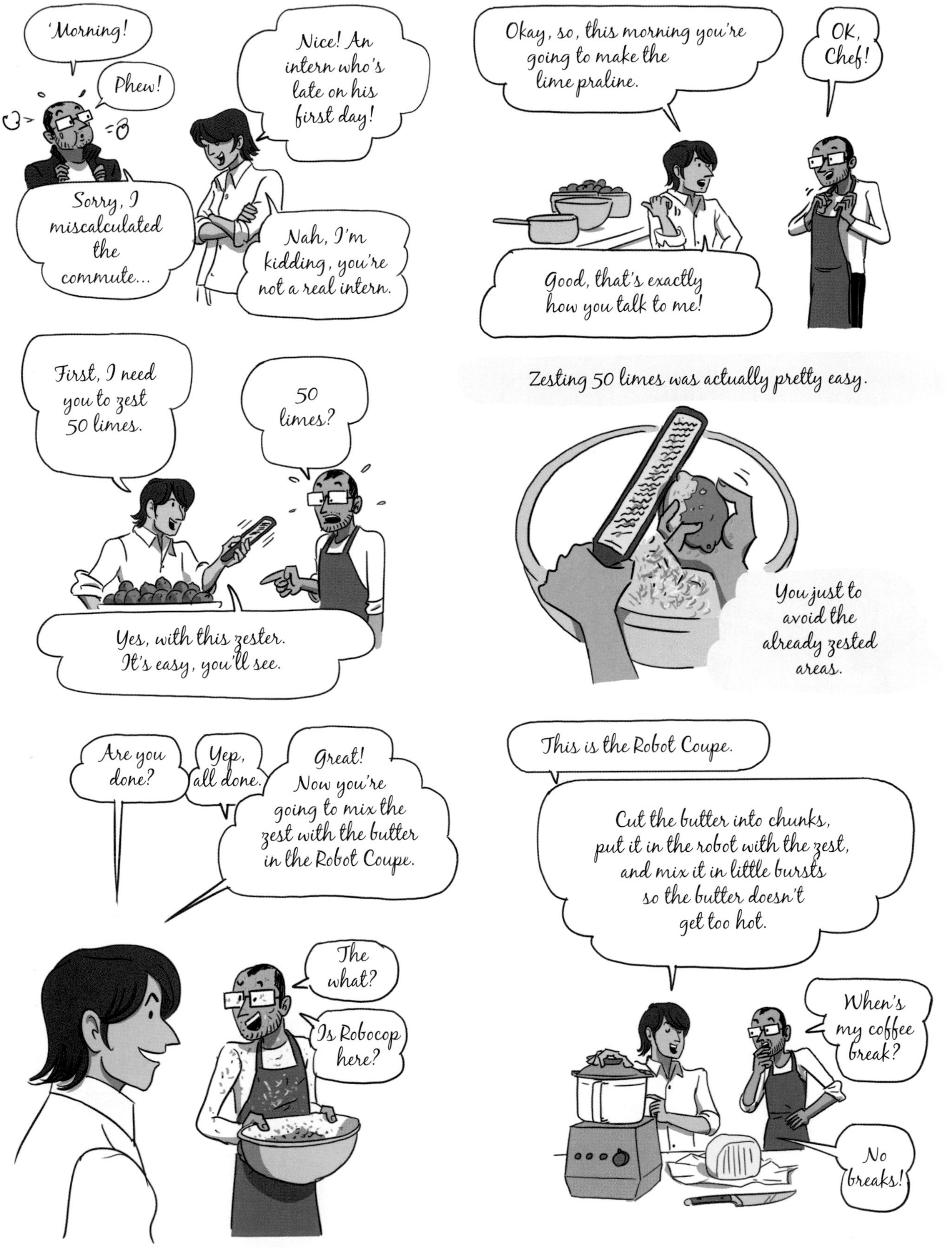

'Morning!
Phew!
Nice! An intern who's late on his first day!
Sorry, I miscalculated the commute...
Nah, I'm kidding, you're not a real intern.
Okay, so, this morning you're going to make the lime praline.
OK, Chef!
Good, that's exactly how you talk to me!
First, I need you to zest 50 limes.
50 limes?
Yes, with this zester. It's easy, you'll see.
Zesting 50 limes was actually pretty easy.
You just to avoid the already zested areas.
Are you done?
Yep, all done.
Great! Now you're going to mix the zest with the butter in the Robot Coupe.
The what?
Is Robocop here?
This is the Robot Coupe.
Cut the butter into chunks, put it in the robot with the zest, and mix it in little bursts so the butter doesn't get too hot.
When's my coffee break?
No breaks!

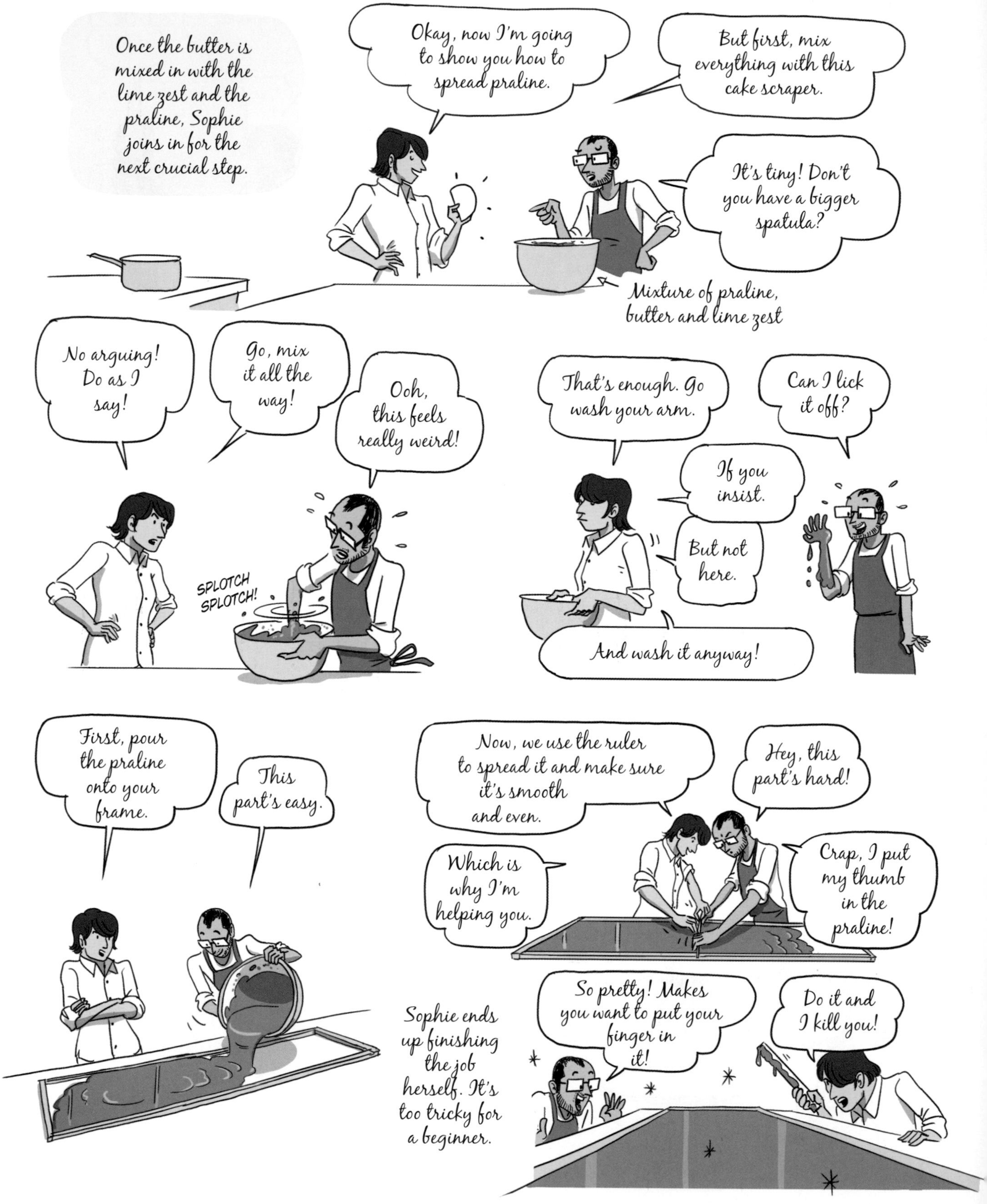
Once the butter is mixed in with the lime zest and the praline, Sophie joins in for the next crucial step.
Okay, now I'm going to show you how to spread praline.
But first, mix everything with this cake scraper.
It's tiny! Don't you have a bigger spatula?
Mixture of praline, butter and lime zest
No arguing! Do as I say!
Go, mix it all the way!
Ooh, this feels really weird!
SPLOTCH SPLOTCH!
That's enough. Go wash your arm.
Can I lick it off?
If you insist.
But not here.
And wash it anyway!
First, pour the praline onto your frame.
This part's easy.
Now, we use the ruler to spread it and make sure it's smooth and even.
Hey, this part's hard!
Which is why I'm helping you.
Crap, I put my thumb in the praline!
Sophie ends up finishing the job herself. It's too tricky for a beginner.
So pretty! Makes you want to put your finger in it!
Do it and I kill you!

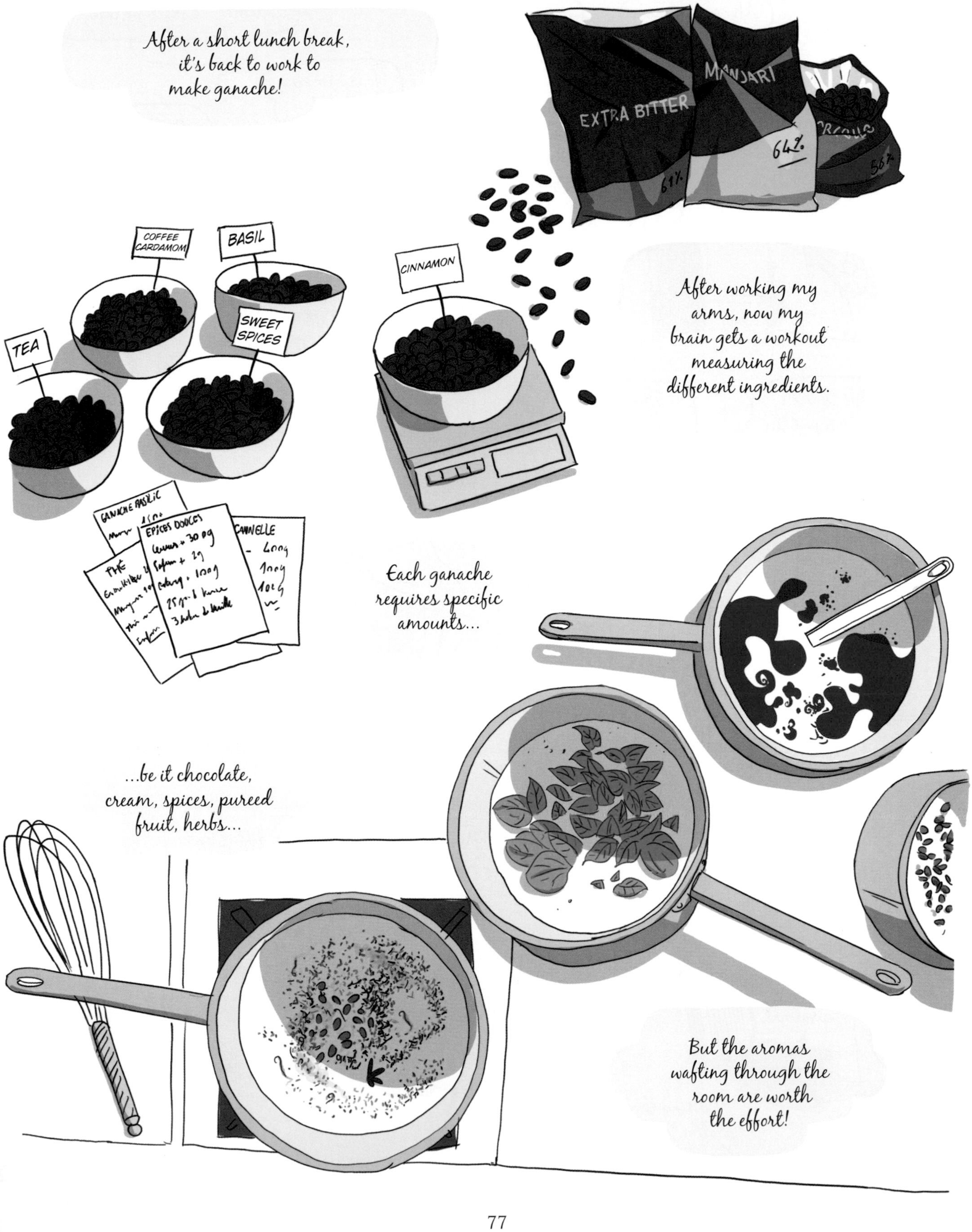
After a short lunch break, it's back to work to make ganache!
EXTRA BITTER
61%
MANJARI
64%
COFFEE CARDAMOM
BASIL
TEA
SWEET SPICES
CINNAMON
After working my arms, now my brain gets a workout measuring the different ingredients.
GANACHE BASILIC
EPICES DOUCES
CANNELLE
THE
Each ganache requires specific amounts...
...be it chocolate, cream, spices, pureed fruit, herbs...
But the aromas wafting through the room are worth the effort!

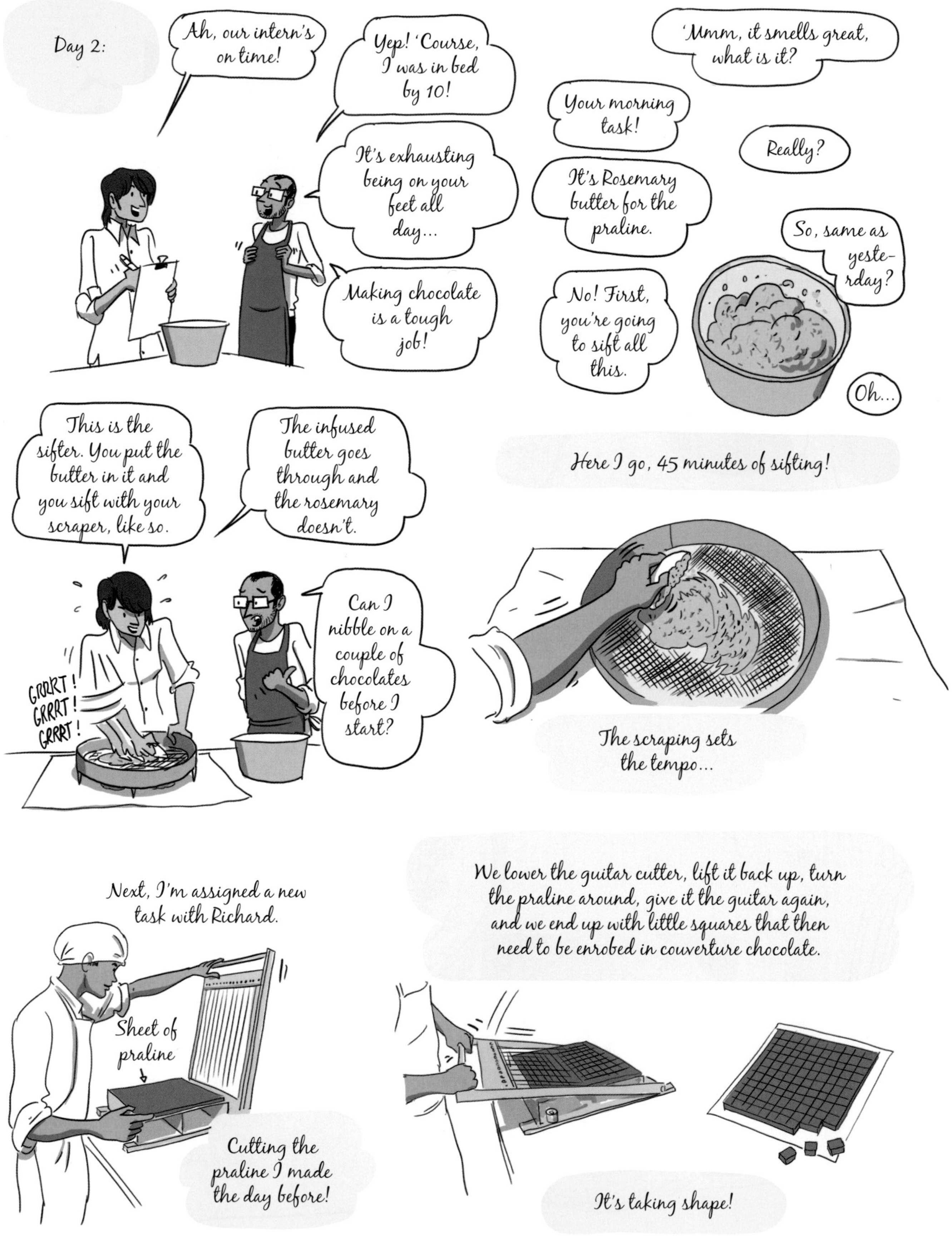
Day 2:
Ah, our intern's on time!
Yep! 'Course, I was in bed by 10!
It's exhausting being on your feet all day...
Making chocolate is a tough job!
'Mmm, it smells great, what is it?
Your morning task!
Really?
It's Rosemary butter for the praline.
So, same as yesterday?
No! First, you're going to sift all this.
Oh...
This is the sifter. You put the butter in it and you sift with your scraper, like so.
The infused butter goes through and the rosemary doesn't.
Can I nibble on a couple of chocolates before I start?
GRRRT! GRRRT! GRRRT!
Here I go, 45 minutes of sifting!
The scraping sets the tempo...
Next, I'm assigned a new task with Richard.
Sheet of praline
Cutting the praline I made the day before!
We lower the guitar cutter, lift it back up, turn the praline around, give it the guitar again, and we end up with little squares that then need to be enrobed in couverture chocolate.
It's taking shape!

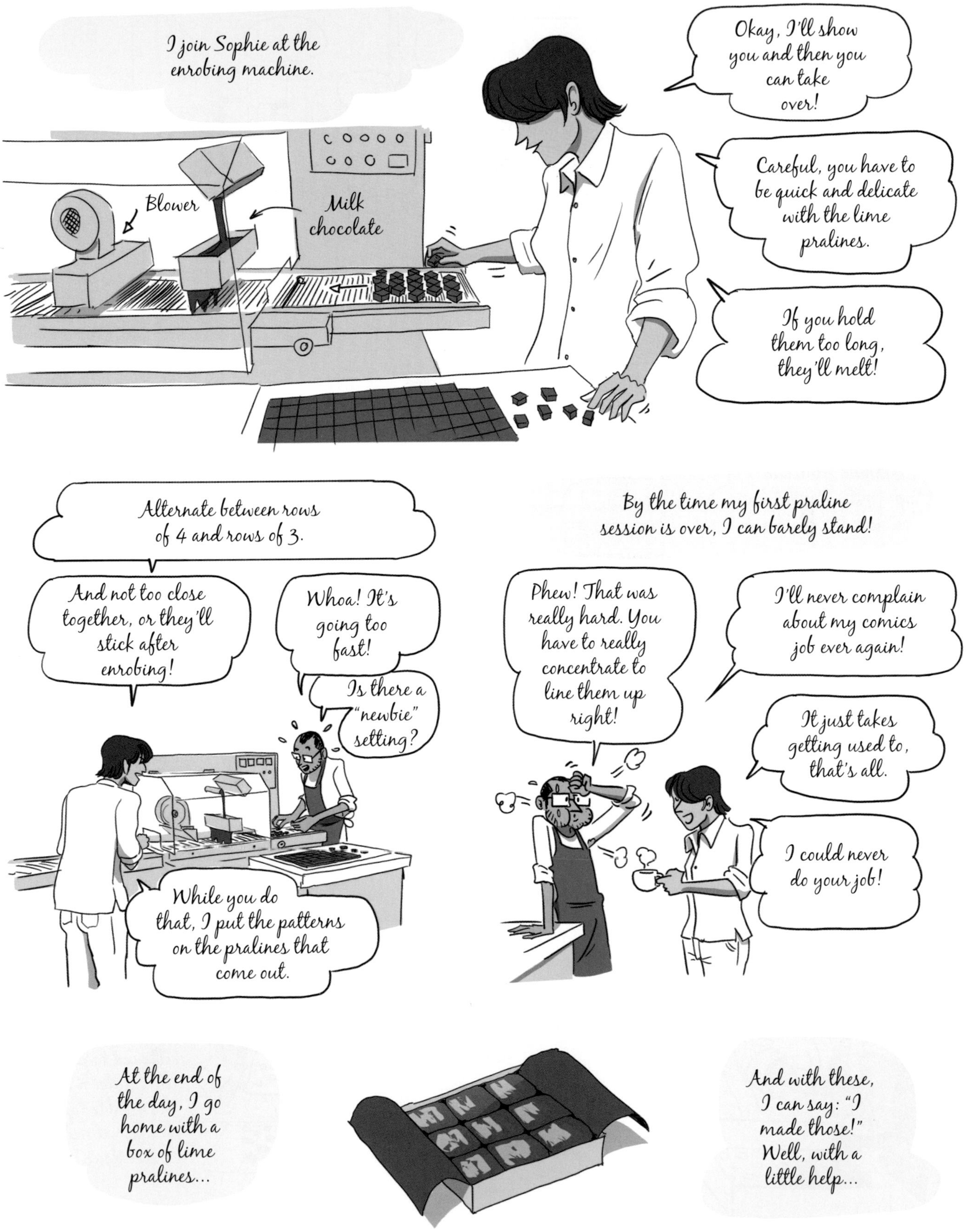
I join Sophie at the enrobing machine.
Okay, I'll show you and then you can take over!
Careful, you have to be quick and delicate with the lime pralines.
If you hold them too long, they'll melt!
Blower
Milk chocolate
Alternate between rows of 4 and rows of 3.
And not too close together, or they'll stick after enrobing!
Whoa! It's going too fast!
Is there a "newbie" setting?
While you do that, I put the patterns on the pralines that come out.
By the time my first praline session is over, I can barely stand!
Phew! That was really hard. You have to really concentrate to line them up right!
I'll never complain about my comics job ever again!
It just takes getting used to, that's all.
I could never do your job!
At the end of the day, I go home with a box of lime pralines...
And with these, I can say: "I made those!" Well, with a little help...

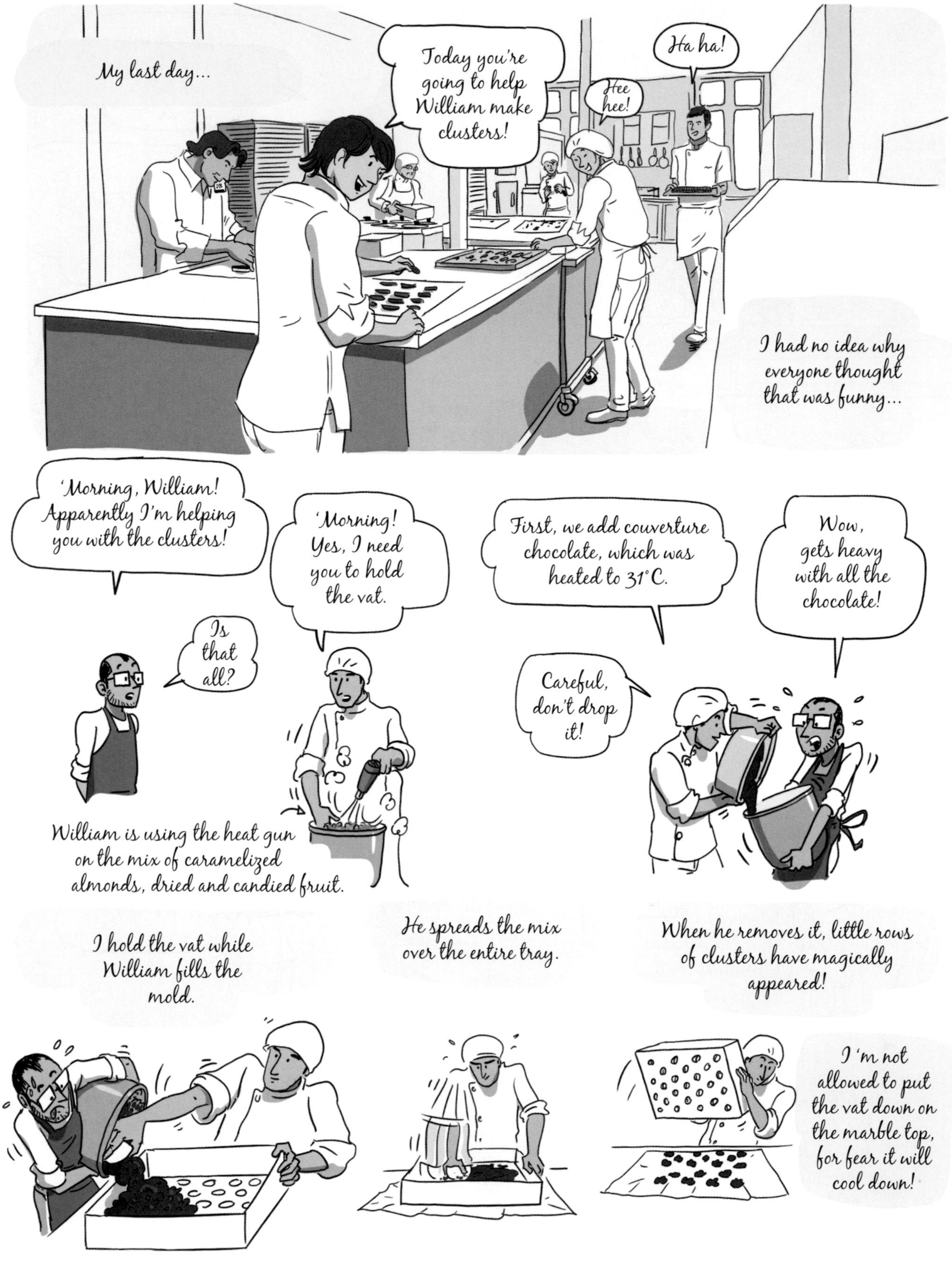

My last day...
Today you're going to help William make clusters!
Hee hee!
Ha ha!
I had no idea why everyone thought that was funny...
'Morning, William! Apparently I'm helping you with the clusters!
Is that all?
'Morning! Yes, I need you to hold the vat.
William is using the heat gun on the mix of caramelized almonds, dried and candied fruit.
First, we add couverture chocolate, which was heated to 31°C.
Careful, don't drop it!
Wow, gets heavy with all the chocolate!
I hold the vat while William fills the mold.
He spreads the mix over the entire tray.
When he removes it, little rows of clusters have magically appeared!
I'm not allowed to put the vat down on the marble top, for fear it will cool down!

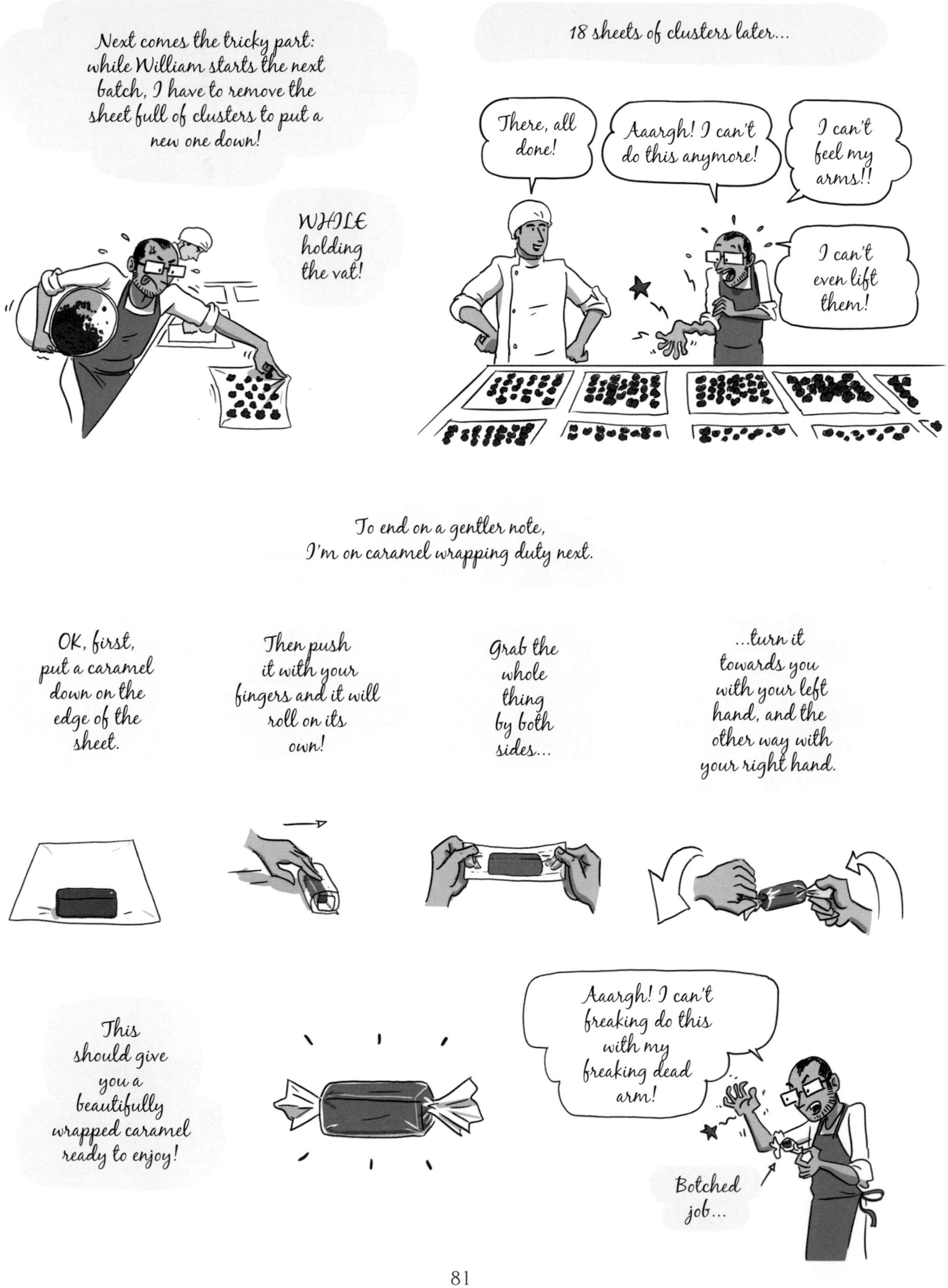
Next comes the tricky part: while William starts the next batch, I have to remove the sheet full of clusters to put a new one down!
WHILE holding the vat!
18 sheets of clusters later...
There, all done!
Aaargh! I can't do this anymore!
I can't feel my arms!!
I can't even lift them!
To end on a gentler note, I'm on caramel wrapping duty next.
OK, first, put a caramel down on the edge of the sheet.
Then push it with your fingers and it will roll on its own!
Grab the whole thing by both sides...
...turn it towards you with your left hand, and the other way with your right hand.
This should give you a beautifully wrapped caramel ready to enjoy!
Aaargh! I can't freaking do this with my freaking dead arm!
Botched job...

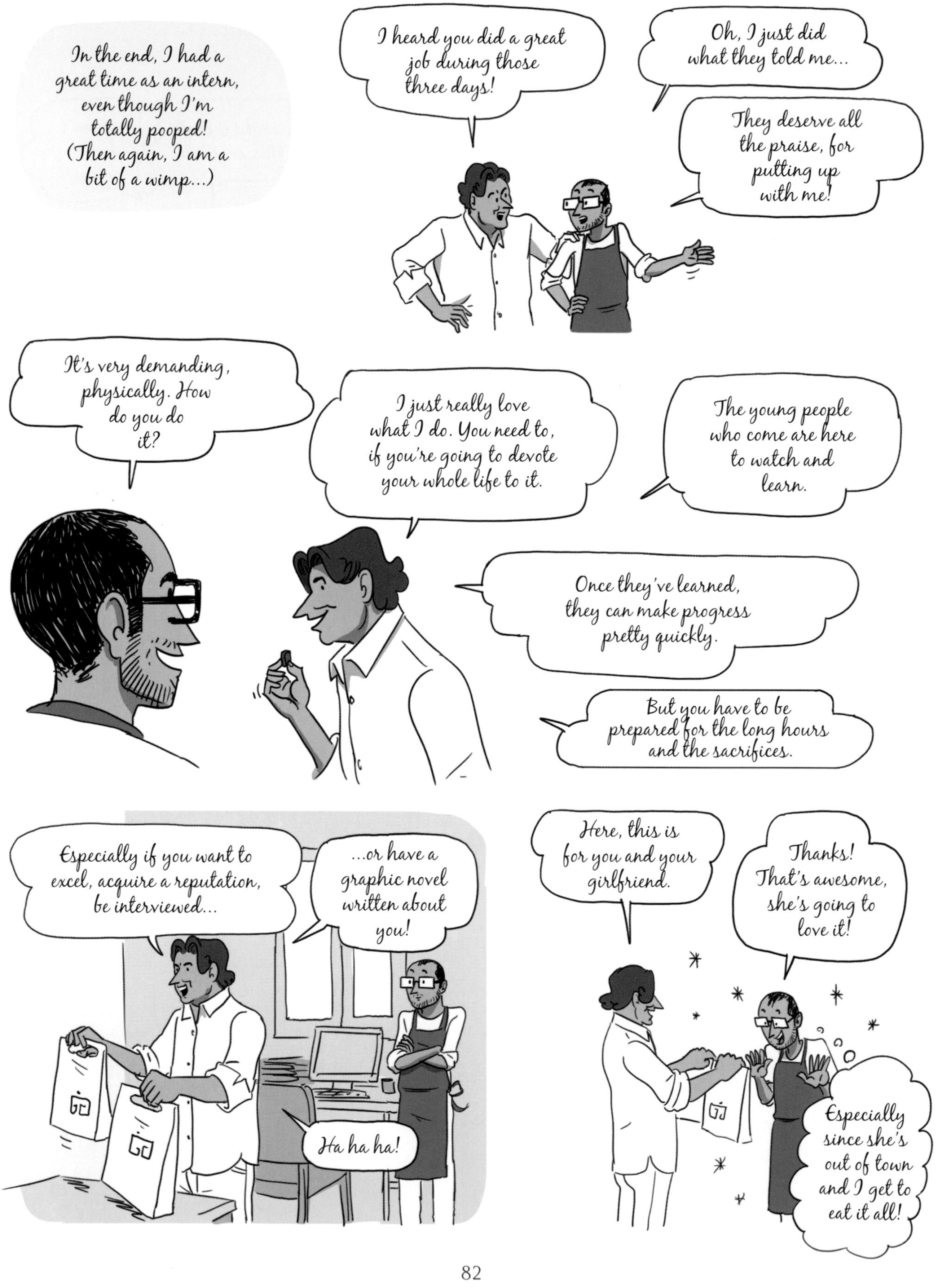
In the end, I had a great time as an intern, even though I'm totally pooped! (Then again, I am a bit of a wimp...)
I heard you did a great job during those three days!
Oh, I just did what they told me...
They deserve all the praise, for putting up with me!
It's very demanding, physically. How do you do it?
I just really love what I do. You need to, if you're going to devote your whole life to it.
The young people who come are here to watch and learn.
Once they've learned, they can make progress pretty quickly.
But you have to be prepared for the long hours and the sacrifices.
Especially if you want to excel, acquire a reputation, be interviewed...
...or have a graphic novel written about you!
Ha ha ha!
Here, this is for you and your girlfriend.
Thanks! That's awesome, she's going to love it!
Especially since she's out of town and I get to eat it all!

TASTE
THE SOURCE OF PLEASURE

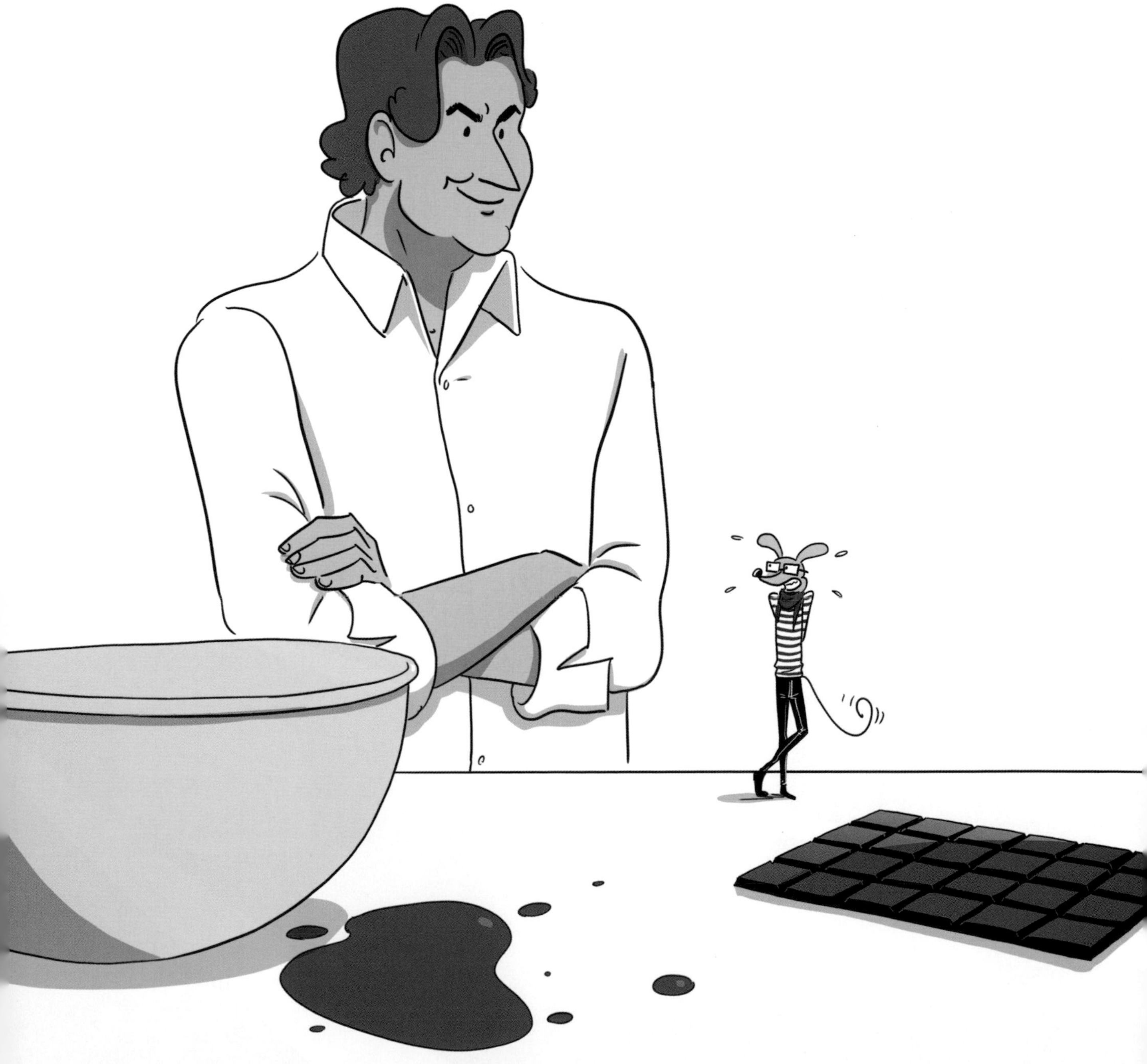

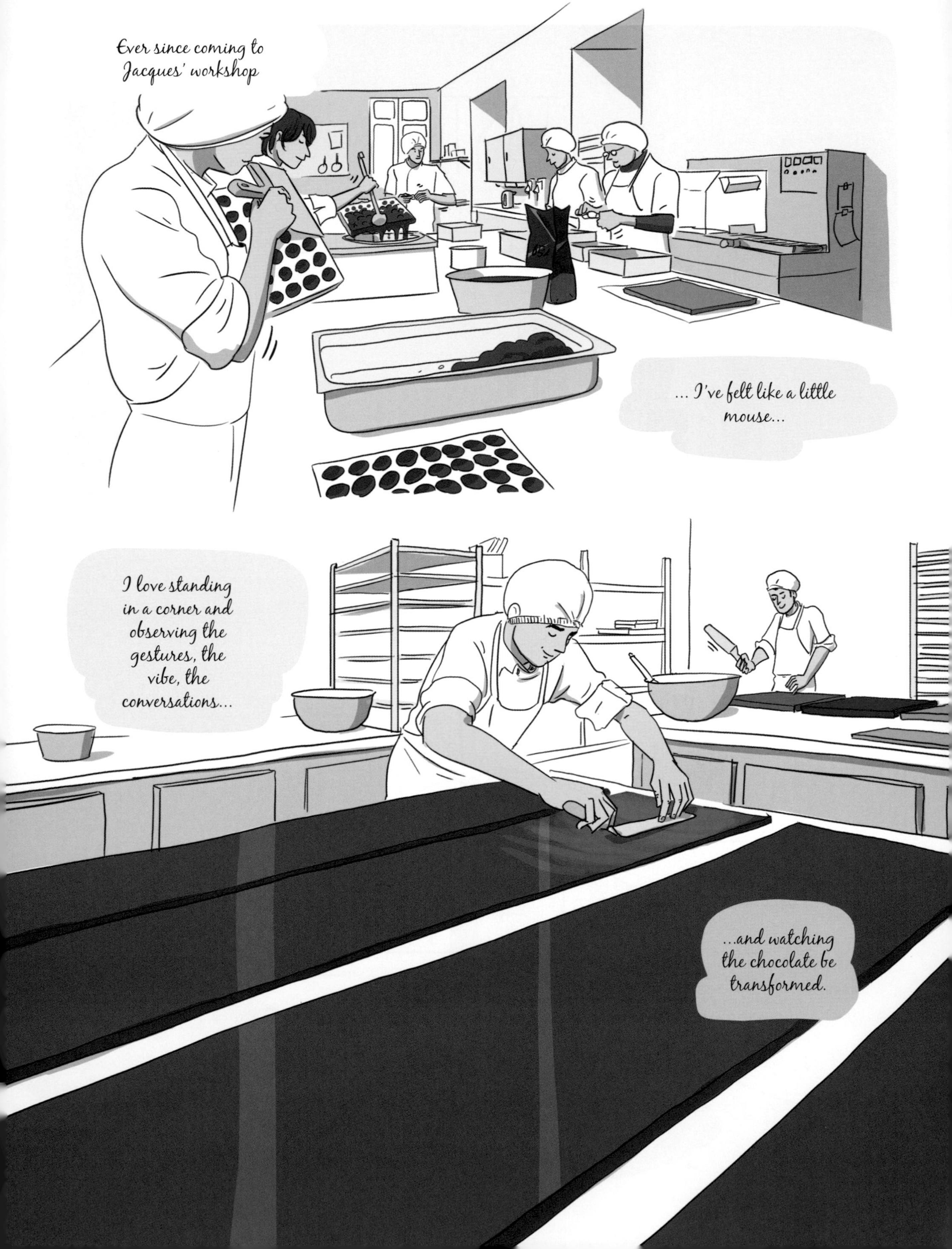
Ever since coming to Jacques' workshop
... I've felt like a little mouse...
I love standing in a corner and observing the gestures, the vibe, the conversations...
...and watching the chocolate be transformed.

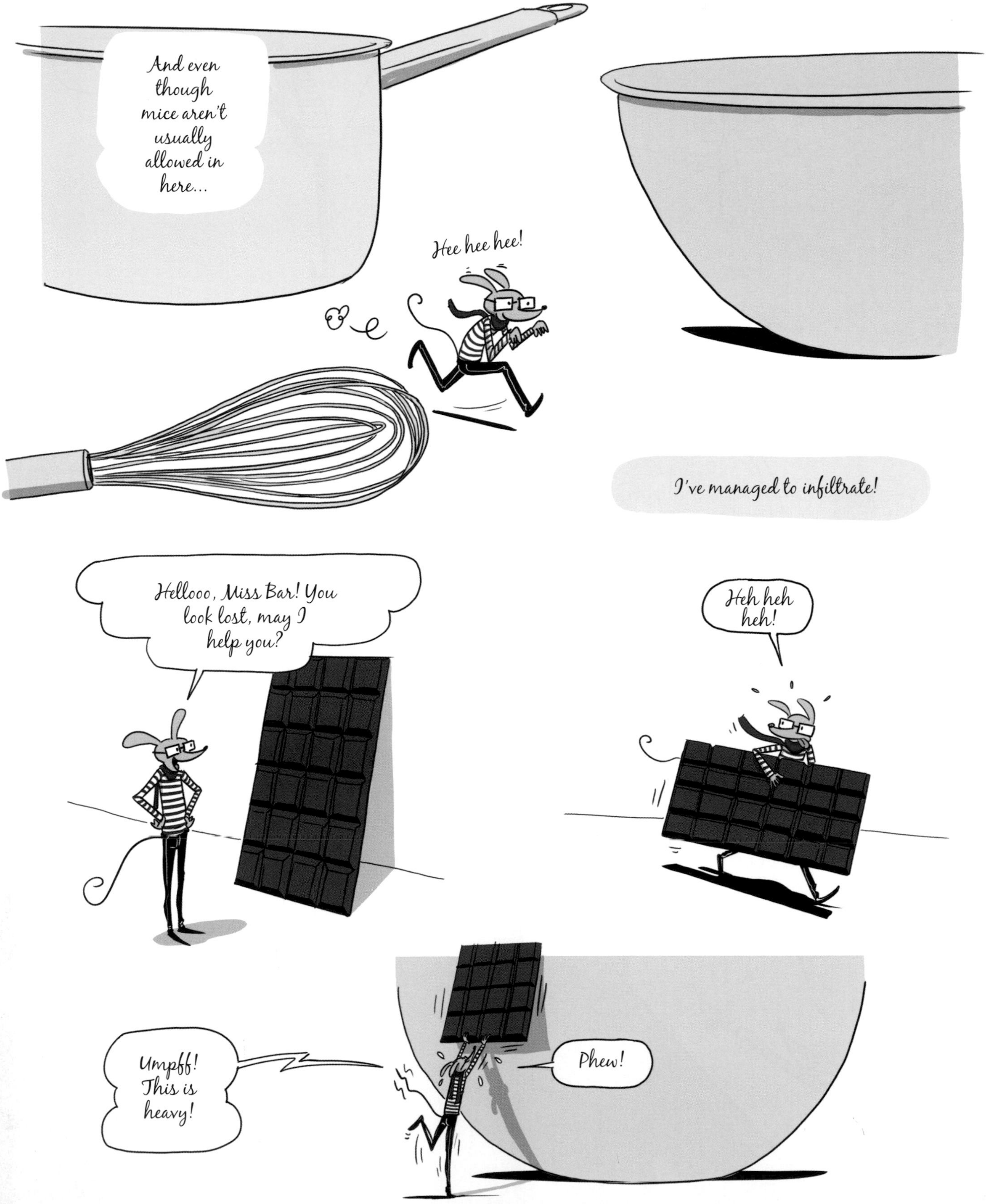
And even though mice aren't usually allowed in here...
Hee hee hee!
I've managed to infiltrate!
Hellooo, Miss Bar! You look lost, may I help you?
Heh heh heh!
Umpff! This is heavy!
Phew!

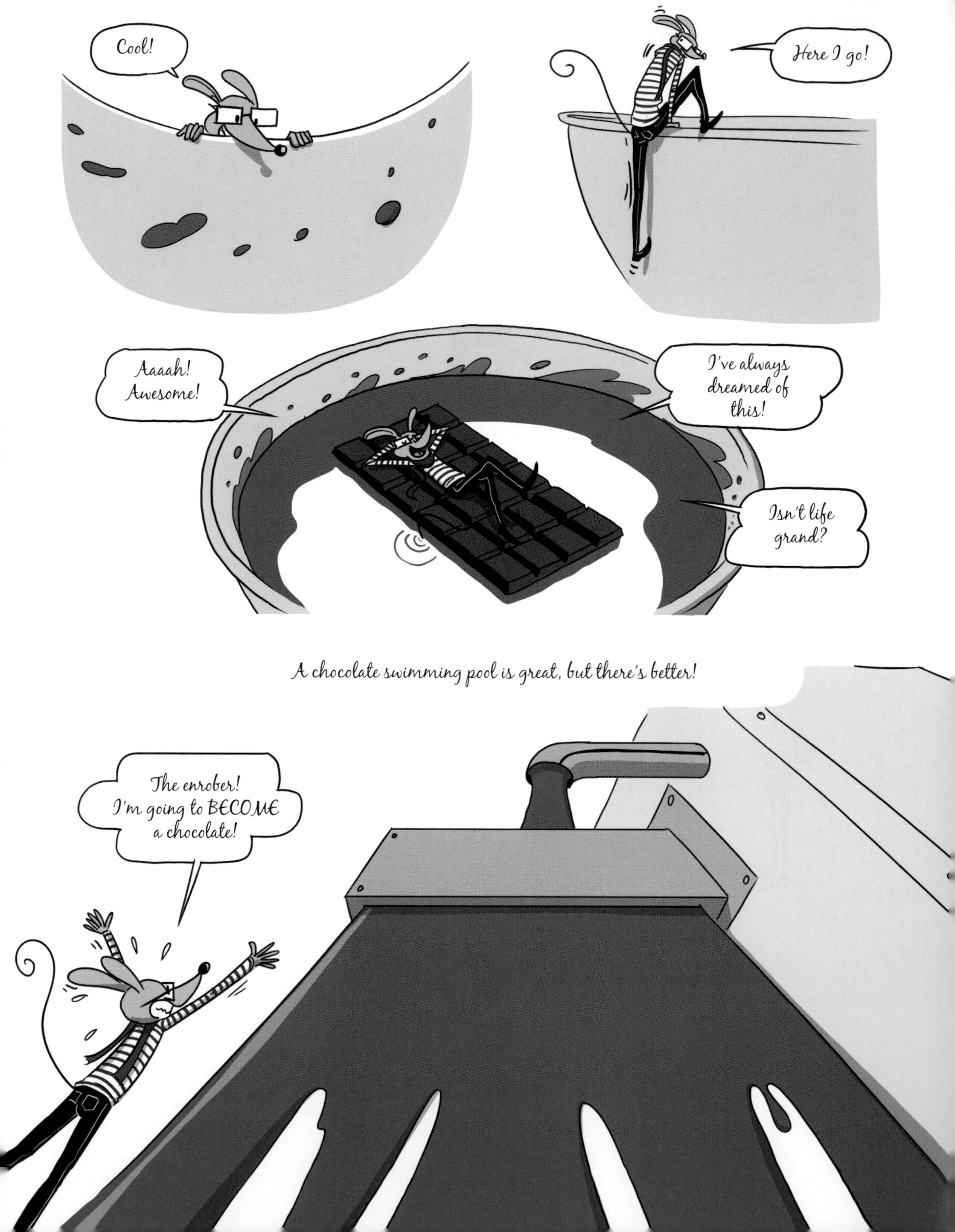
Cool!
Here I go!
Aaaah! Awesome!
I've always dreamed of this!
Isn't life grand?
A chocolate swimming pool is great, but there's better!
The enrober! I'm going to BECOME a chocolate!

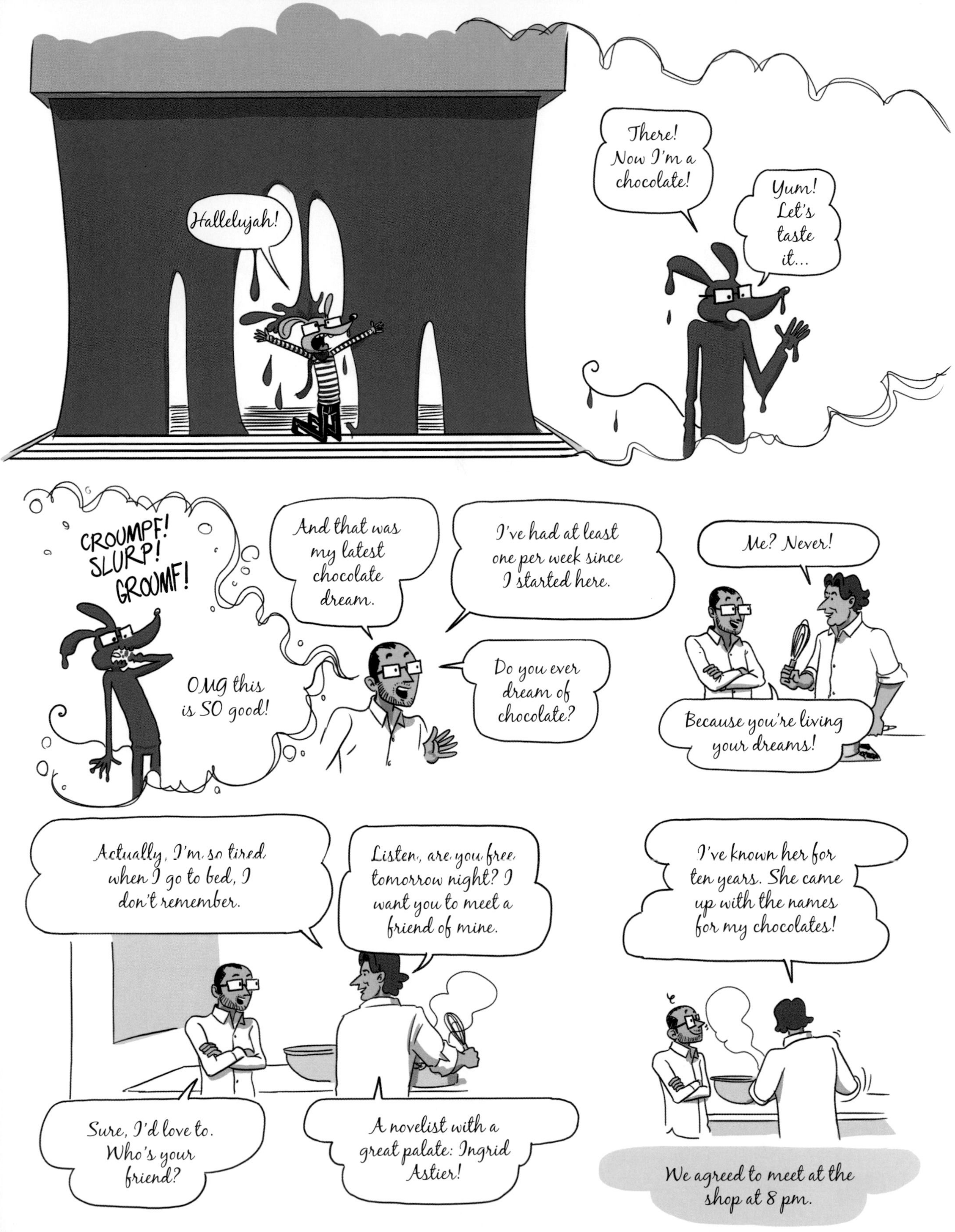
Hallelujah!
There! Now I'm a chocolate!
Yum! Let's taste it...
CROUMPF! SLURP! GROUMF!
OMG this is SO good!
And that was my latest chocolate dream.
I've had at least one per week since I started here.
Do you ever dream of chocolate?
Me? Never!
Because you're living your dreams!
Actually, I'm so tired when I go to bed, I don't remember.
Listen, are you free tomorrow night? I want you to meet a friend of mine.
Sure, I'd love to. Who's your friend?
A novelist with a great palate: Ingrid Astier!
I've known her for ten years. She came up with the names for my chocolates!
We agreed to meet at the shop at 8 pm.

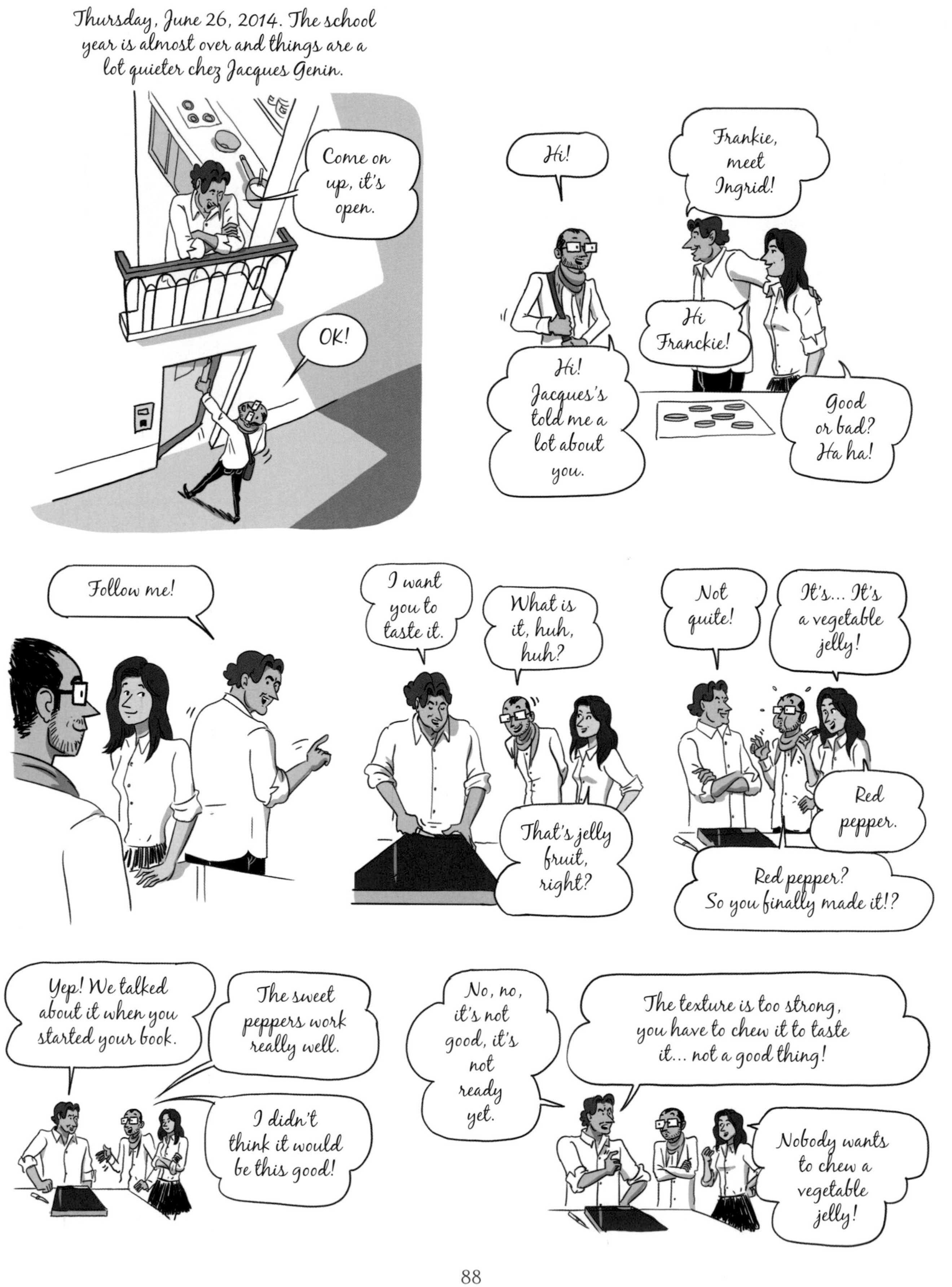
Thursday, June 26, 2014. The school year is almost over and things are a lot quieter chez Jacques Genin.
Come on up, it's open.
OK!
Hi!
Frankie, meet Ingrid!
Hi Franckie!
Hi! Jacques's told me a lot about you.
Good or bad? Ha ha!
Follow me!
I want you to taste it.
What is it, huh, huh?
That's jelly fruit, right?
Not quite!
It's... It's a vegetable jelly!
Red pepper.
Red pepper? So you finally made it!?
Yep! We talked about it when you started your book.
The sweet peppers work really well.
I didn't think it would be this good!
No, no, it's not good, it's not ready yet.
The texture is too strong, you have to chew it to taste it... not a good thing!
Nobody wants to chew a vegetable jelly!

We leave the shop and head for the Café des Musées.

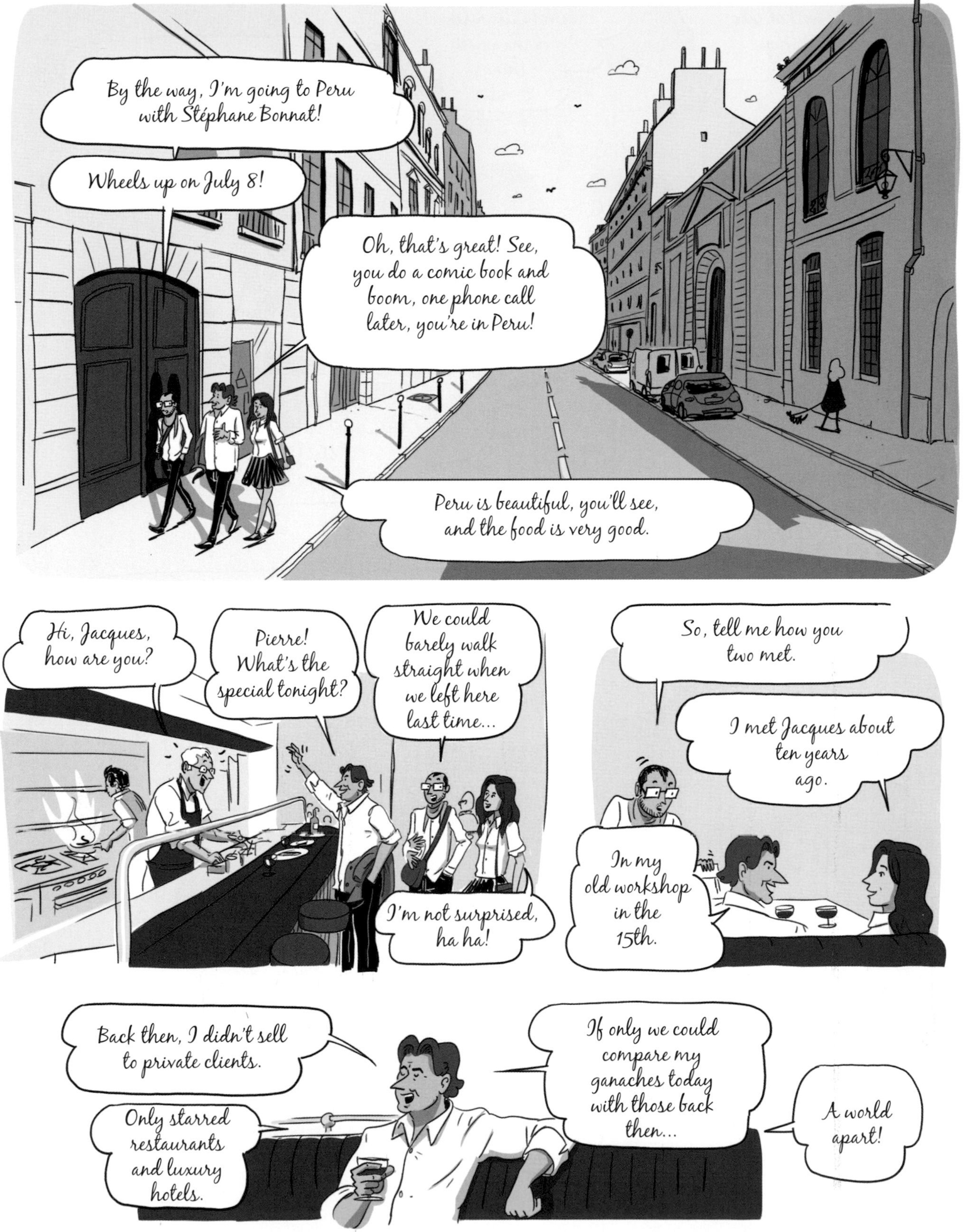
By the way, I'm going to Peru with Stéphane Bonnat!
Wheels up on July 8!
Oh, that's great! See, you do a comic book and boom, one phone call later, you're in Peru!
Peru is beautiful, you'll see, and the food is very good.
Hi, Jacques, how are you?
Pierre! What's the special tonight?
We could barely walk straight when we left here last time...
I'm not surprised, ha ha!
So, tell me how you two met.
I met Jacques about ten years ago.
In my old workshop in the 15th.
Back then, I didn't sell to private clients.
Only starred restaurants and luxury hotels.
If only we could compare my ganaches today with those back then...
A world apart!

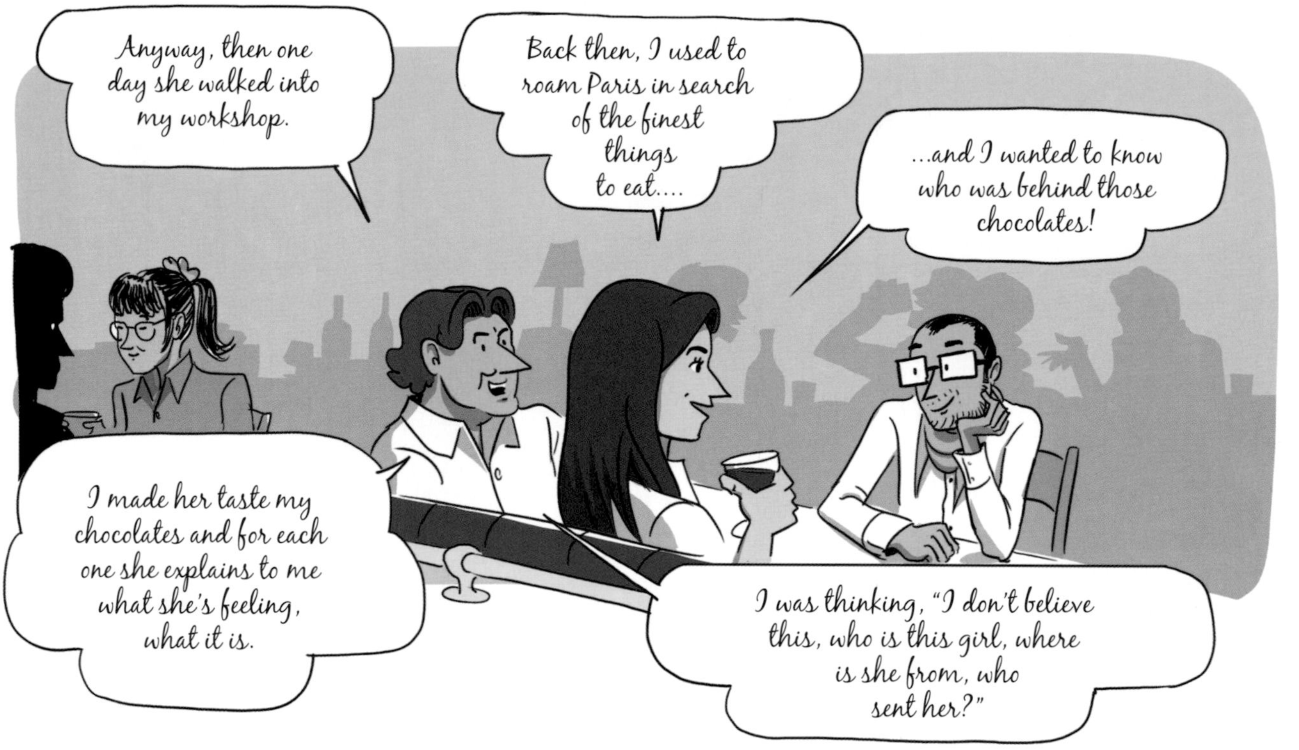
Anyway, then one day she walked into my workshop.
Back then, I used to roam Paris in search of the finest things to eat....
...and I wanted to know who was behind those chocolates!
I made her taste my chocolates and for each one she explains to me what she's feeling, what it is.
I was thinking, "I don't believe this, who is this girl, where is she from, who sent her?"

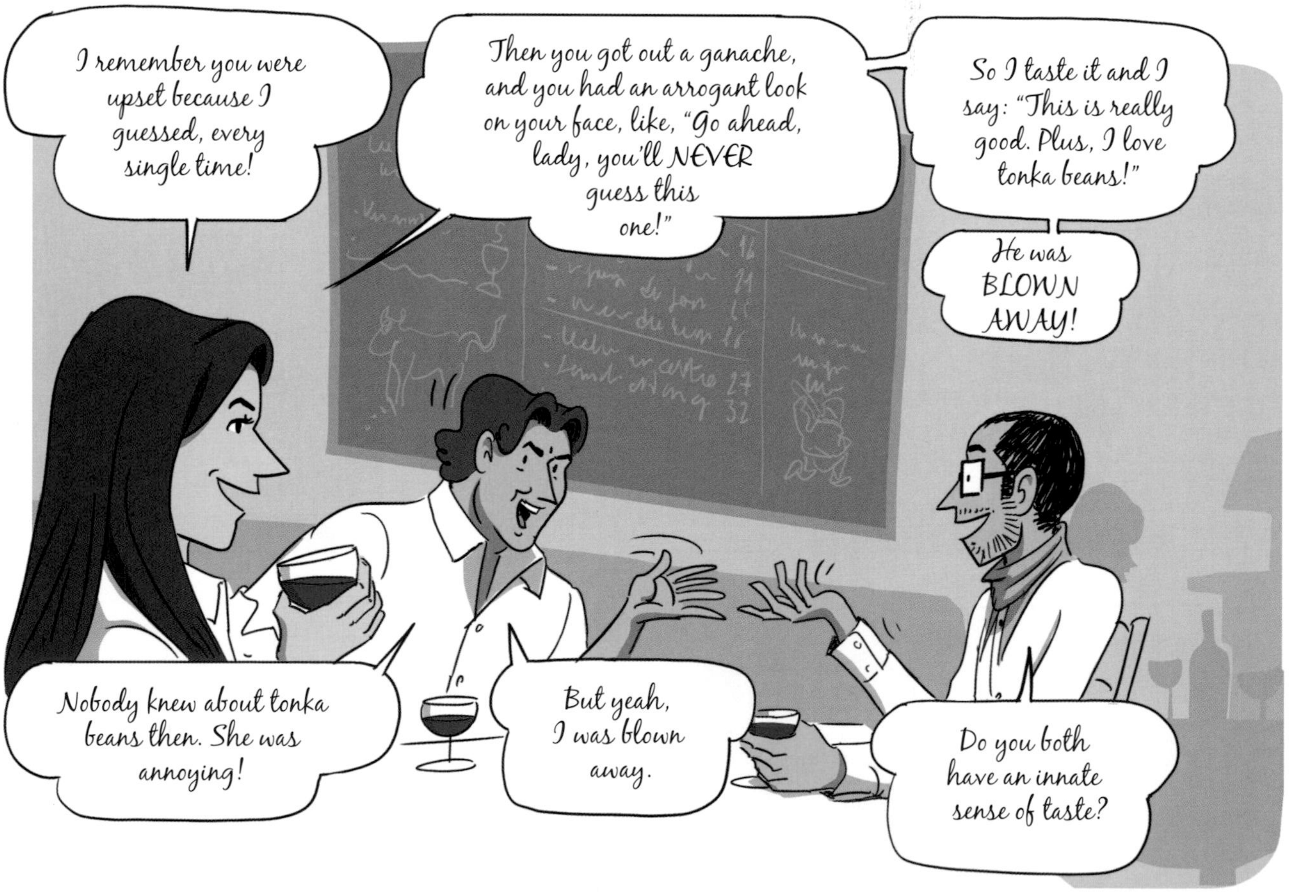
I remember you were upset because I guessed, every single time!
Then you got out a ganache, and you had an arrogant look on your face, like, "Go ahead, lady, you'll NEVER guess this one!"
So I taste it and I say: "This is really good. Plus, I love tonka beans!"
He was BLOWN AWAY!
Nobody knew about tonka beans then. She was annoying!
But yeah, I was blown away.
Do you both have an innate sense of taste?

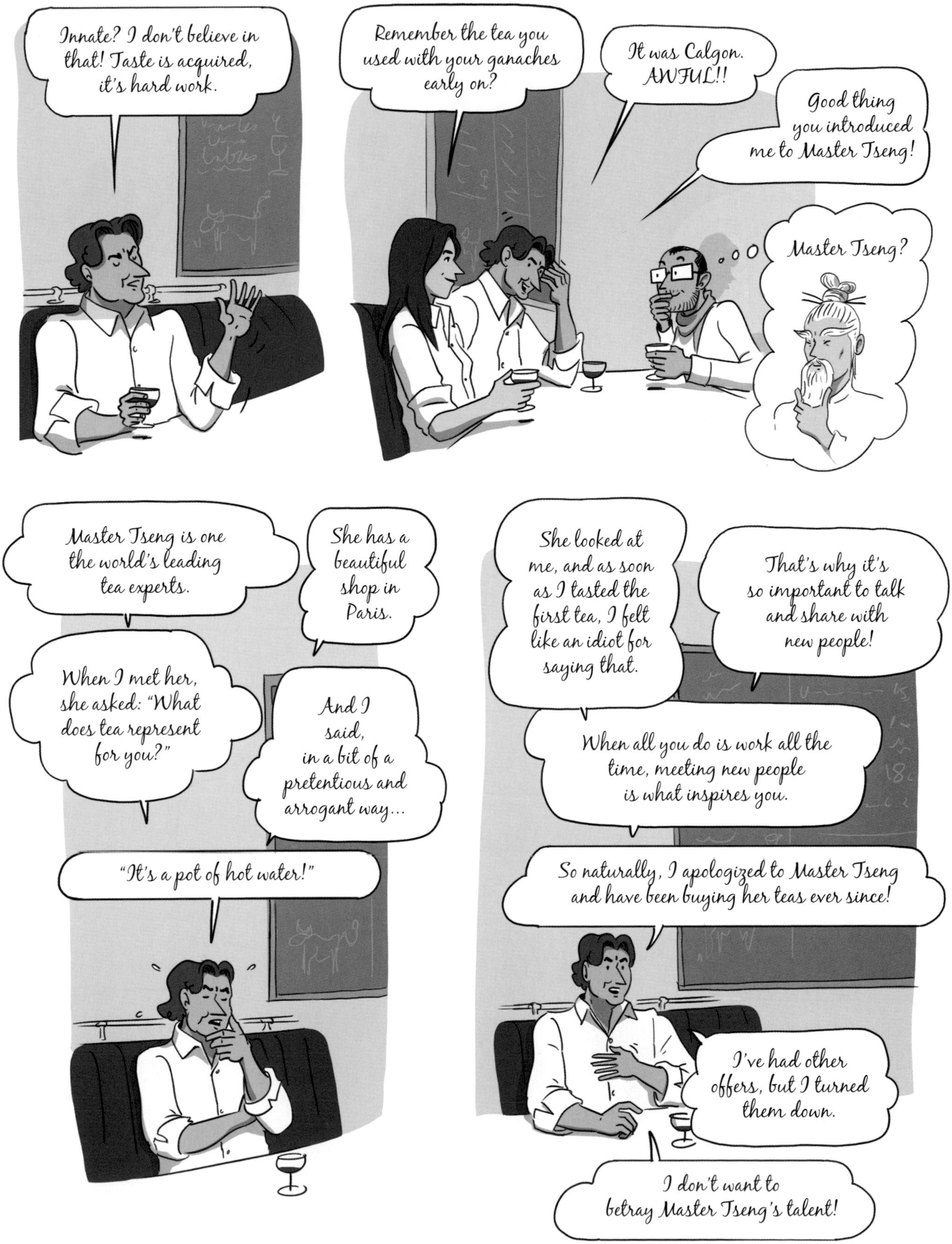
Innate? I don't believe in that! Taste is acquired, it's hard work.
Remember the tea you used with your ganaches early on?
It was Calgon. AWFUL!!
Good thing you introduced me to Master Tseng!
Master Tseng?
Master Tseng is one the world's leading tea experts.
She has a beautiful shop in Paris.
When I met her, she asked: "What does tea represent for you?"
And I said, in a bit of a pretentious and arrogant way...
"It's a pot of hot water!"
She looked at me, and as soon as I tasted the first tea, I felt like an idiot for saying that.
That's why it's so important to talk and share with new people!
When all you do is work all the time, meeting new people is what inspires you.
So naturally, I apologized to Master Tseng and have been buying her teas ever since!
I've had other offers, but I turned them down.
I don't want to betray Master Tseng's talent!

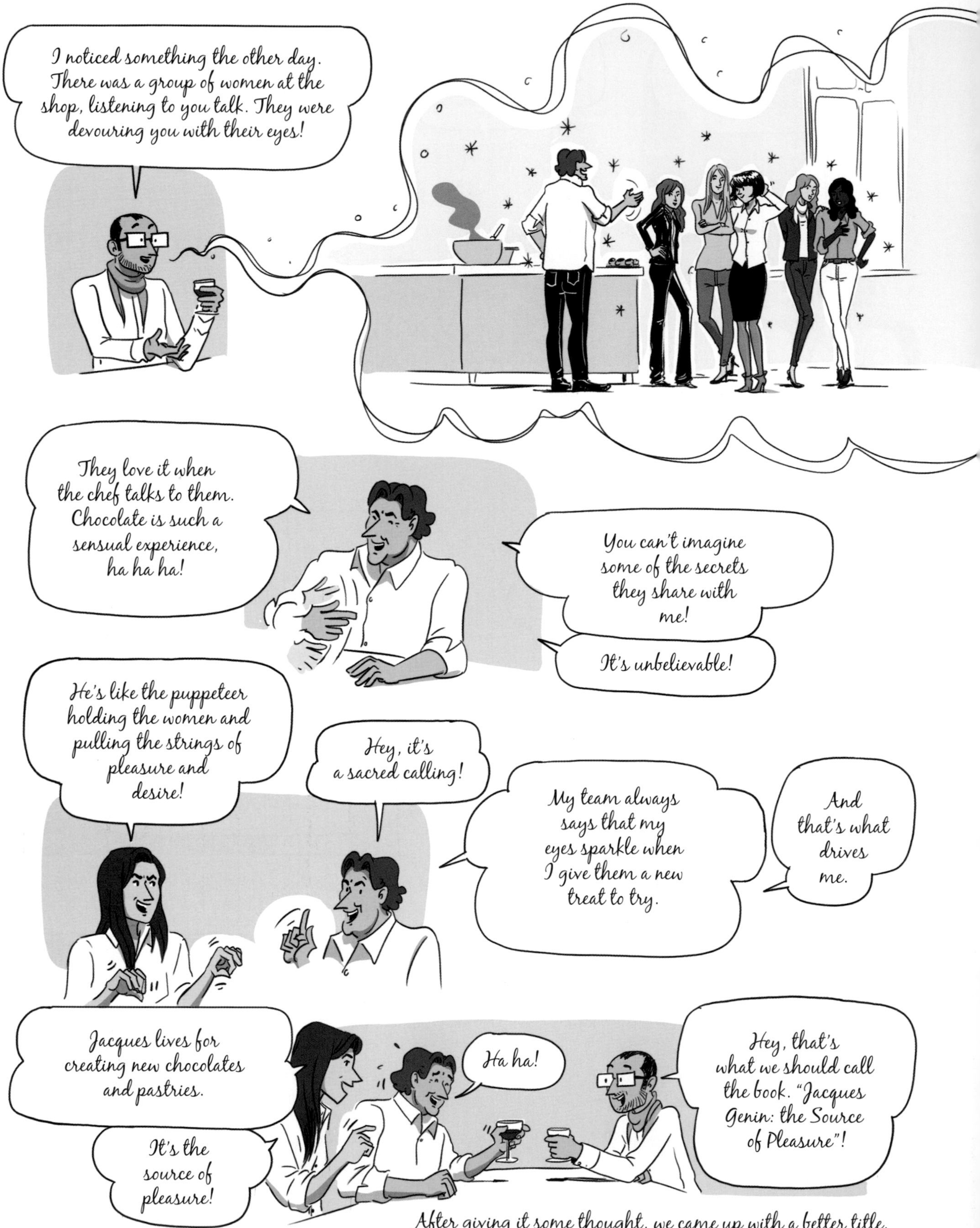
I noticed something the other day. There was a group of women at the shop, listening to you talk. They were devouring you with their eyes!
They love it when the chef talks to them. Chocolate is such a sensual experience, ha ha ha!
You can't imagine some of the secrets they share with me!
It's unbelievable!
He's like the puppeteer holding the women and pulling the strings of pleasure and desire!
Hey, it's a sacred calling!
My team always says that my eyes sparkle when I give them a new treat to try.
And that's what drives me.
Jacques lives for creating new chocolates and pastries.
It's the source of pleasure!
Ha ha!
Hey, that's what we should call the book. "Jacques Genin: the Source of Pleasure"!
After giving it some thought, we came up with a better title.

COCOA
THE ORIGINS OF CHOCOLATE

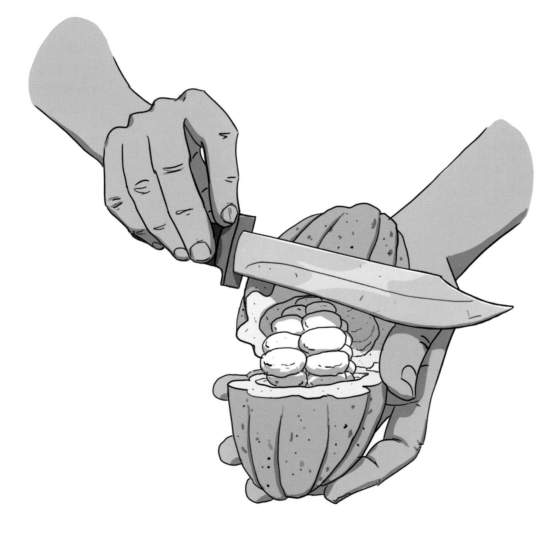

Tuesday, July 8, Charles de Gaulle airport, 6 A.M. I'm flying out to go meet Stéphane Bonnat in Lima and to visit a chocolate plantation in the Amazon jungle!

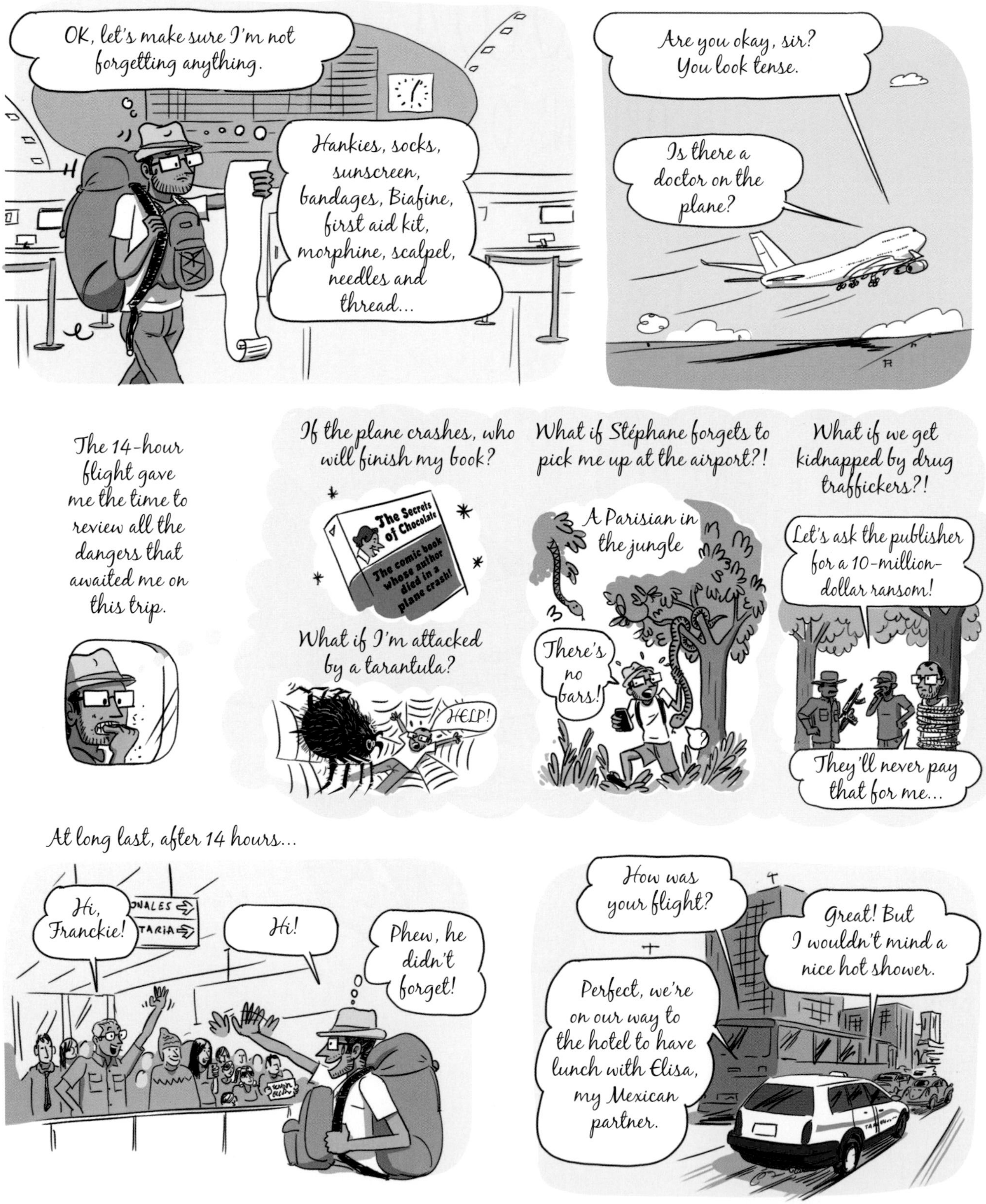

OK, let's make sure I'm not forgetting anything.
Hankies, socks, sunscreen, bandages, Biafine, first aid kit, morphine, scalpel, needles and thread...
Are you okay, sir? You look tense.
Is there a doctor on the plane?
The 14-hour flight gave me the time to review all the dangers that awaited me on this trip.
If the plane crashes, who will finish my book?
The Secrets of Chocolate
The comic book whose author died in a plane crash!
What if I'm attacked by a tarantula?
HELP!
What if Stéphane forgets to pick me up at the airport?!
A Parisian in the jungle
There's no bars!
What if we get kidnapped by drug traffickers?!
Let's ask the publisher for a 10-million-dollar ransom!
They'll never pay that for me...
At long last, after 14 hours...
Hi, Franckie!
Hi!
Phew, he didn't forget!
How was your flight?
Great! But I wouldn't mind a nice hot shower.
Perfect, we're on our way to the hotel to have lunch with Elisa, my Mexican partner.

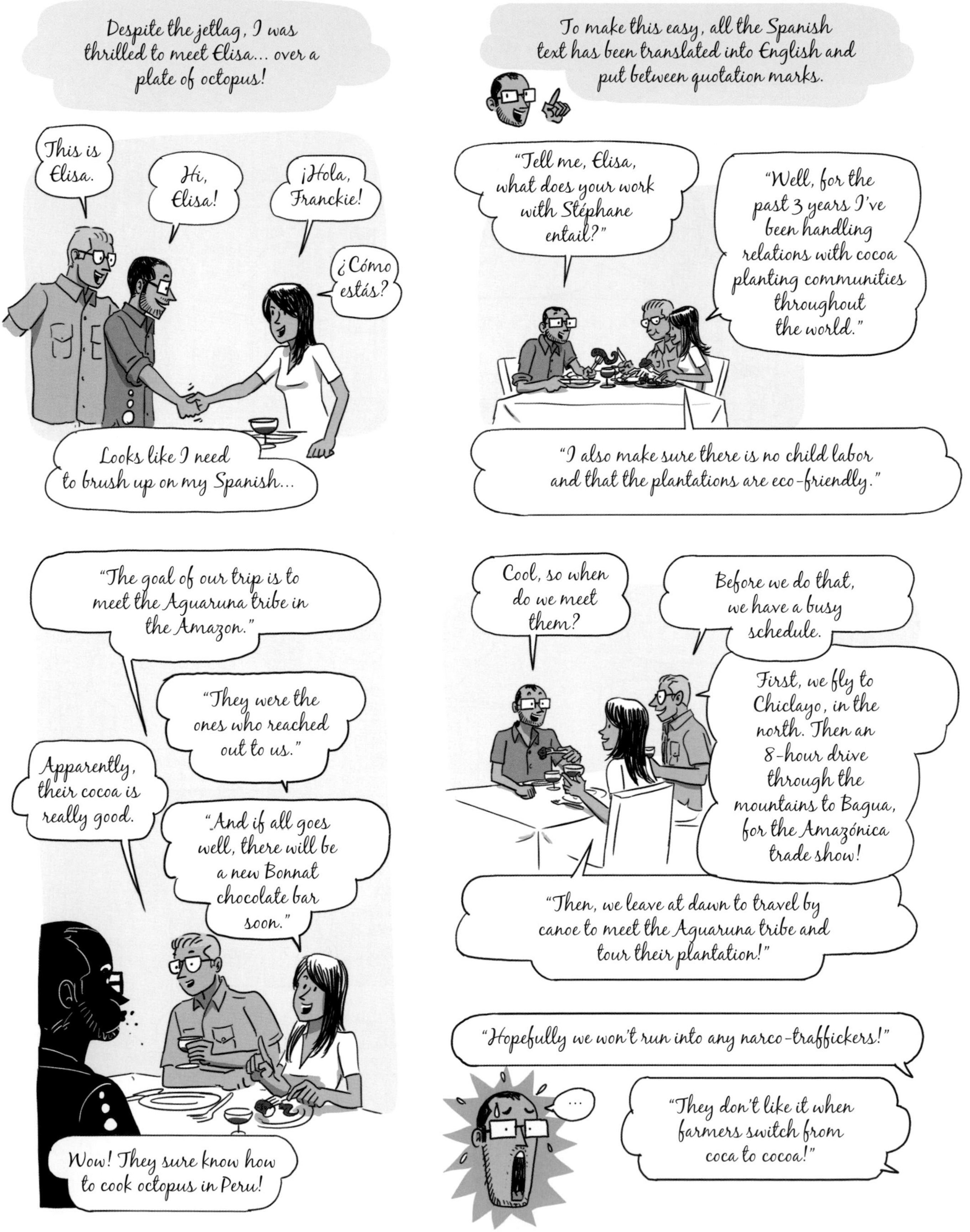
Despite the jetlag, I was thrilled to meet Elisa... over a plate of octopus!
This is Elisa.
Hi, Elisa!
¡Hola, Franckie!
¿Cómo estás?
Looks like I need to brush up on my Spanish...
To make this easy, all the Spanish text has been translated into English and put between quotation marks.
"Tell me, Elisa, what does your work with Stéphane entail?"
"Well, for the past 3 years I've been handling relations with cocoa planting communities throughout the world."
"I also make sure there is no child labor and that the plantations are eco-friendly."
"The goal of our trip is to meet the Aguaruna tribe in the Amazon."
"They were the ones who reached out to us."
Apparently, their cocoa is really good.
"And if all goes well, there will be a new Bonnat chocolate bar soon."
Wow! They sure know how to cook octopus in Peru!
Cool, so when do we meet them?
Before we do that, we have a busy schedule.
First, we fly to Chiclayo, in the north. Then an 8-hour drive through the mountains to Bagua, for the Amazónica trade show!
"Then, we leave at dawn to travel by canoe to meet the Aguaruna tribe and tour their plantation!"
"Hopefully we won't run into any narco-traffickers!"
...
"They don't like it when farmers switch from coca to cocoa!"

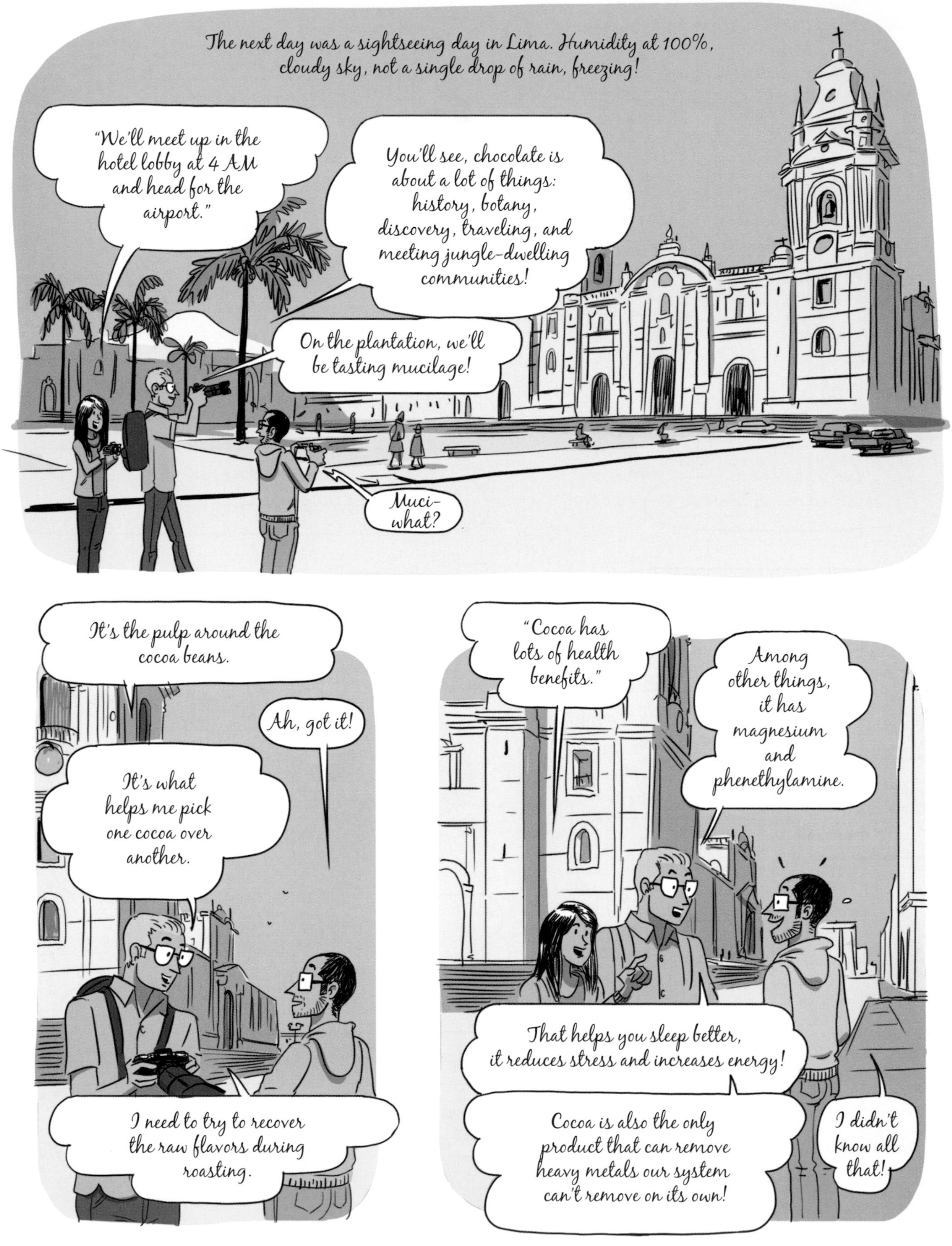
The next day was a sightseeing day in Lima. Humidity at 100%, cloudy sky, not a single drop of rain, freezing!
"We'll meet up in the hotel lobby at 4 AM and head for the airport."
You'll see, chocolate is about a lot of things: history, botany, discovery, traveling, and meeting jungle-dwelling communities!
On the plantation, we'll be tasting mucilage!
Muci-what?
It's the pulp around the cocoa beans.
Ah, got it!
It's what helps me pick one cocoa over another.
I need to try to recover the raw flavors during roasting.
"Cocoa has lots of health benefits."
Among other things, it has magnesium and phenethylamine.
That helps you sleep better, it reduces stress and increases energy!
Cocoa is also the only product that can remove heavy metals our system can't remove on its own!
I didn't know all that!

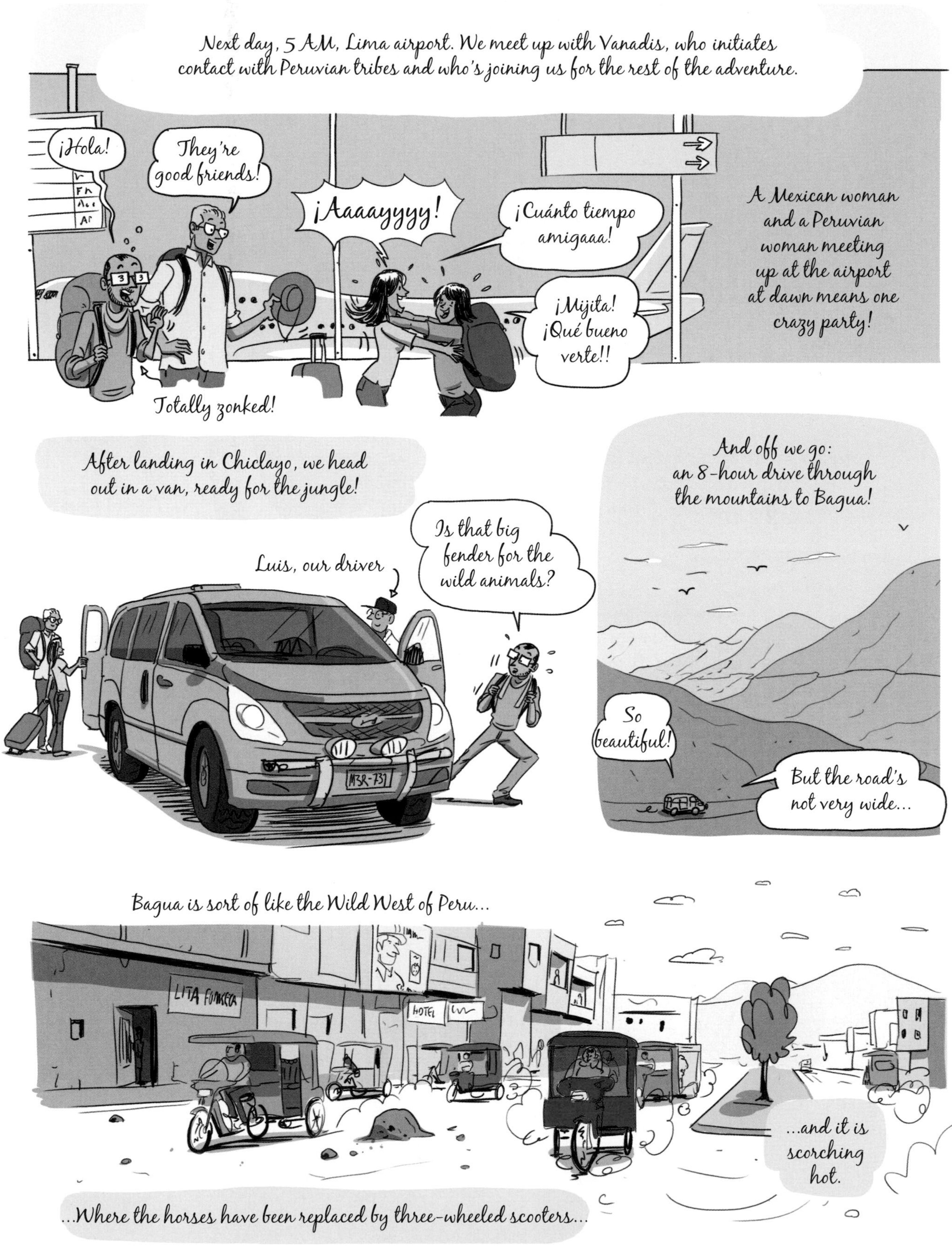
Next day, 5 AM, Lima airport. We meet up with Vanadis, who initiates contact with Peruvian tribes and who's joining us for the rest of the adventure.
¡Hola!
They're good friends!
Totally zonked!
¡Aaaayyyy!
¡Cuánto tiempo amigaaa!
¡Mijita! ¡Qué bueno verte!!
A Mexican woman and a Peruvian woman meeting up at the airport at dawn means one crazy party!
After landing in Chiclayo, we head out in a van, ready for the jungle!
Luis, our driver
Is that big fender for the wild animals?
And off we go: an 8-hour drive through the mountains to Bagua!
So beautiful!
But the road's not very wide...
Bagua is sort of like the Wild West of Peru...
HOTEL
...and it is scorching hot.
...Where the horses have been replaced by three-wheeled scooters...

After a good night's rest under the fan in our hotel room, we head for the Amazónica trade show, a forum for all the farming sectors in Peruvian Amazonia.

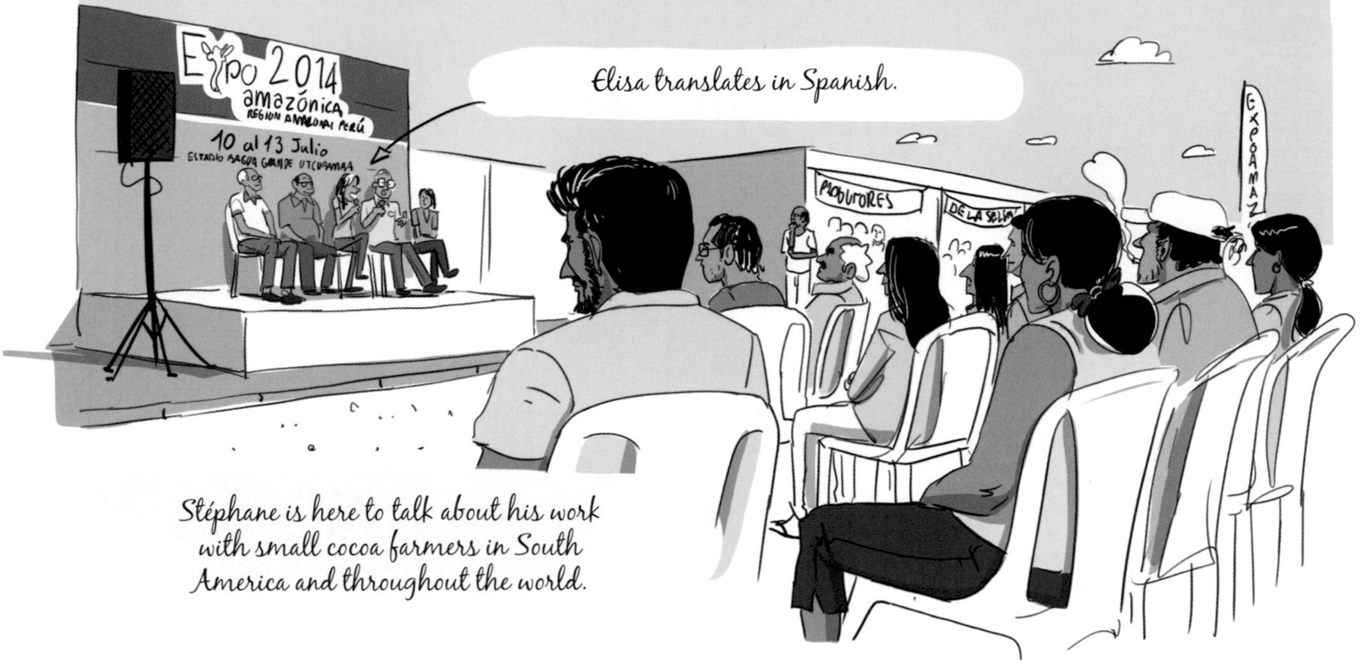
Elisa translates in Spanish.
Expo 2014
amazónica
PRODUCTORES
DE LA SELVA

Stéphane is here to talk about his work with small cocoa farmers in South America and throughout the world.

After the conference, Vanadis gives me a tour of the stands, where we sample local products: coffee, cheese, yogurt, cocoa, canned and dried Amazon fish, grilled guinea pig, chorizo... I even pose for a few pictures!

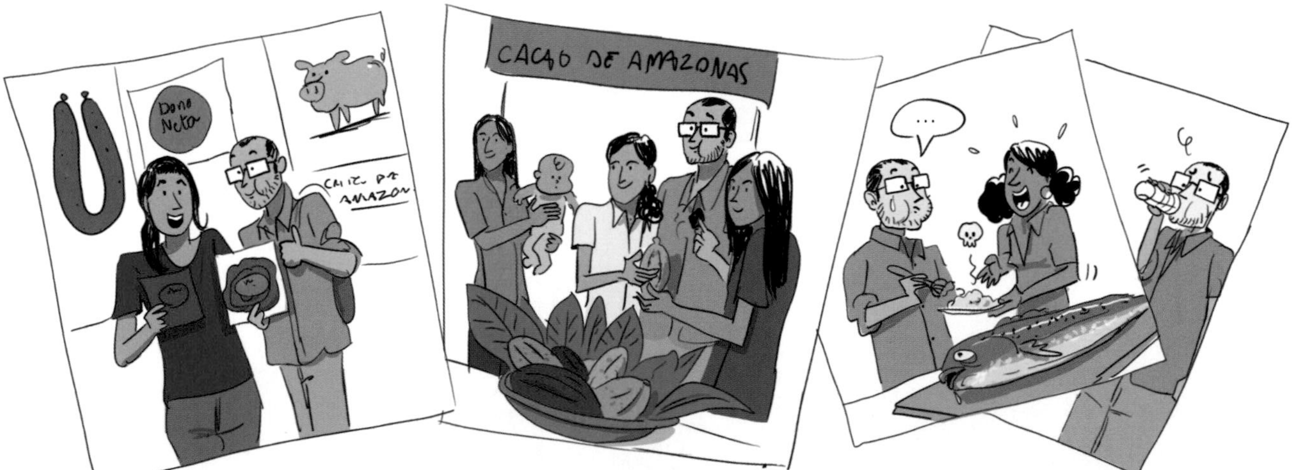
CACAO DE AMAZONAS
...

I feel like the president at the Agriculture Trade Show! (Later, my ego took quite a blow: they passed me off as Stéphane, who had to go meet the local press!)

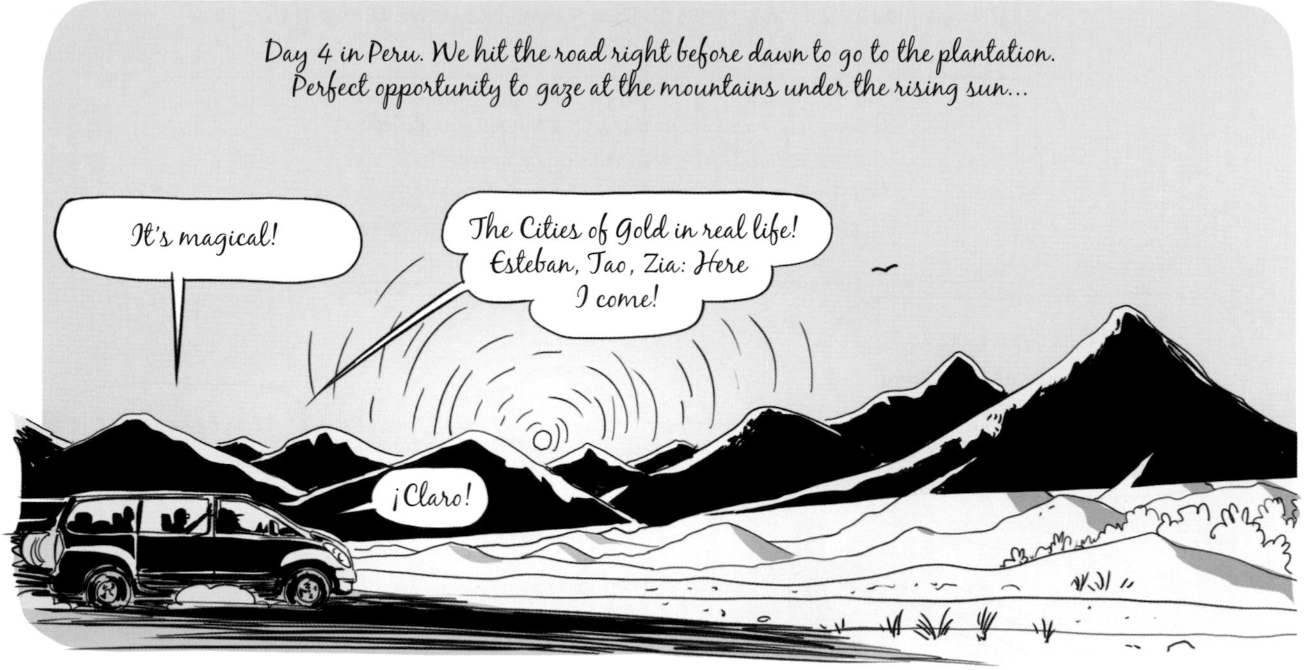
Day 4 in Peru. We hit the road right before dawn to go to the plantation.
Perfect opportunity to gaze at the mountains under the rising sun...
It's magical!
The Cities of Gold in real life! Esteban, Tao, Zia: Here I come!
¡Claro!

Around 11 AM, we arrive at a village deep in the jungle to board our canoe.

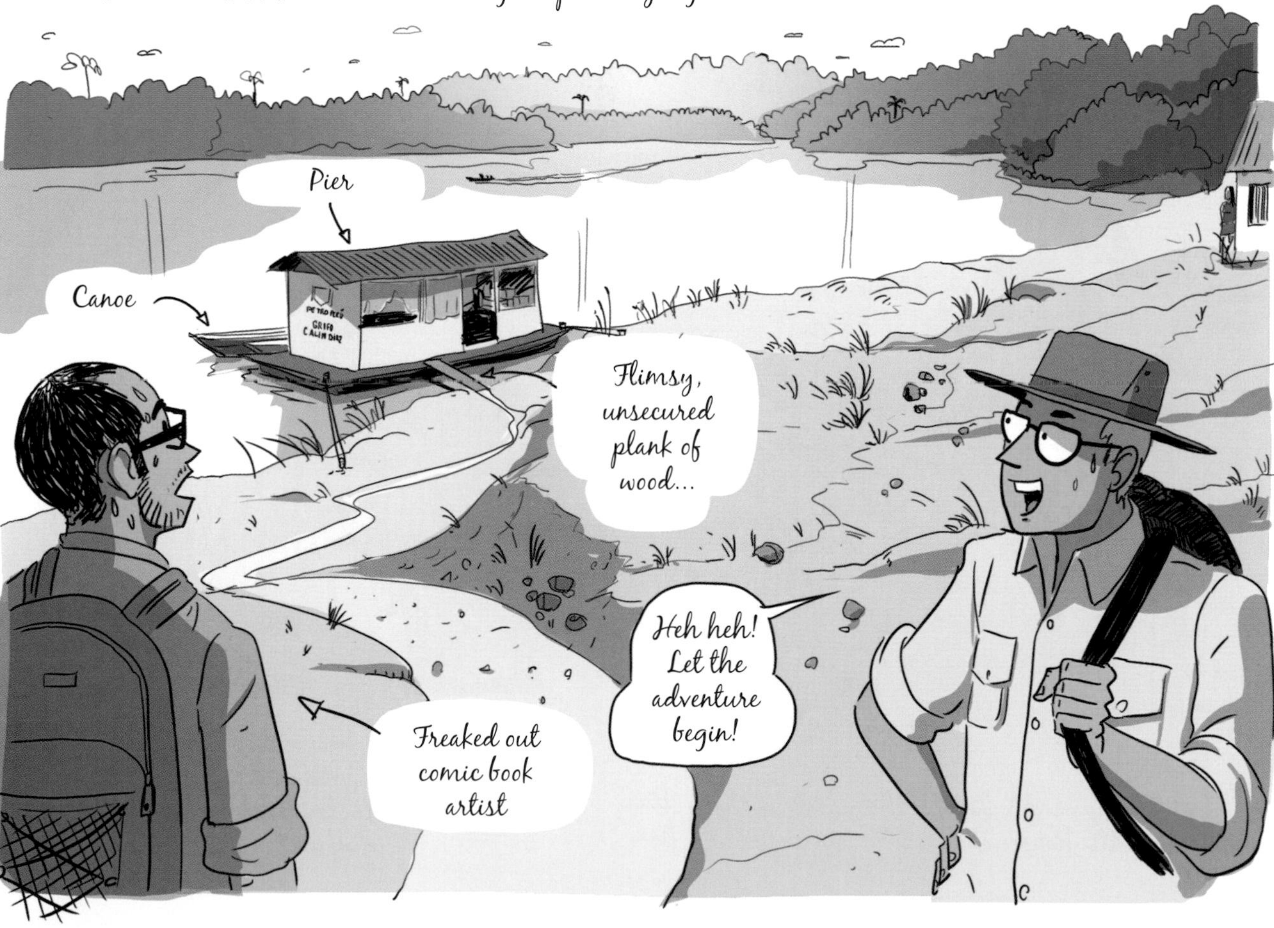
Pier
Canoe
Flimsy, unsecured plank of wood...
Heh heh! Let the adventure begin!
Freaked out comic book artist

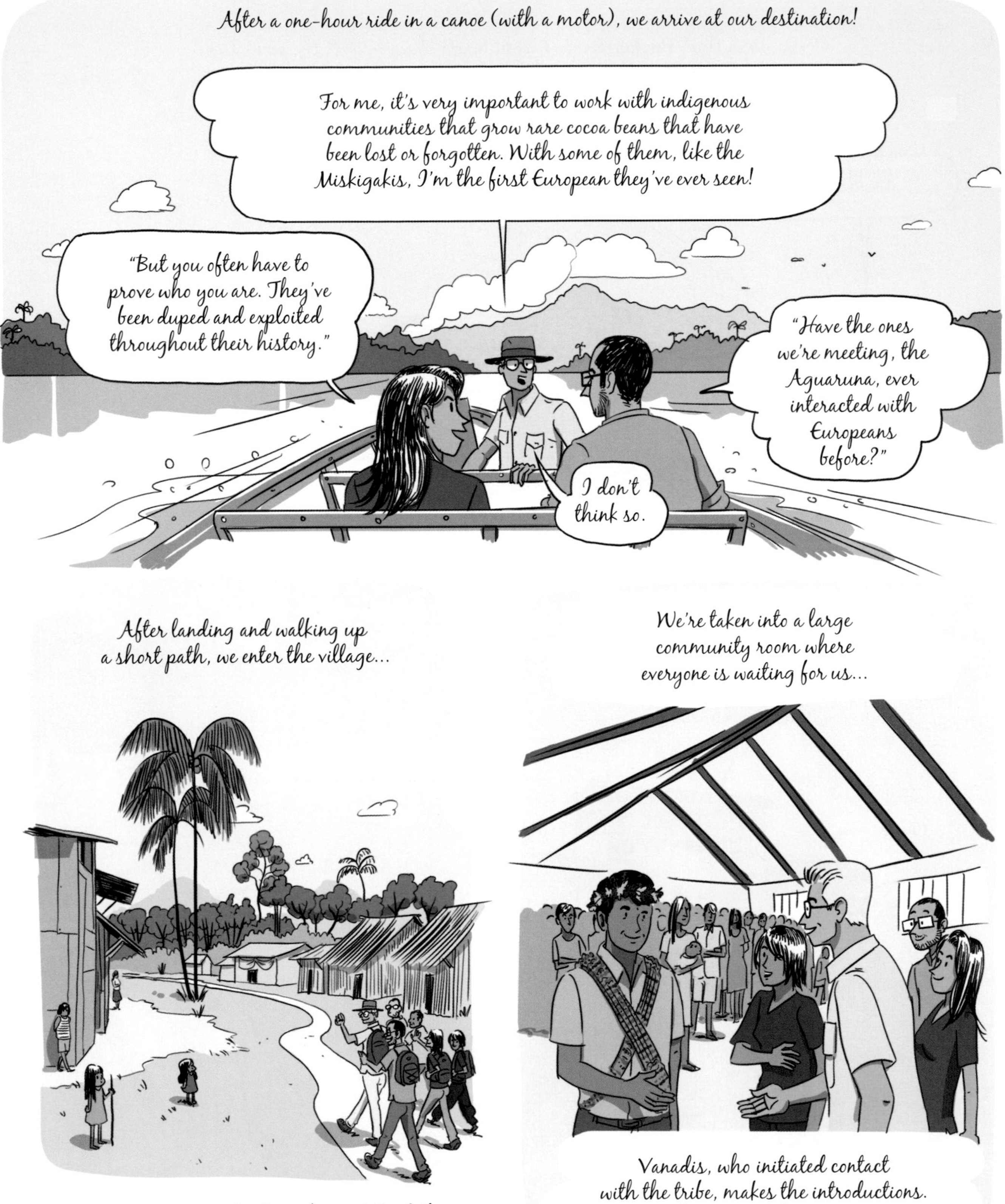
After a one-hour ride in a canoe (with a motor), we arrive at our destination!
For me, it's very important to work with indigenous communities that grow rare cocoa beans that have been lost or forgotten. With some of them, like the Miskigakis, I'm the first European they've ever seen!
"But you often have to prove who you are. They've been duped and exploited throughout their history."
"Have the ones we're meeting, the Aguaruna, ever interacted with Europeans before?"
I don't think so.
After landing and walking up a short path, we enter the village...
I'm surprised to find, in the middle of the jungle, little houses and children staring at us...
We're taken into a large community room where everyone is waiting for us...
Vanadis, who initiated contact with the tribe, makes the introductions. The leader welcomes us in official attire!

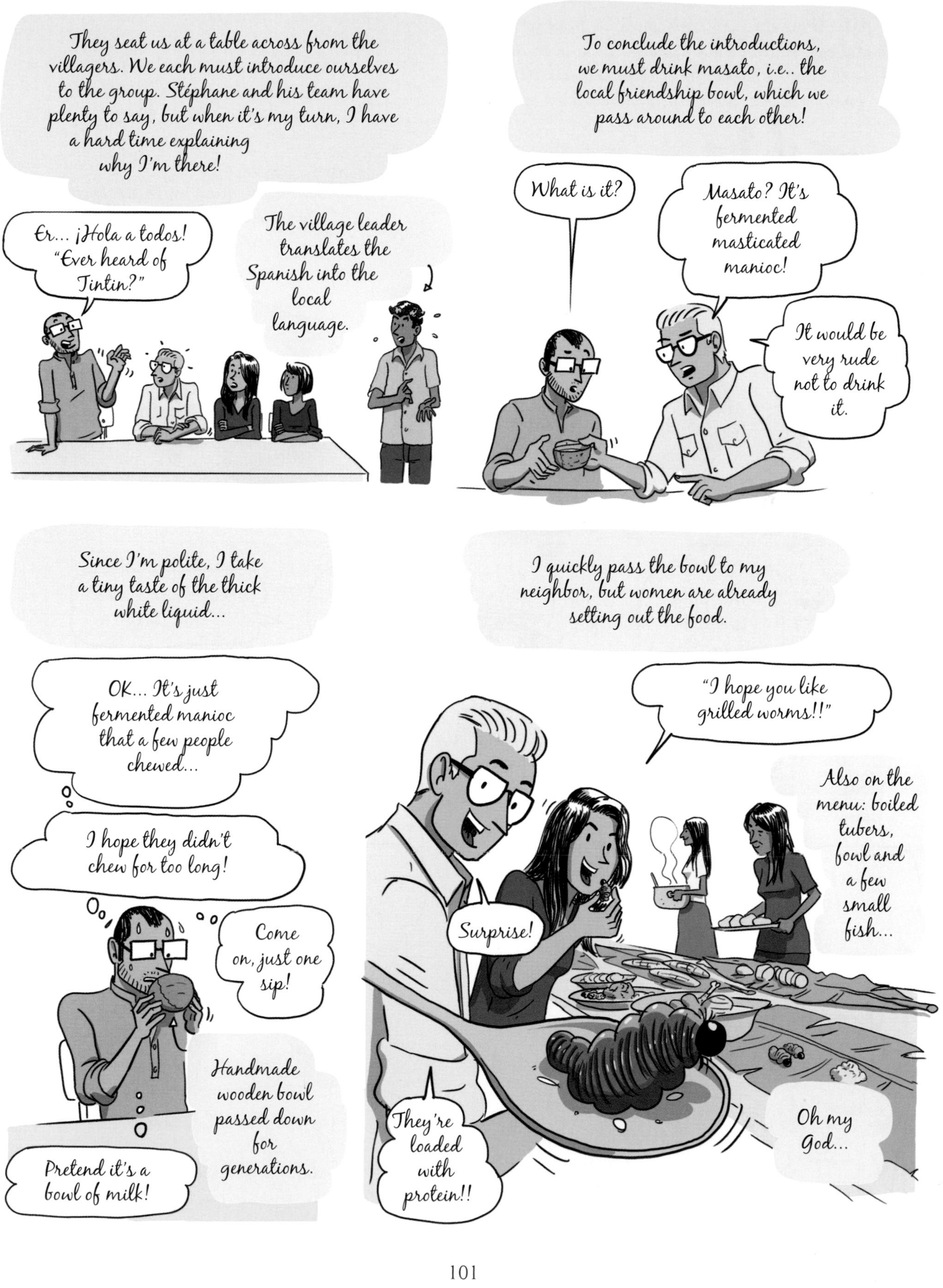
They seat us at a table across from the villagers. We each must introduce ourselves to the group. Stéphane and his team have plenty to say, but when it's my turn, I have a hard time explaining why I'm there!
Er... ¡Hola a todos! "Ever heard of Tintin?"
The village leader translates the Spanish into the local language.
To conclude the introductions, we must drink masato, i.e.. the local friendship bowl, which we pass around to each other!
What is it?
Masato? It's fermented masticated manioc!
It would be very rude not to drink it.
Since I'm polite, I take a tiny taste of the thick white liquid...
OK... It's just fermented manioc that a few people chewed...
I hope they didn't chew for too long!
Come on, just one sip!
Handmade wooden bowl passed down for generations.
Pretend it's a bowl of milk!
I quickly pass the bowl to my neighbor, but women are already setting out the food.
"I hope you like grilled worms!!"
Also on the menu: boiled tubers, fowl and a few small fish...
Surprise!
They're loaded with protein!!
Oh my God...

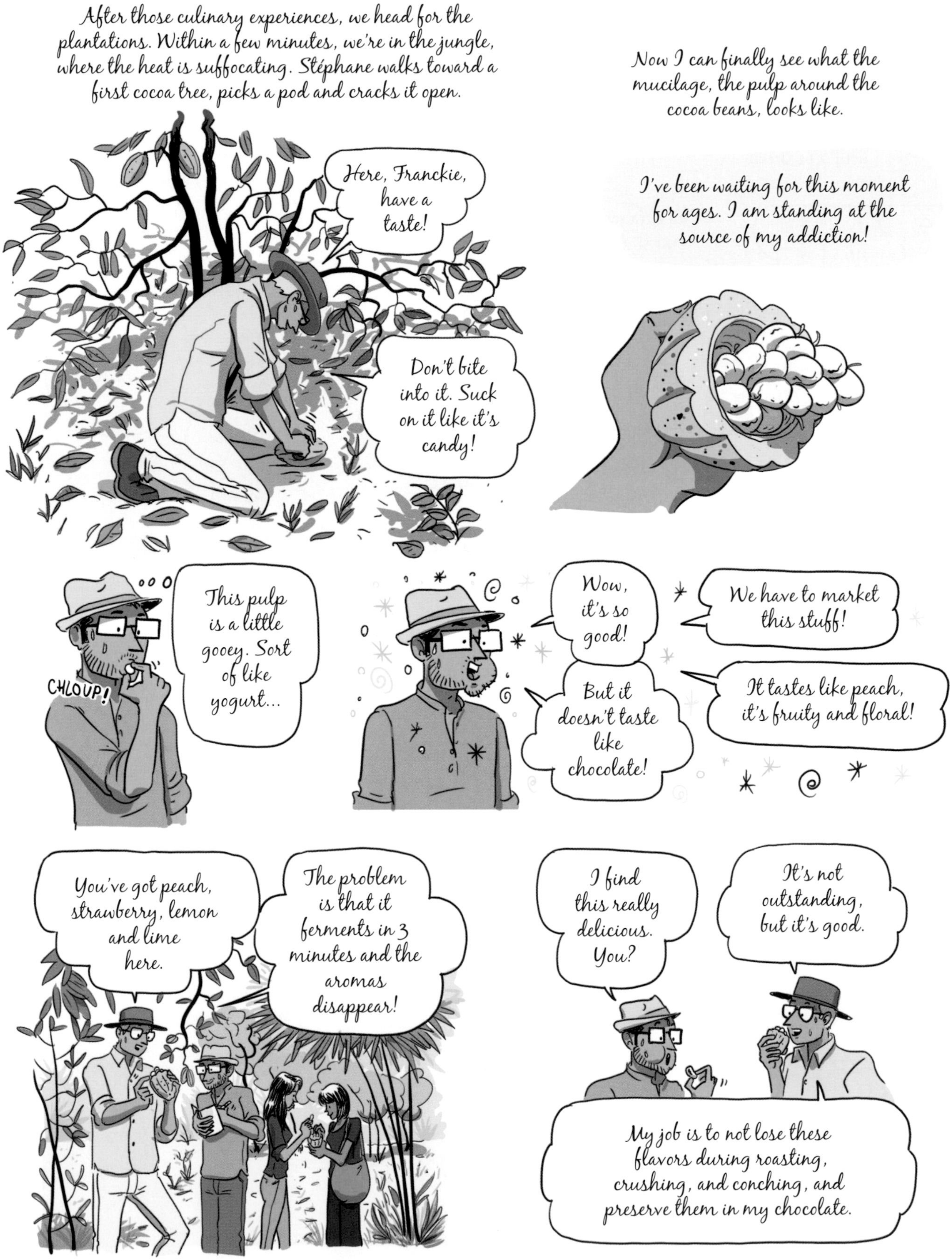

After those culinary experiences, we head for the plantations. Within a few minutes, we're in the jungle, where the heat is suffocating. Stéphane walks toward a first cocoa tree, picks a pod and cracks it open.
Here, Franckie, have a taste!
Don't bite into it. Suck on it like it's candy!
Now I can finally see what the mucilage, the pulp around the cocoa beans, looks like.
I've been waiting for this moment for ages. I am standing at the source of my addiction!
CHLOUP!
This pulp is a little gooey. Sort of like yogurt...
Wow, it's so good!
But it doesn't taste like chocolate!
We have to market this stuff!
It tastes like peach, it's fruity and floral!
You've got peach, strawberry, lemon and lime here.
The problem is that it ferments in 3 minutes and the aromas disappear!
I find this really delicious. You?
It's not outstanding, but it's good.
My job is to not lose these flavors during roasting, crushing, and conching, and preserve them in my chocolate.

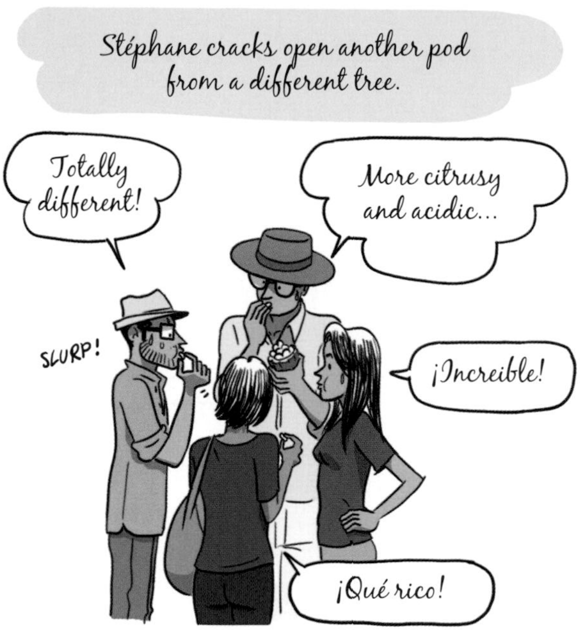
Stéphane cracks open another pod from a different tree.
Totally different!
More citrusy and acidic...
SLURP!
¡Increible!
¡Qué rico!

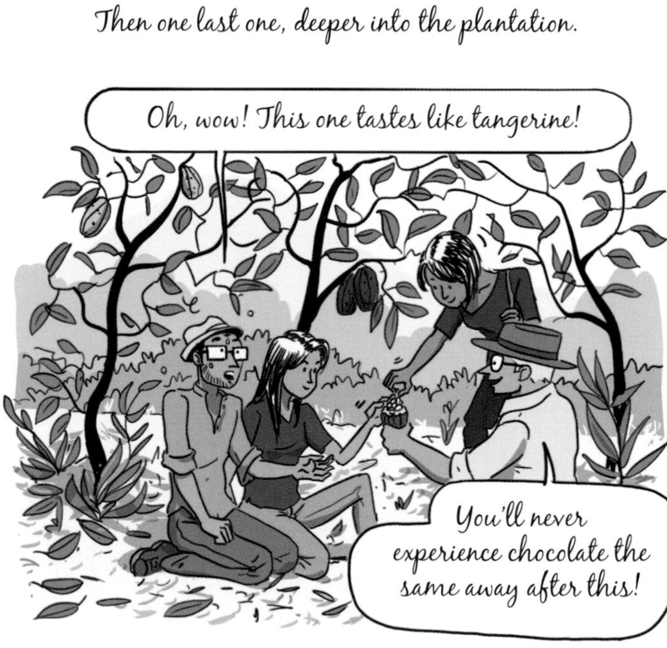
Then one last one, deeper into the plantation.
Oh, wow! This one tastes like tangerine!
You'll never experience chocolate the same away after this!

We go back to the village. I ask Stéphane about the harvest in the plantations he works with.

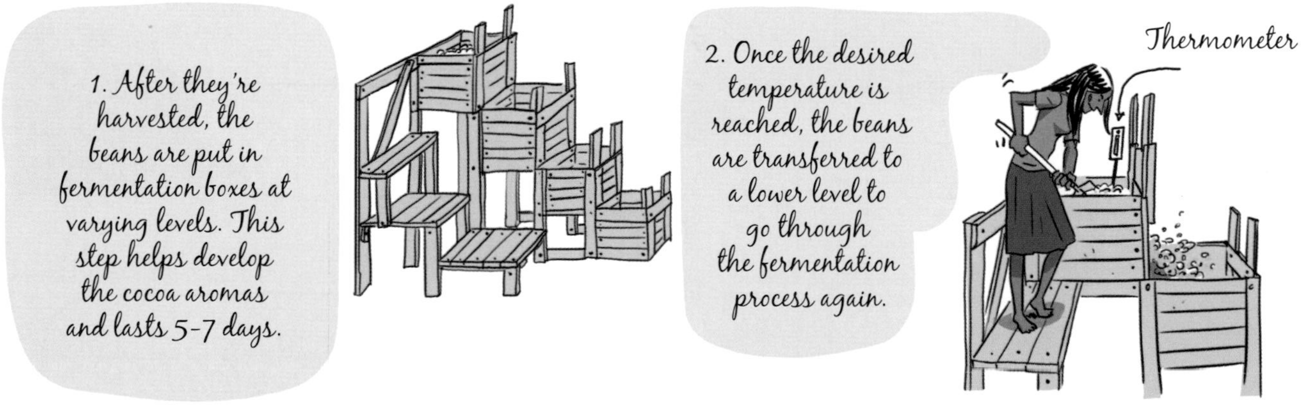
1. After they're harvested, the beans are put in fermentation boxes at varying levels. This step helps develop the cocoa aromas and lasts 5-7 days.
2. Once the desired temperature is reached, the beans are transferred to a lower level to go through the fermentation process again.
Thermometer

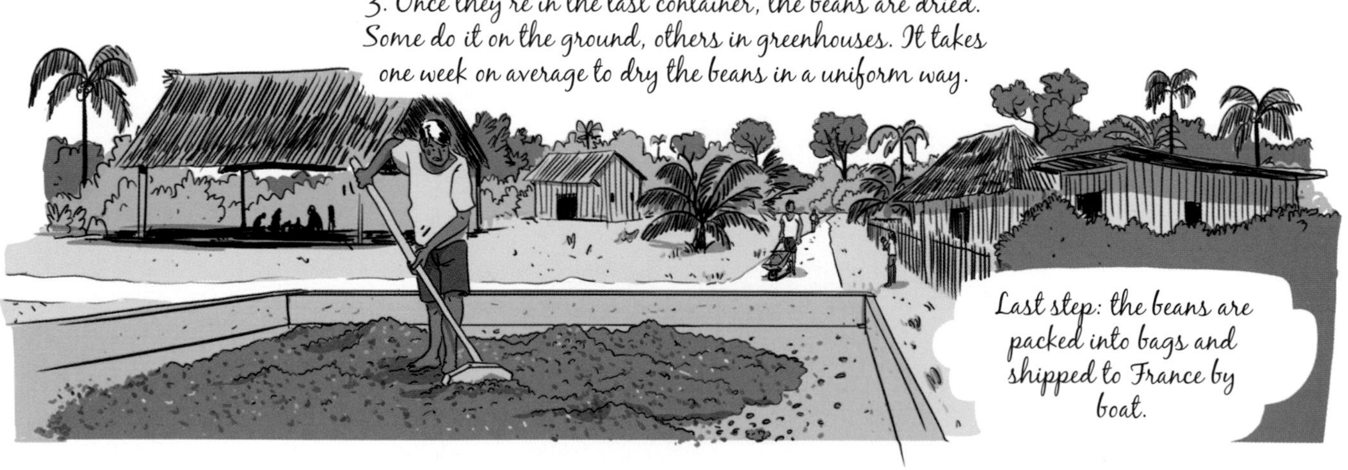
3. Once they're in the last container, the beans are dried. Some do it on the ground, others in greenhouses. It takes one week on average to dry the beans in a uniform way.
Last step: the beans are packed into bags and shipped to France by boat.

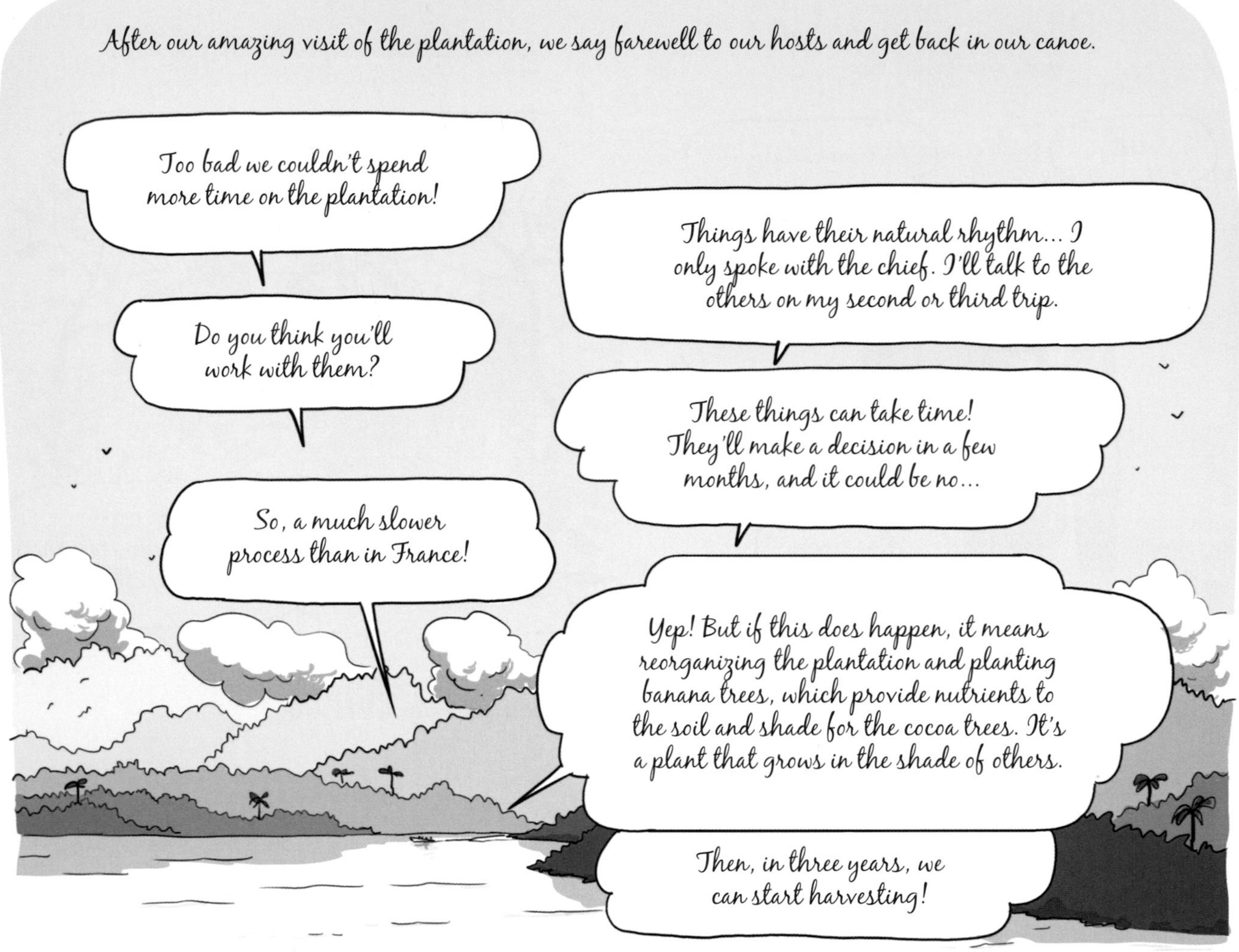
After our amazing visit of the plantation, we say farewell to our hosts and get back in our canoe.
Too bad we couldn't spend more time on the plantation!
Things have their natural rhythm... I only spoke with the chief. I'll talk to the others on my second or third trip.
Do you think you'll work with them?
These things can take time! They'll make a decision in a few months, and it could be no...
So, a much slower process than in France!
Yep! But if this does happen, it means reorganizing the plantation and planting banana trees, which provide nutrients to the soil and shade for the cocoa trees. It's a plant that grows in the shade of others.
Then, in three years, we can start harvesting!

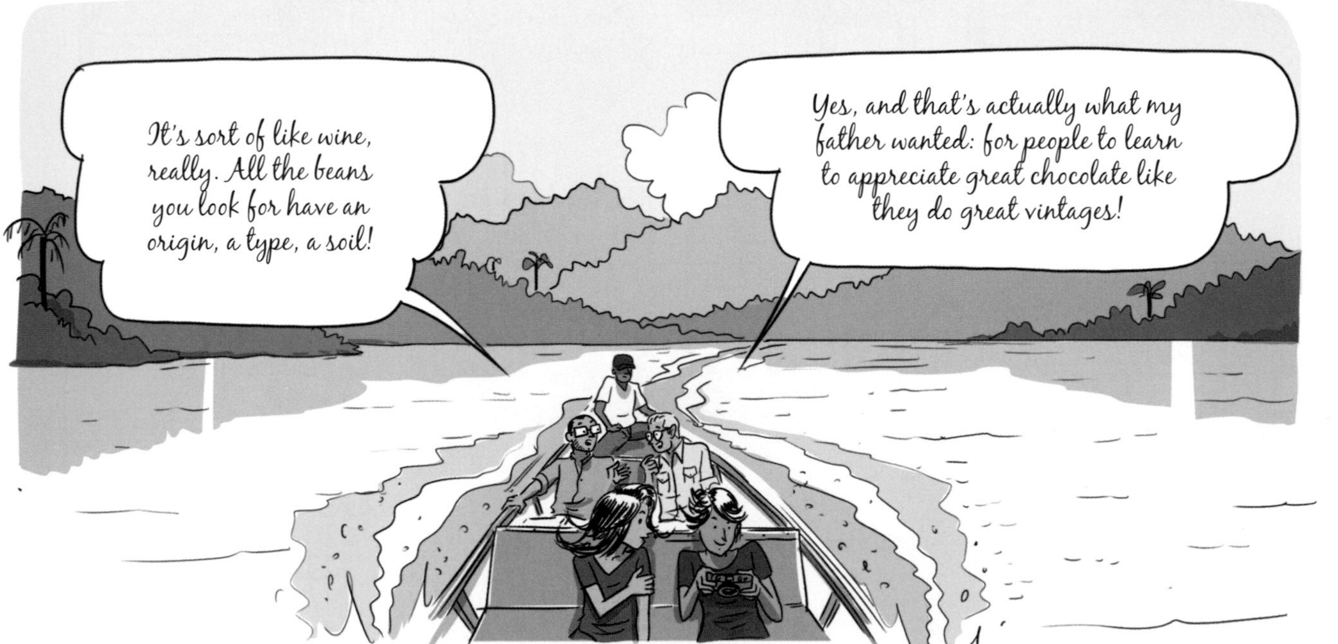
It's sort of like wine, really. All the beans you look for have an origin, a type, a soil!
Yes, and that's actually what my father wanted: for people to learn to appreciate great chocolate like they do great vintages!

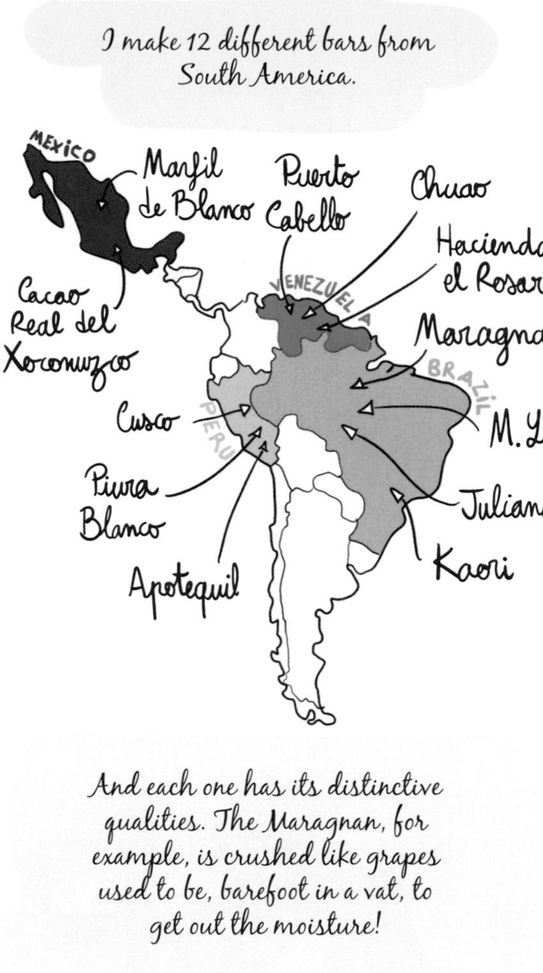
I make 12 different bars from South America.
MEXICO
Marfil de Blanco
Puerto Cabello
Chuao
Hacienda el Rosario
VENEZUELA
Cacao Real del Xoconuzco
Maragnan
BRAZIL
Cusco
PERU
M. Libânio
Piura Blanco
Juliana
Kaori
Apotequil
And each one has its distinctive qualities. The Maragnan, for example, is crushed like grapes used to be, barefoot in a vat, to get out the moisture!

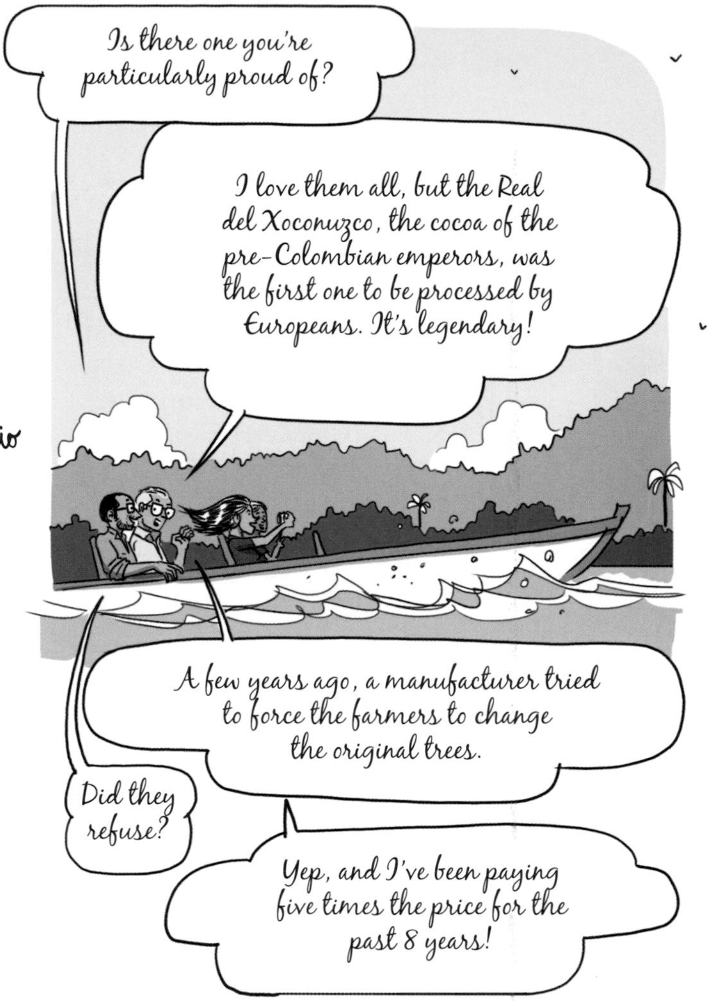
Is there one you're particularly proud of?
I love them all, but the Real del Xoconuzco, the cocoa of the pre-Colombian emperors, was the first one to be processed by Europeans. It's legendary!
A few years ago, a manufacturer tried to force the farmers to change the original trees.
Did they refuse?
Yep, and I've been paying five times the price for the past 8 years!

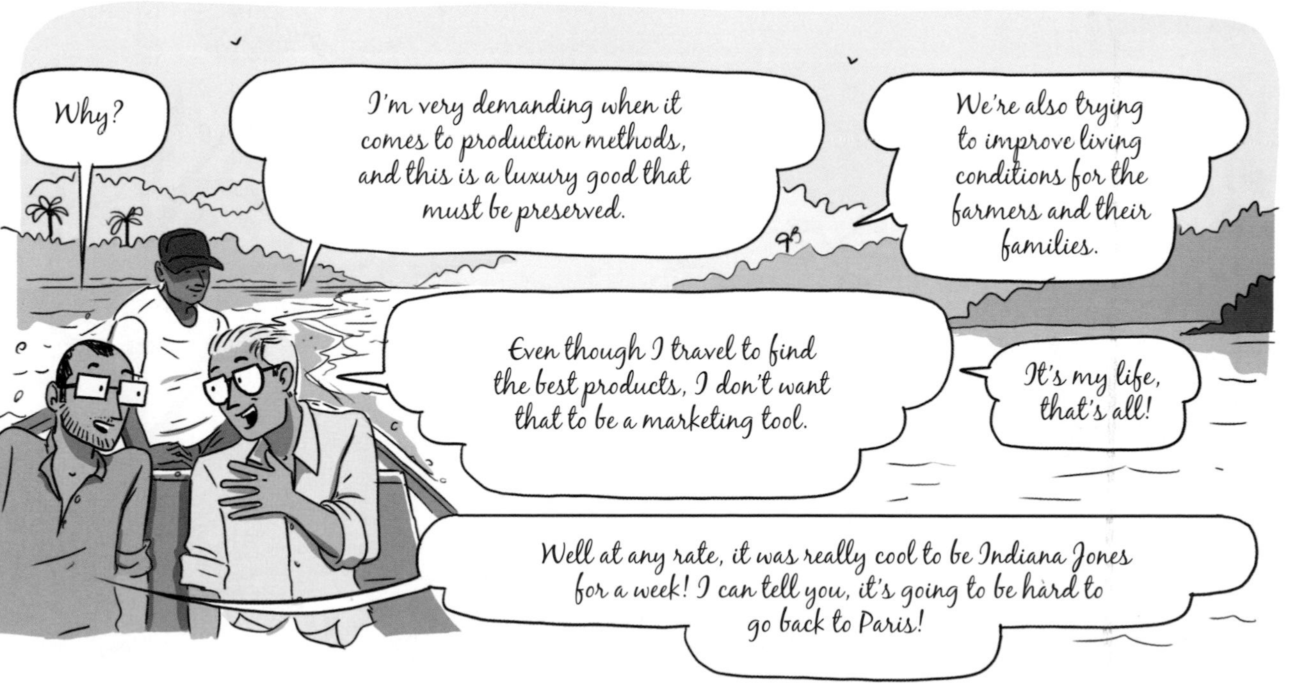
Why?
I'm very demanding when it comes to production methods, and this is a luxury good that must be preserved.
We're also trying to improve living conditions for the farmers and their families.
Even though I travel to find the best products, I don't want that to be a marketing tool.
It's my life, that's all!
Well at any rate, it was really cool to be Indiana Jones for a week! I can tell you, it's going to be hard to go back to Paris!

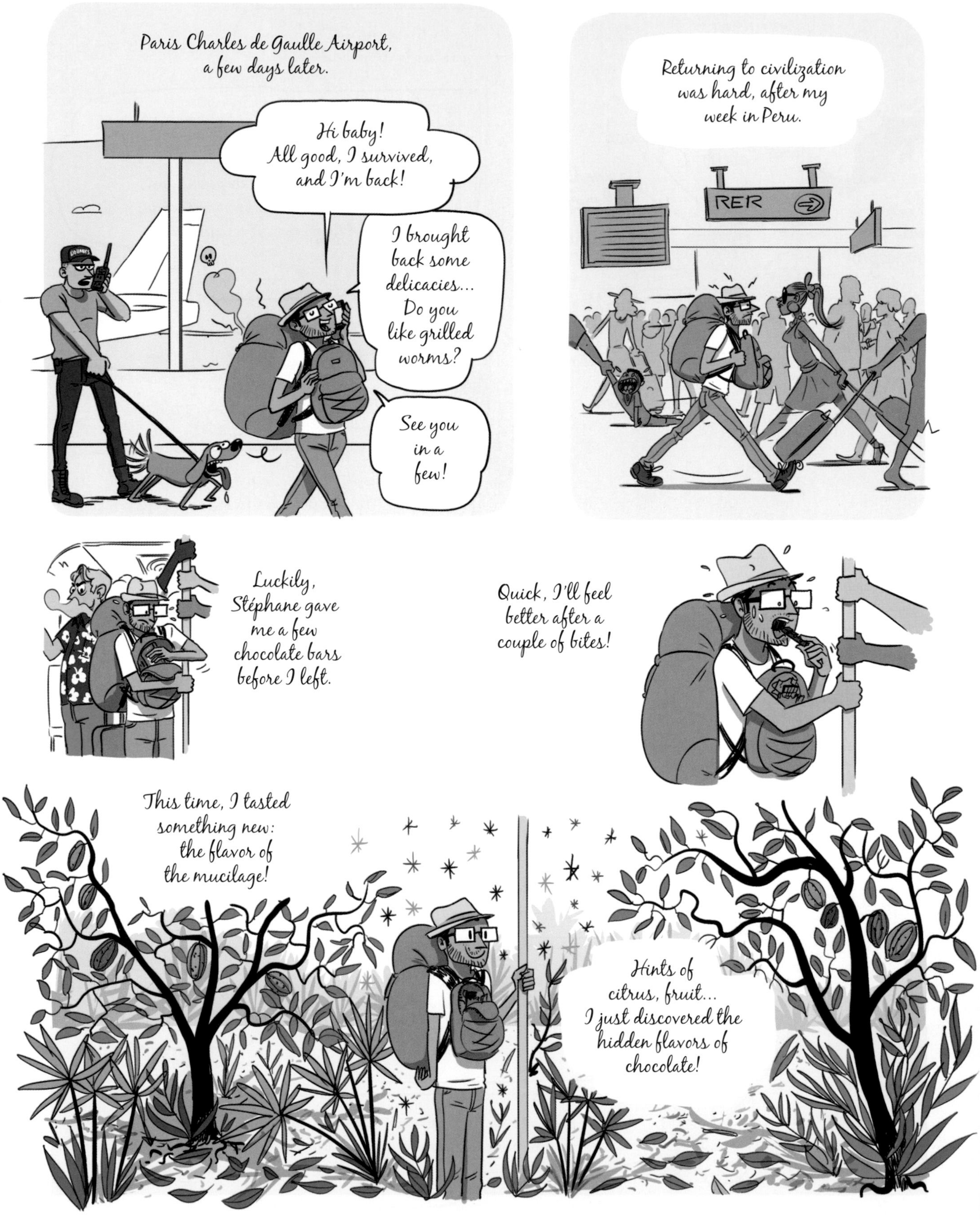
Paris Charles de Gaulle Airport, a few days later.
Hi baby! All good, I survived, and I'm back!
I brought back some delicacies... Do you like grilled worms?
See you in a few!
Returning to civilization was hard, after my week in Peru.
RER
Luckily, Stéphane gave me a few chocolate bars before I left.
Quick, I'll feel better after a couple of bites!
This time, I tasted something new: the flavor of the mucilage!
Hints of citrus, fruit... I just discovered the hidden flavors of chocolate!

PARTING WORDS

AN ALL-CONSUMING PASSION

Friday, August 29 2014. I pay one last visit to Jacques. Yannick, who supervises the product lines, and Ingrid are there as well. We all read the 110 pages of the book together...

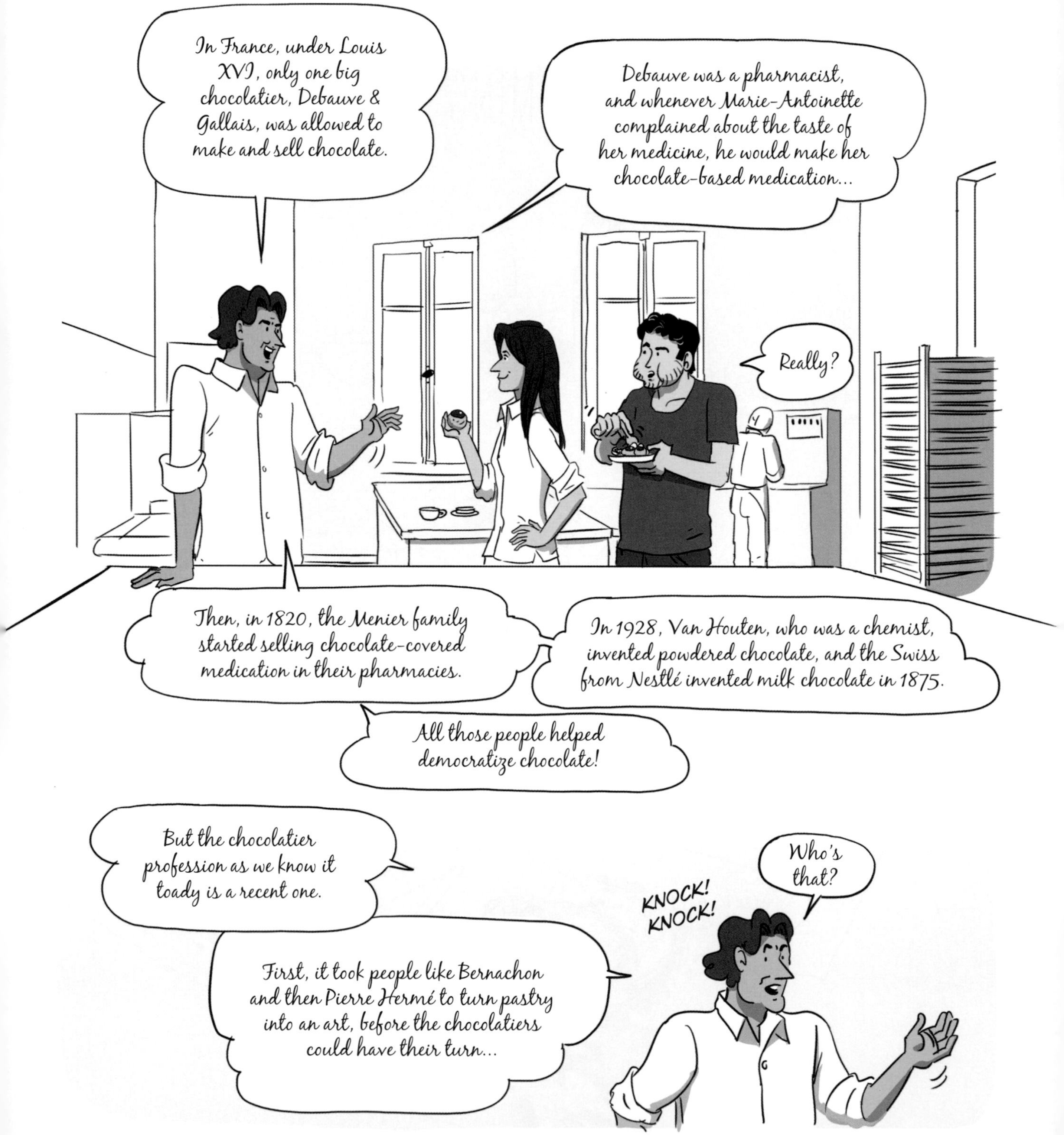

In France, under Louis XVI, only one big chocolatier, Debauve & Gallais, was allowed to make and sell chocolate.
Debauve was a pharmacist, and whenever Marie-Antoinette complained about the taste of her medicine, he would make her chocolate-based medication...
Really?
Then, in 1820, the Menier family started selling chocolate-covered medication in their pharmacies.
In 1928, Van Houten, who was a chemist, invented powdered chocolate, and the Swiss from Nestlé invented milk chocolate in 1875.
All those people helped democratize chocolate!
But the chocolatier profession as we know it toady is a recent one.
First, it took people like Bernachon and then Pierre Hermé to turn pastry into an art, before the chocolatiers could have their turn...
KNOCK! KNOCK!
Who's that?

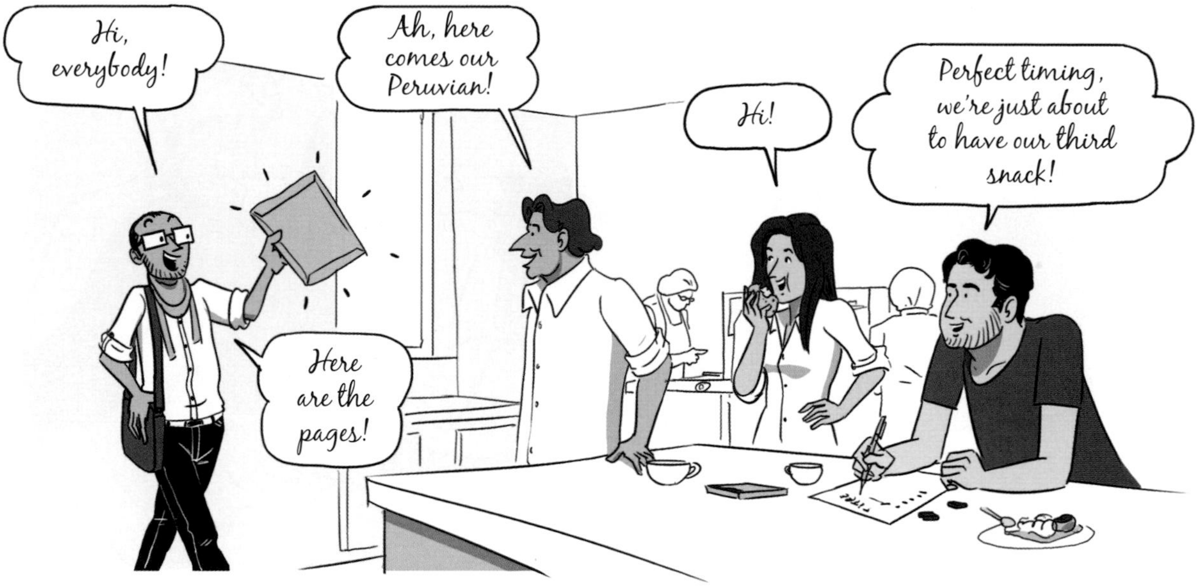
Hi, everybody!
Ah, here comes our Peruvian!
Hi!
Perfect timing, we're just about to have our third snack!
Here are the pages!

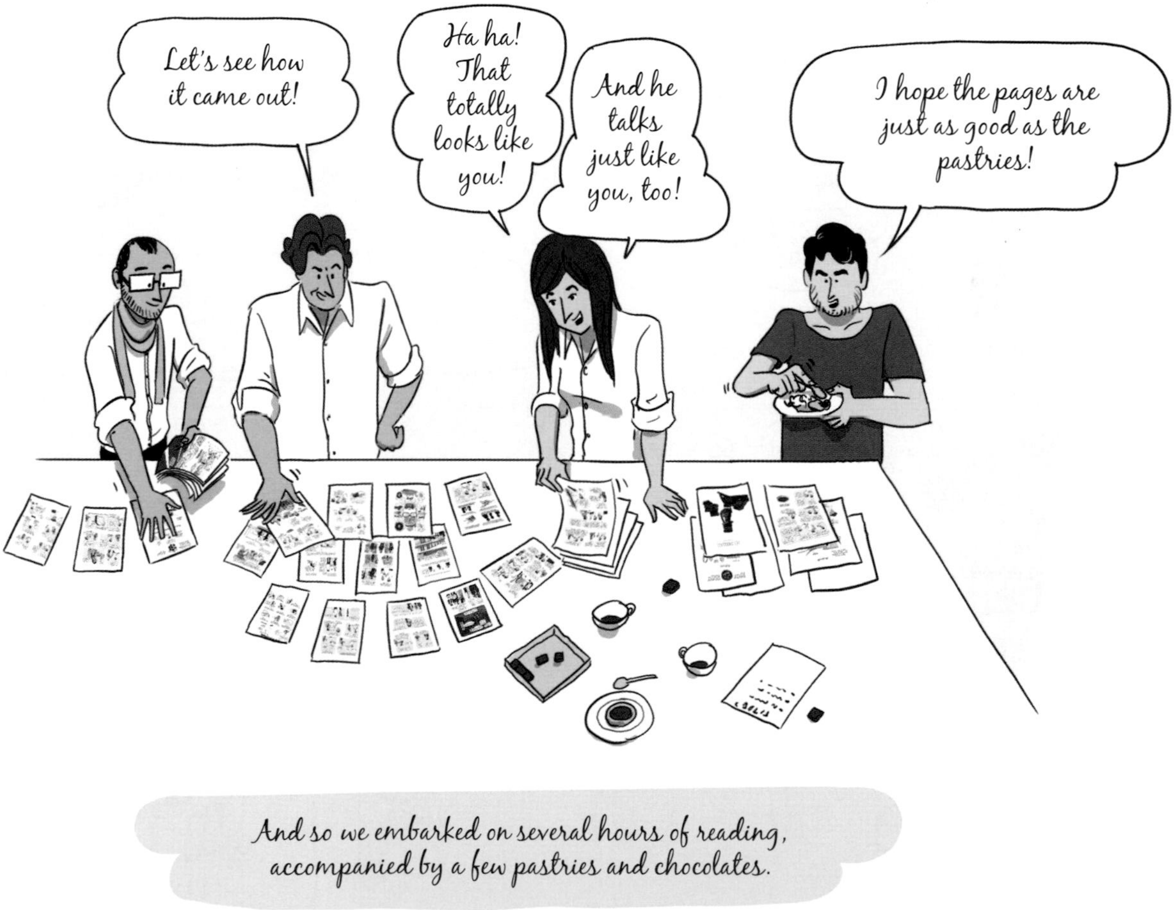
Let's see how it came out!
Ha ha! That totally looks like you!
And he talks just like you, too!
I hope the pages are just as good as the pastries!
And so we embarked on several hours of reading, accompanied by a few pastries and chocolates.

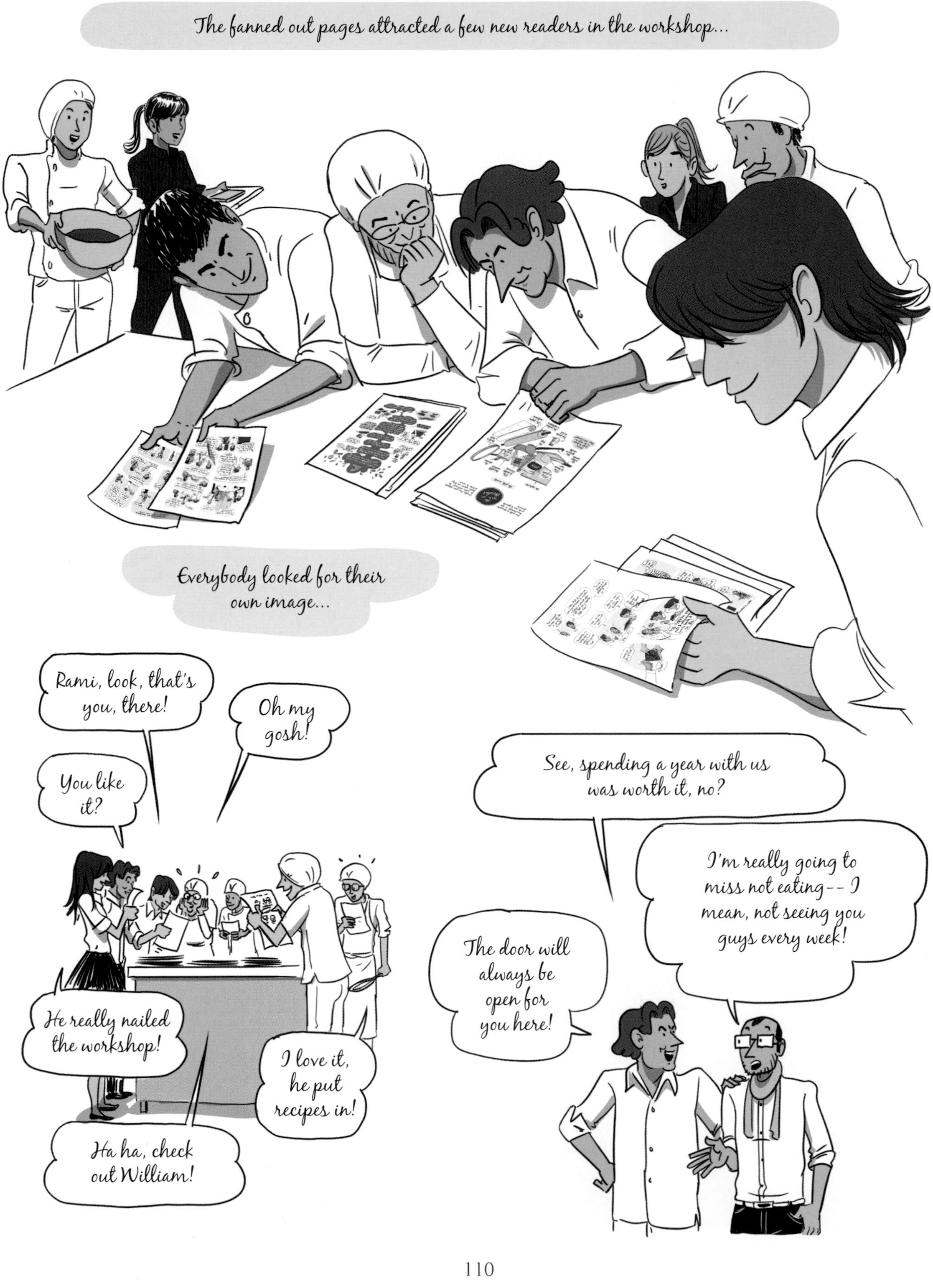

The fanned out pages attracted a few new readers in the workshop...
Everybody looked for their own image...
Rami, look, that's you, there!
Oh my gosh!
You like it?
He really nailed the workshop!
I love it, he put recipes in!
Ha ha, check out William!
See, spending a year with us was worth it, no?
I'm really going to miss not eating-- I mean, not seeing you guys every week!
The door will always be open for you here!

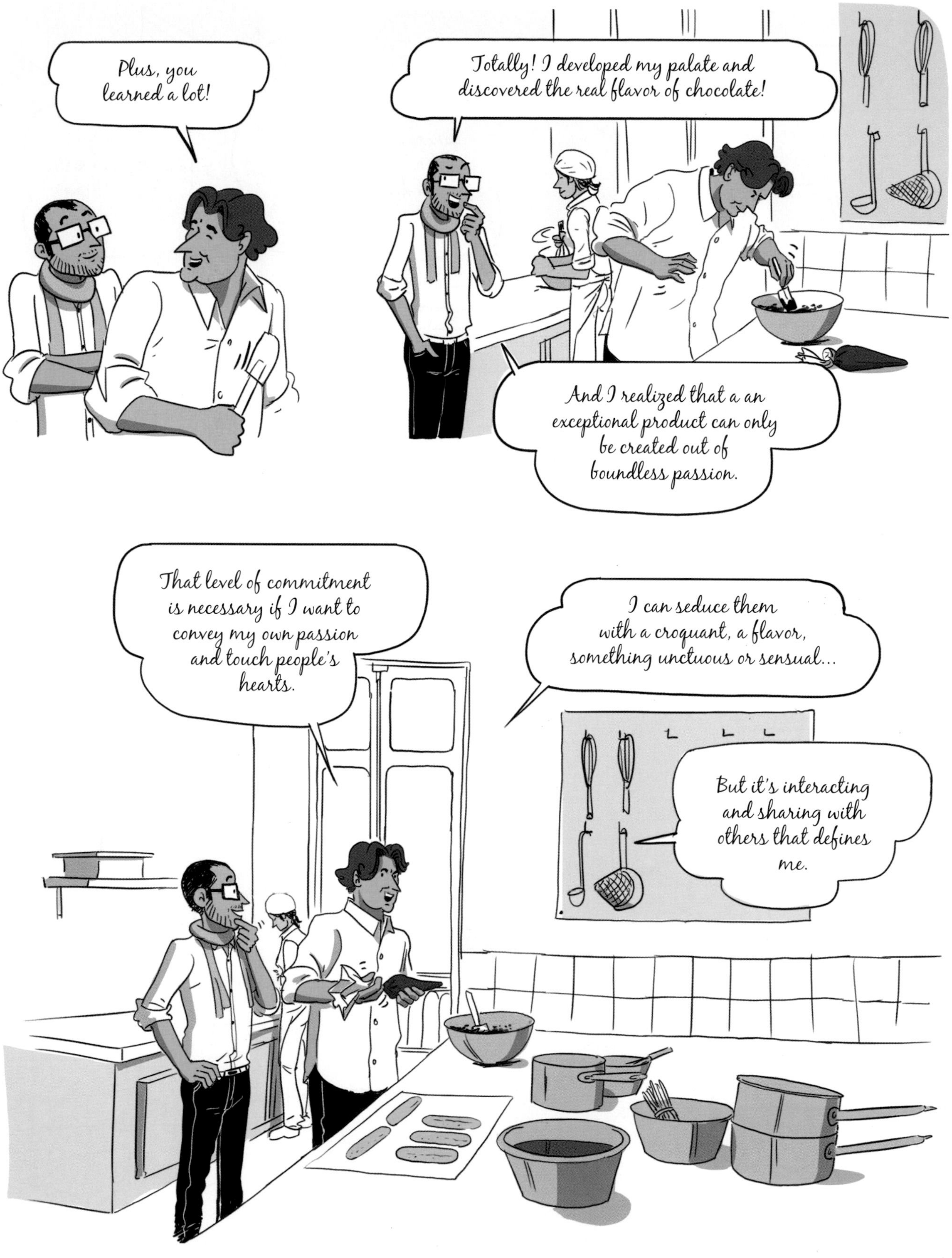
Plus, you learned a lot!
Totally! I developed my palate and discovered the real flavor of chocolate!
And I realized that a an exceptional product can only be created out of boundless passion.
That level of commitment is necessary if I want to convey my own passion and touch people's hearts.
I can seduce them with a croquant, a flavor, something unctuous or sensual...
But it's interacting and sharing with others that defines me.

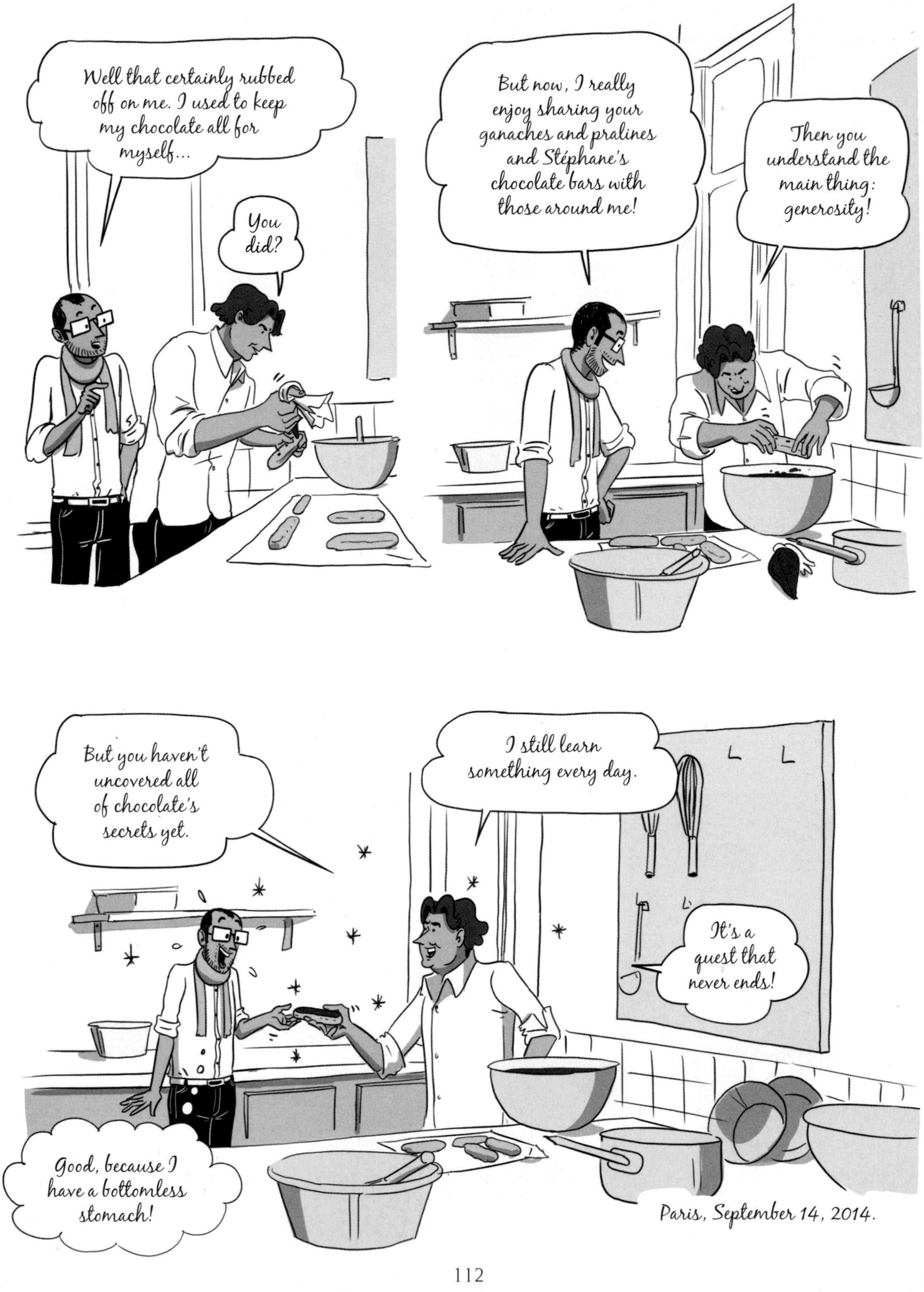
Well that certainly rubbed off on me. I used to keep my chocolate all for myself...
You did?
But now, I really enjoy sharing your ganaches and pralines and Stéphane's chocolate bars with those around me!
Then you understand the main thing: generosity!
But you haven't uncovered all of chocolate's secrets yet.
I still learn something every day.
It's a quest that never ends!
Good, because I have a bottomless stomach!
Paris, September 14, 2014.